CURRIES AND BUGLES

A MEMOIR AND COOKBOOK OF THE BRITISH RAJ

Jiena Kennie

1990

CURRIES AND BUGLES

A Memoir and a Cookbook of the British Raj

•

WRITTEN AND ILLUSTRATED BY

JENNIFER BRENNAN

HarperCollins*Publishers*

FIRST EDITION

Designed by Dinah Benson

Library of Congress Cataloging-in-Publication Data

Brennan, Jennifer.
Curries and bugles : memoirs and cookbook of the British Raj / Jennifer Brennan.

p. cm.
ISBN 0-06-016434-4
1. Cookery, Indic.   2. Cookery, British.   3. British—India—Social life and customs.   I. Title.
TX724.5.I4B74   1990   89-46519
394.1′2′08921054—dc20

90 91 92 93 94   MPC   10 9 8 7 6 5 4 3 2 1

CONTENTS

V

CONTENTS

To My Father
Major-General G. A. T. Pritchard, CBE
Known as "Pritch"

PREFACE

This is an intensely personal book. It celebrates the food, people and places of the British Raj in India. You are what you eat *but* your choice of food is also determined by what you have become. What follows, therefore, is my tribute to the sense of adventure and wonder in all of us.

As both a child and grandchild of the British Raj in India, and a member of that rapidly dwindling, anachronistic group, it is inevitable that, one day, I would turn again to the misty island which bore me, and to that other vivid and exotic country in which I was raised, to recapture and record what that long-ago life was like: how the colonialists and empire-builders lived; why they worked, struggled and often died far away from their own land; what they did in their daily lives; how they entertained and what they ate.

Our family is part of that saga. My maternal great-grandfather sailed for the East India Company on a ship called *Tiger*. His daughter, my grandmother, was born in Calcutta, as was my mother. My maternal grandfather ran away to sea from England as a young lad and sailed on the tea clippers, which brought him to Calcutta where he met my grandmother. My father, as a dashing and very junior officer in the Royal Engineers, served for many years on the North-west Frontier – the provincial, tribal buffer between what was then India (now Pakistan) and Afghanistan.

In those days, an officer in the British Army was not allowed to marry until he was thirty, and only then with his commanding officer's permission and approval of the fiancée. My father met my mother in Kashmir. After the requisite year's engagement period, she was invited to spend the weekend in Peshawar with my father's CO and his wife for the ritual pre-nuptial inspection. She passed muster. They were married in the little church in Sargodha which my grandfather (at the time district engineer) had built.

I

My parents decided, however, that I should be born in England and so I was. My mother, quite naturally accompanied by the now Captain Gordon Arthur Thomas Pritchard, went to Aldershot, home of the British Army, to give birth at the Louise Margaret Hospital. Shortly thereafter my father received a letter from his faithful Pathan manservant, patiently awaiting the Captain's return to the Frontier. A fierce tribesman but typically illiterate, he had hired the services of a local letter-writer. His two-page, congratulatory epistle – in vivid green ink on coarse paper – began, "Esteemed Sahib," and continued with flowery felicitations. However, at the close, the simple, rough-hewn Muslim surfaced: "PS, Sir, if it had been a boy, I would have written three pages."

My early childhood was spent between the North-west Frontier Province, the Punjab and Kashmir. And the memories are with me to this day: sights of the heaven-thrusting ice peaks of the Himalayas and the parched brown infinity of the plains; the soft soughing of wind through the pines of the hill stations and the plaintive call of the brain-fever bird (harbinger of hot weather); the acrid but strangely pleasing aroma of the burning dung of village fires; the heady perfume from the ceremonial garlands in the bazaar and the unforgettable smell of the first hard drops of monsoon rain on the thirsting earth.

India assaults the senses. There is nothing subtle about her. It is the same with the food. The sensuality of texture, vivid colours, pungent aromas and tingling tastes demand attention, even one's total concentration. The hardy and open-minded culinary explorers are weeded out from the mere voyeurs and dilettantes. In the same manner, there were those who sought to be part of the British Raj but whose sensibilities were offended by the challenge. Those who accepted and adapted survived and went on to love the vast subcontinent and all it had to offer. Among them I count my extraordinary and beloved family.

Jennifer Brennan

Yokohama, Japan

For the convenience of our American cousins the more singular (but charming) measurements of the British Raj have been converted where possible to the nearest sensible equivalent. Your forbearance and common sense are earnestly requested. Do remember to use your standard marked measuring cup for liquids.

J. B.

INTRODUCTION

No one could say that the relationship between India and England began as love at first sight. Nevertheless, it has enjoyed, in changing form, an astonishing longevity and style.

Imagine India as a talented and beautiful young girl, living in a rural area, remote from the focus of western civilization. She is discovered and then wooed by a cluster of impetuous, headstrong European gallants, who fight each other for her. Gradually one young Albion, resplendent in his East India Company regalia, prevails. He declares that he intends to make her his wife and proceeds to overpower her, stifling her objections.

Of course, upon marriage her dowry becomes his property – it was probably what attracted him to her in the first place. Naturally he reserves the right to administer it according to his own dictates and self-avowed superior wisdom, as he also assumes the prerogative of changing her life to conform to his own habits and ideals.

Their union lasts for a considerable period – more or less comfortably. Certainly Albion is satisfied; he is becoming middle-aged and staid and, as fitting all proper liaisons of the period, he feels he has worked hard for her benefit and maintenance. Madam India, however, is maturing and blossoming. Albion's support has undeniably helped her, but the bonds of wedlock are chafing and confining. She feels a burgeoning sense of her own identity and begins to agitate for more independence. Albion pays her little heed. He is tired, beset with business worries outside the home. India

---

1. Alec Hugh, bearer, his *ayah* and *dooley*, Gulmarg, 1937; 2. Guard at a Frontier Camp, Michni Kandao; 3. The youngest of the Whitburns in the family car, Sargodha; 4. Attock Bridge, North-West Frontier side; 5. Houseboats, Srinagar, Kashmir; 6. Taj Mahal, and the Ganges, 1939; 7. An open air market, Darjeeling; 8. *Dhobis* at Bangalore; 9. Rajasthani women with water pots at a festival, Ghanerao.

refuses to perform her household duties until he listens to her. There follows a painful series of marital upsets and a divorce ensues. Subsequently, India's offspring leave home, causing fresh distress.

After the first flush of freedom, India discovers she was more influenced by Albion than she realized. They have shared much through the years and interchanged customs, habits, language and foods. Now, in their mature years, though living permanently apart, they regard each other with respect and a certain fondness. Napoleon may have called Albion perfidious, but he and India have sustained a relationship for nearly 400 years.

Flyspecks in the pepper

The story behind the allegory dates back to the time of Good Queen Bess of the scarlet hair and temperament to match. When the Dutch gained a temporary monopoly on pepper and the cost of the spice rose fourfold – from two shillings and eightpence to eight shillings per pound – the Queen was affronted by the impudent Hollanders and, on 31 December 1600, granted a charter to a small group of merchants for a trading corporation. It was hastily formed under the grandiose title of The Governor and Company of Merchants of London Trading into the East Indies. The fledgeling concern was to operate on a voyage-to-voyage basis to secure England its own supply of pepper and other spices. A Captain James Lancaster promptly sailed for the Indies to return three years later with a cargo of 1 million pounds of pepper, which he had purchased in Sumatra at less than sixpence a pound. It earned him a knighthood from his grateful monarch, and for the merchants a handsome profit. The East India Company was in business.

Thereafter, English eyes were fixed firmly upon the fabled wealth of spices in the East Indies; India was merely regarded as a way station for cotton goods to be bartered later with the spice growers. It was a major contribution to the myth of the successful British amateur. England had the good fortune to be in the right place at the right time for the wrong reasons.

An English embassy was established in India at the court of the Mogul emperor, Jahangir, but it was not until the Dutch virtually barred the Company from the East Indies that the merchants focused on the sub-continent. Then, although a right to trade and establish factories in return for naval protection was negotiated by ambassador Sir Thomas Roe, English mercantile aims were thwarted until they ousted the Portuguese from India. (Portugal did retain a small enclave, Goa.)

Sugar and spice, and everything nice

The Company's affairs began to prosper. Madras, Gujarat, Bengal and Bombay supplied cotton, indigo, silk, sugar and saltpetre, and the Malabar coast of southern India provided spices. The factories flourished and forts were erected to protect them from nearby princes and marauders – sometimes with consequences that exceeded the wildest expectations of the builders. In 1690 a trading post was founded on a mud flat in Bengal, blessed with a deep anchorage for ships. A fort was built to protect the post and named after William III, who then ruled England. The little village originally on the site had been called Kali Ghat, after the goddess of death, who also protected the mud flats. Kali must have been well pleased with all the activity for the village expanded into a town and, down the years, into a vast city, Calcutta.

But commerce was not enough for the diligent factors of the East India Company. They quickly learned the art of political negotiation with the Mogul emperors and further areas of India were brought under English control. The influence of the Moguls was waning and their golden empire dying. France now saw its own opportunities in the subcontinent, which was becoming increasingly attractive to would-be colonialists, so the English art of bargaining was rapidly backed by force of arms against Gallic ambitions. One young factor with the Company, Robert Clive, discovered that his martial talents exceeded his commercial skills when, in 1751, he seized the fort at Arcot, west of Madras. With a cadre of 200 Europeans and 300 Indians, he successfully withstood a fifty-one-day siege by a French-backed Mogul prince. French dreams of dominating India evaporated. Young Clive ultimately became Governor of Bengal and his meteoric career and influence marked the real beginning of the British Empire in India.

The Company proud and the Company disallowed

The complex web of British interests expanded rapidly under the pressure of the commercial goals of the East India Company. Commercial expansion became inextricably entwined with the political tactics that enabled it to function. Coupled with this was determined and, sometimes, brilliant military action in the name of protection. Governors-general, whose names headlined the history books of generations of British – Hastings, Cornwallis and Wellesley – became hammer strokes in the forging of an empire.

The British were able to control and conquer with relative ease because the post-Mogul Hindu or Muslim rulers of the princedoms hated and feared each other more than they disliked the British. Casting envious eyes on the flourishing trade in areas already under the Company's flag, they enlisted British support in their internecine rivalries and, one after the other, allied themselves and lost their autonomy, sometimes their thrones.

Ironically, as the East India Company prospered, it signed its own death warrant. The Company's "servants" became so wealthy through private trade and the taking of presents (to be delicate) that, motivated by greed, they separated themselves from British standards and social restraints. No revenue collection, mercantile transaction nor, indeed, any form of commerce occurred but through their sticky hands. Moreover, the wretched Indian merchants had to pay these British profiteers for protection from harassment. Under the old Mogul Empire, the title of a deputy ruler or viceroy was *nawab*. This term was corrupted and applied to these *nouveaux riches* who returned to England at the end of their tenure with vast fortunes and purchased estates, country seats and memberships of parliament. They were contemptuously nicknamed "nabobs" by the envious but geographically disadvantaged. The British government took notice of the flagrant abuses and decided that the wings of the East India Company should be clipped. In 1818 some 360 disparate areas of British influence, scattered all over India like pieces of a broken jigsaw puzzle, became the British Empire of India; power was gradually transferred from the Company to the Crown. By 1833 the Company had lost its trade altogether and become a mere governing corporation under the watchful eye of parliament in London. The British government took over the duties and treaty obligations of the Company in 1858, following the disastrous Sepoy rebellion which sparked the Indian Mutiny in the previous year. Sir Charles Canning became the First Viceroy of India.

The Raj triumphant

The period from 1858 until just after the close of World War I was the zenith of the British Raj. The British had not come to the subcontinent as rapacious conquerors nor as zealous missionaries. If they had they probably would never have fared so well. No, it was an example of evolution; a progression initiated by adventurous entrepreneurs, furthered by gifted amateurs and finalized by dedicated administrators. But the Mutiny left a legacy of racial hatred and the seeds of final separation were sown even before the period of greatest triumph. As imperialists, the British began to treat the land and people, so carefully and slowly gathered into the fold, as conquered inferiors. They ruled India with the unshakeable conviction that they were supremely equipped to do so: by a sense of moral rectitude, a certainty of intellectual superiority and a patriotism firmly rooted in their country's interests. In short, a sense of manifest destiny.

Their record of achievement, like the parson's egg, was spotty in places. They turned India from the wealthy exporter they had created into a consumer market for British goods. But the agriculture of the country blossomed. At the height of British rule, 50 percent of the revenues from India were agricultural, but the balance came principally from the illicit opium trade with China and the official monopoly on salt. Between 1858 and 1914, 200 miles of railway tracks spidered out into a network of 35,000 miles, and the locomotives were *locally* manufactured and the trains *ran on time*. There were universities and schools, roads, bridges and canals, a painstaking civil service and an excellent system of irrigation; but the poor remained virtually destitute and the religious and cultural differences between caste, race and sect were as pronounced as they had been for centuries.

Yes, but I wouldn't have one to tea

By the Victorian era, the British in India had become *pukka sahibs*: stuffy, overbearing and, definitely, snobbish. The Frontier syndrome of the previous century – boom towns, interracial marriages, colourful adventures and instant fortunes – had ended in the humdrum gentility of civil administration. The brave scarlets of the regiments were to be found more on the parade grounds than charging through jungles and galloping over plains.

Except for the mountainous rim of the Empire, life became civilized. The easy camaraderie of Britisher and native crumbled with the distrust engendered by the Mutiny. Upon the completion of the Suez Canal, the passage to India was cut from three months to as many weeks, and English-women arrived in multiplying numbers to marry and domesticate their surroundings. Military cantonments, originally built outside the cities and towns to house the expanded and re-formed army, became enclaves of the British and symbols of the separation between ruler and subject. The natives were not to be fraternized with; an exception could be made for a maharaja. The club became the central focus of social life and an exclusively British and white preserve. The term "Anglo-Indian," which formerly applied to those Europeans whose careers caused them to spend their lives in India, became a pejorative name for the offspring of mixed marriages.

The British who spent their entire lives in India became, in their advancing years, "old India hands" (that is to say, somewhat opinionated experts on all things Indian). Seasoned and weathered by floods, riots, droughts, insurrections and deaths of both friends and enemies alike, they resembled venerable oak trees, surviving in alien soil. It was their custom upon entering a house (theirs or anyone else's) to throw their *topee*, or pith helmet, on to the hall table and shout, "*Kohai!*" – meaning literally, "Who's there?" But, in truth, the peremptory call was a demand for the nearest Indian servant to come running. This idiosyncrasy earned for them the – not always affectionate – nickname "old *kohais*."

Although the Frontier and the newly annexed Punjab had their share of "old *kohais*" and bigots, they were still places of adventure and areas of comparative personal freedom away from the stultifying and rigid social snobbery of the large cities. Loyalty, trust and camaraderie still existed on an interpersonal level between the British and the tribespeople and warriors. Border wars and skirmishes blew across the mountains and down the valleys but the air was free from corruption and hypocrisy – people breathed a little easier. This was the country my family inherited.

The gilded time warp

While Europe and America leapt into modernization in the early decades of this century, India progressed at a slower, more leisurely pace. In the 1920s and 1930s the life of the "servants" of the British Empire remained essentially as it had during the previous fifty years. The Edwardian strictures of social conduct were, even then, largely adhered to.

As little as sixty years ago, the British in outlying stations and cantonments happily endured kerosene lamps and charcoal cooking stoves (of course, they tended neither), and an icebox was exactly that. Electricity had not reached the rural areas and, as a small child, even I remember visiting homes where servants pulled the ropes of *punkahs*, or fans, to stir the heat-laden air.

In 1935, the same year that I was born, the Pan American Airways China Clipper flying boat operated for the first time from San Francisco to Manila, polyethylene was developed by ICI in England, nylon by Du Pont in America, and the first tape recorder to use plastic tape by AEG in Berlin. But the British Raj still travelled to and from India on the slow and majestic liners of the Peninsular & Oriental Company, their cotton and silk clothes were sewn for them by the *durzis*, or tailors, from the bazaars and they played Cole Porter at 78 r.p.m. on wind-up gramophones. What life lacked in amenities it made up for in graciousness. The engraved calling cards on the silver salvers of hall tables were an open sesame to the social life of the Raj.

The climate – the cool weather, the hot weather and the rains – dictated lifestyle and activities and even where one lived. From November to March, after the heat and the monsoon, when the weather was sunny, dry and cool (cold in north Punjab and on the Frontier), the social season swung into a whirl of activity. Riding, tennis, picnics, gymkhanas, hunts and shoots, luncheons, Government House garden parties, cricket matches and teas filled the daylight hours. Dinner parties, fancy dress or costume masquerades, dances, mess-night dinners and balls occupied and illuminated the nights.

The "fishing fleet" of marriageable young ladies sailed out to India each year for the Season. There was definitely no shortage of bachelors: officers from the regiments; employees of the Indian Civil Service (ICS), or "heaven-born" as they were lightly termed; young gentlemen carving out careers in commerce as future *burra sahibs* of large trading companies. Those unfortunate females who did not ensnare husbands sailed disconsolately back to England at the close of the Season, unkindly referred to as "returned empties."

At the beginning of the hot season, around the end of March, the families went up to the "hills." In some cases the British seat of government moved up to summer quarters but, more often, the men stayed down on the plains working, snatching the occasional week or weekend when they could join their wives in cooler climes. Every major town in which the British lived had its nearby hill station or range of accessible resorts. Kashmir was universally favoured for its beauty and amenities.

Darjeeling, Gulmarg, Simla, Murree, Ootacamund: each had its own character and qualities, but generally a hill station was a nucleus of little wooden structures on relatively level ground with the outskirts spreading over the steep mountainsides like toy blocks spilled hugga-mugga down a slope, lodging where they came to rest. The roof of one house would be the ground-level of the next. The post office, church, main shops and, perhaps, the railway station, if the narrow-gauge mountain train went that far, would anchor the haphazard and precarious town layout.

However, the prevailing impressions of the hill stations were of pines and cedars, half-veiled by the mists of low clouds that slumbered among the mountains, waking and rising to reveal the magnificence of the gigantic Himalayas so far up in the sky that they mimicked a panoramic mirage. The air moved with the gentle calls of wood pigeons and doves, the tinkling of goat bells and the ever-present sighing of the wind stirring the branches of the pines. The smells recall it best. The hot and intrusive smells of the plains were replaced by the elusive waft of wood smoke and the resinous scent of sunwarmed pine needles as they were pressed under the hooves of horses and the footsteps of people on the steep and wandering mountain paths.

Life in the hills was simple and slow-paced – strings of riders wound their way around wooded hillsides and from the tennis courts the gentle blat of racquet hitting ball was heard throughout the day. To discover one's own picnic spot was a high priority; wicker hampers were stuffed with *naan* bread, steamroller chicken, potato cutlets and cold ham. Beer, ginger beer and lemonade completed the occasion. Many a dress or pair of jodhpurs was carefully plucked over at the end of an afternoon to remove its clinging cargo of pine needles.

There were few social obligations, except in Simla. For one thing, wives did not entertain formally without their husbands. For another, the household staff was left down in the plains and only a personal bearer, or manservant, accompanied the family. Most people stayed in modest resort hotels, primitive by today's standards. Sometimes there were bachelor officers up on leave and the community would buzz with gossip about the summer liaison of a wandering wife. The pace of life would quicken when the husbands arrived: shooting parties for black partridge or wild duck would be organized; the evenings would ring with gramophone music and laughter after dinner parties.

In September, down on the plains, the houses were dusted out and the lawns mown by the *malis* (gardeners) and all the servants lined the entrances to welcome the returning families. The bearer, resplendent in his white tunic and *puggaree* (turban), both banded with diagonal sashes striped with the household colours, hurried around giving orders to the *ayah* or personal maid, and superintending the unpacking of the boxes; the *khansamer* (cook) would sharpen knives in the outdoor kitchen prior to the evening meal, allotting tasks to the *masalchi* (scullery boy); the *bhisti* (water-carrier) padded on bare feet with swaying, dripping buckets with water for the baths. The sweeper gave a few extra strokes to the already immaculate verandas, and the *syces* (grooms) curried the horses once more, for they knew that the *sahib* and *memsahib* would soon come out to see the animals after the long summer separation. The families were home.

Mistress of all she surveys

The mistress of the house, or *burra mem*, was not a housewife as we understand the term. She had the imposing task of managing a household staff numbering between eight and thirty servants, ostensibly employed to take care of the domestic chores with the lubricated efficiency of a well-run luxury hotel and so lighten the white woman's burden. In reality the arrangement did not reach that pinnacle of achievement. The servants' interpersonal relationships, religious taboos and caste-bound job definitions would make a present-day shop steward or personnel manager resign and start collecting matchboxes. As Charles Allen wrote in *Plain Tales from the Raj*:

Status – and a highly developed sense of demarcation – also contributed to the general superabundance of domestics, who were there "not because you need them but because they were very strict about their own little trade unions."

The lack of modern conveniences also affected the size of the household. For instance, before widespread electrification, when fans were manually operated instead of merely switched on for a rush of air, the old *punkah* fan – resembling a hanging, wooden-framed, medieval banner – was moved by a rope which disappeared through a hole in the wall to the veranda outside. There sat the *punkah wallah*, alternately pulling and slacking on the rope. (The contraption was reminiscent of a Heath-Robinson/Rube Goldberg sketch.) If the boy was sleepy, he would lie down and tie the rope around his toe, languidly waving his foot. Sometimes the fan stopped, and the sweating occupant of the room would rush outside to find that the boy was asleep or had gone for a drink of water, or that the rope had broken – a frequent occurrence since the channel through which the rope passed was often the neck of a broken bottle. As an average of three rooms often needed cooling at once and as the *punkah* boys naturally had to work in shifts, up to nine people could be employed for a simple process that we take for granted – moving air.

The servants formed an extended family. (Indeed, some had their own families living with them.) Their quarrels had to be arbitrated, their grievances listened to and their misfortunes commiserated with. The wisdom of Solomon was frequently required to adjudicate real or perceived injustices: the indoor servants were generally Muslim, the gardeners and *dhobis* (laundrymen) Hindu, the *syces* for the horses were of either faith, and the sweeper – who also looked after the dogs – was an "untouchable," the lowest category within the caste system. The head bearer, who was usually long in service and well trusted, was second-in-command to the mistress and a wise woman would leave the hiring of replacement servants to him; the subsequent harmony of the household then became his concern. The cook, however, was outside the bearer's influence, being a person of individual status and in sole charge of the kitchen.

My grandmother, born and raised to become a *burra mem*, took the command of the household in her stride. Her large bunch of keys was necessary both as a prevention against theft and as a symbol of her status; indeed, most Indian and some English women wore them hanging from chatelaines on their belts. Every morning after breakfast, her household duties began. She met the *khansamer* (cook) outside the store cupboard near the pantry, unlocked the room and, with due ceremony, gave out measured quantities of flour, tea, sugar and other imperishables in the amounts required for the meals of the day. Earlier that morning the *khansamer* had done the shopping for the day's requirements of perishables, meats and vegetables, hailing a passing *tonga* – a horse-drawn, two-wheeled carriage for hire – for the several-mile journey to the native bazaar. There was an understanding between mistress and cook that a perquisite of his job was to be allowed to purchase at a discount from the Indian merchants and charge her retail price, with the proviso that his profits did not become too exorbitant. The *khansamer* presented his accounts book, or *hissab*, to my grandmother, who scrutinized it carefully. The menus for the following day were then discussed and she gave him a sum of *rupees* for his future shopping requirements.

Meals were elaborate in framework but simple in content. The majority of the British in India came from middle-class homes with straightforward tastes in food. There were always several courses to a meal. This concept even extended to breakfast which, whether taken buffet-style from hot-plates on the sideboard or cooked to order, contained a choice of dishes.

The cooks were talented, mostly. Goanese, Nepalese, Madrassi or Bengali, they had served long apprenticeships with a variety of families and were well used to the idiosyncrasies of British tastes. The more accomplished *khansamers* acquired a repertoire of French dishes and all could, naturally, produce a wide range of Indian food, accented by the regional tastes of their home provinces. In truth, I suspect that the talents of most cooks were somewhat under-utilized. Individual tastes, preferences and methods of preparation were transmitted back and forth between mistress and cook so the resultant complexion of the fare reflected many cross-cultural influences. However, once a meal was ordered, it was not done for any *memsahib* to interfere in the kitchen.

Dinner, the crowning meal and signal event of the day, was served late, around 9 p.m., and normally consisted of soup, followed by fish, then meat. Desserts were predictable and were mostly puddings, sometimes a trifle or a fruit salad. Our family was particularly fond of Indian food and so curries were served very frequently either at lunch or at dinner. Vegetables were only available seasonally, owing to lack of refrigeration, and we celebrated with a variety of squashes, "ladies' fingers"/okra (*bhindi*) and leafy greens during the hot weather, while the more traditional peas, beans, cauliflower and cabbages were winter produce. Sometimes the *mali* would nurse a particularly handsome specimen to gargantuan proportions and proudly show it at the annual agricultural fair for the district. If it won an award, he would be allowed to eat the exhibit in celebration while we had to be content with his certificate of merit.

Meat was mostly lamb or chicken (pork was prohibited in the Muslim areas in which we lived), frequently varied with game, such as partridge or pheasant. As there were many shoots during the cold season, little time elapsed before someone presented the family with a brace of birds or even a dressed deer. Mutton, the principal meat of northern India, came from the *dumba*, or fat-tailed sheep, aptly named for their rear appendages which hung like padded plates, thickly layered with fat. The *khansamer* bought meat in bulk, then butchered it into pieces for individual meals. He also rendered the sheep's tails for cooking fat. (There were no bottled cooking oils available except for olive oil, and that was used for dressing salads.)

In the Punjabi winters, when the frost crackled on the grass and the temperature occasionally dropped to 19°F (−7°C), the meat was stored outside in *dooleys* – wooden boxes with mesh-screened sides – which were hung from the branches of trees, out of range of any prowling animals. In the warmer weather perishables were put in the icebox, which was made of wood and lined with tin sheeting. The large blocks of ice for this were purchased from the icehouse by the bearer, wrapped in gunny sacks and placed into the box together with saltpetre. The bearer was also responsible for the non-edible household shopping, candles, cleaning materials, etc., and he presented his daily accounts book in the same manner as the cook.

Cow's milk was delivered daily in large metal churns. When families had children, it was often the practice to own a cow and have it milked daily so that the source of the milk could be checked for contamination. In any event, the milk was always boiled. The dairy also supplied semi-soft farmer's cheese called *paneer*. One of my early memories of my grandmother was of her churning buffalo milk into creamy white butter, which we would spread on *chapattis* and eat with marmalade for breakfast.

Closing the time warp

Every day started with the usual hearty English-style meal, after which the *memsahibs* would probably go for a morning ride, returning to bathe and change before light lunch, or *tiffin*. In the afternoon there would be a quiet period for writing letters, pottering in the garden or taking a brief nap before changing for tennis at the club. After a surprisingly brisk workout on the courts, when lengthening shadows began to stripe the immaculate lawns, everyone would repair to the clubhouse to play bridge or snooker, read the latest periodicals from England (usually months out of date but, nevertheless, perused with earnest study), or gather companionably in the well-worn chintz armchairs to review the latest petty scandals over pink gins, gimlets and whiskies. As the shadows filled, lamps were lighted and it was time to return home, bathe and change into formal clothes for dinner and the night's entertainment.

This comfortable routine occupied the days, which slipped by unnoticed. The gathering storm of World War II in Europe was headlined in the English newspapers but talk of local unrest or of the Mahatma's latest campaign of *satyagraha* – non-violent non-cooperation – was of more immediate concern. And, anyway, human nature being what it is, it was far more fun to hear about the cobra in the district commissioner's bathroom, to discuss the latest indiscretion of young Miss X with a newly arrived captain, or to plan the details of the next gymkhana and dissect what went wrong last year.

Even when war was declared and patriotism ran high, no one thought it would last for long, or saw any reason to change their lifestyle. But the changes were there, if at first barely perceptible. Some of the faces in the billiards-room were missing, having been posted to strategic theatres of war, and there was talk of cutting back on expenses, more from sentiment than need. But the hallowed fixtures of the social seasons continued to preserve the framework of the Raj, even if the flesh was sagging slightly on the bones.

Eventually, as more of the males went off to South-east Asia and then to the Burma Front, life became less formal and the structure loosened. Wives were forced to entertain without their husbands if they wanted any sort of social life. Many families had long-term guests – advisers and specialists assigned to certain areas on hush-hush, temporary duty. There were, of course, the perfunctory air-raid drills, voluntary work, and at the local hospitals first-aid training and bandage-rolling exercises. There were anxious faces and whispers about an invasion of India. There was also a constant influx of young officers at the clubs – officers whom the local, self-appointed social arbiters declared "would never have been allowed in before the war" – as the army increased in size and mobility under the exigencies of war. The same momentum brought modernization with it and the time warp closed.

By the end of the war, many families had left India. For those who stayed behind, there was tremendous anxiety and uncertainty about the future. The unthinkable had happened. Life in India was no longer to be taken for granted.

Requiem for the Raj

Independence, followed by the partition of India and Pakistan, left the peoples of the subcontinent with a mixed sense of jubilation and bewilderment. The *sahibs* were gone. The British no longer ruled the land. After the din of fireworks and mass celebrations died away and the turmoil of resettlement finally subsided, emptiness remained.

Dust devils blew across the parade grounds. Spiders fastened cobwebs over the doors of the echoing bungalows of the civil lines. The lawn-mowers rusted. Solar *topees* and pith helmets sat in forlorn piles on the shelves of the shops – the last ones sold had been cast into the foaming wake of the ocean liners and bobbed for a little on the waves before they sank. The vacuum left by the Raj was both psychological and physical.

A station master looked at his cooling cup of tea in front of him, rose and marched out to the head of the platform. He blew his whistle long and loud. "Damnit! The *sahibs*, they were always saying that the trains should be running on time, my God." He adjusted his *topee* to a more commanding angle.

In his office, an adjutant called a sergeant and barked out a series of commands in flawless Oxford English. "Let's have a parade. Can't have the men getting slack. We have the reputation of the Indian Army to think of!"

The provincial civil servants moved their families into the bungalows and planted more zinnias and marigolds.

The British went home, many to a land they had never seen. The reality of a rapidly changing post-war England was not the fabric of their colonial dreams. They built suburban bungalows for themselves and fastened gleaming brass nameplates on the gates: "Dalhousie," "Dehra Dun" and "Dun-roamin." They erected tall, white-painted flagstaffs and flew the Union Jack every day, ceremoniously lowering it each night and to half-mast on appropriate occasions. They sat in cramped drawing-rooms with Kashmir *dhurries* and Kashan rugs on the floor. They polished their Benares brass tables. They mounted their photographs in albums and wrote meticulous captions. They wrote autobiographies, some of which were published. They met in pubs and raised pint tankards to the Good Old Days and invited each other to endless curry *tiffins* on Sundays.

The Raj had ended.

Colours

The dawn chorus of birds rising from the banyan tree . . .

Distant commands blowing in the breeze from the parade ground . . .

The whinnying of the horses from the stables . . .

The rhythmic slapping of twisted, wet cloth as the *dhobi*-women beat the laundry on the river rocks . . .

The pungent smell of burning dung from the village fires . . .

The aroma of curries from the servants' quarters . . .

The splish-splash of water and the squeaking of the handles of the *bhisti*'s buckets . . .

The crack of the polo ball and the muffled kettledrums of horses' hooves . . .

The gentle click of a cricket ball . . .

The plaintive rising scale of the brain-fever bird, heralding the heat . . .

The stealthy waft of incense from a temple . . .

The bazaar bouquet of sandalwood, roasted cumin, frying onions, jasmine . . .

Sweating leather and hookah smoke . . .

The clang of the coppersmith's hammer . . .

The burst of fresh dampness as the first monsoon raindrops hit the parched earth . . .

The geometric flowerbeds ablaze with cannas . . .

The regular cry of the hoopoe bird . . .

Vivid clashes of magenta, yellow, scarlet and pink of the zinnias echoing the swaying saris in the crowded streets of the Old Quarter . . .

The buzzing of flies . . .

The planned explosions of the flame-of-the-forest trees and purple jacarandas lining the broad Mall . . .

The newly washed white of the government buildings set back behind clipped green lawns and banks of bougainvillaea . . .

The howl and yip of a jackal serenading the sleepless on a hot night . . .

The remote bugles at dawn and dusk . . .

India Britannica.

1

THE SPICES
AND AROMATICS
OF INDIA

•

Or what it was all about

At the time of the foundation of the East India Company in England, the Elizabethan passion for spices and highly seasoned food matched that of the Indians under the Mogul emperors, although the two countries had little previous contact – except, perhaps, for the occasional wandering English eccentric. Maybe it was the Romans who had tantalized the early Britons with visions of sugar plums and the legend that every legionnaire marched with a leather pouch of spices strapped to his belt. Perhaps it was roving Celts up from Spain with spicy tales of foods and perfumes of Araby. Then again, it could have been the Normans with Gallic culinary arrogance and wicked hints of superior continental cuisines. Whoever started the mischief in the English kitchen, the gingering and peppering of every dish, together with the pinches of ground cloves, gratings of nutmegs and sprinklings of allspice, was enough to make a stranger believe that every wealthy Englishman grew spices at the bottom of his kitchen garden. Well, there *was* a spice garden, but it was at the other side of the world and the Dutch were tilling it for vast profit.

---

1. Vegetable market, Darjeeling, *c*.1940; 2. Gathering the harvest, 1916; 3. Arab traders, 1921; 4. Vegetable sellers, Sulon, near Ajanta; 5. Pepper vines, Sarawak; 6. Street view, Bombay; 7. Women preparing spices for chutney.

Because the English had convinced themselves that spice was a necessity of life, the enforced rationing of something so prized became an outrage and a challenge to their ingenuity. How dare the Dutch control something that England wanted! Hadn't they just whipped the Spanish for such temerity? So the English displayed their ingenuity and audacity in a bid for mastery over the Dutch and control of that far-off spice garden – the charter of the East India Company.

India, by contrast, had been a producer and consumer of spices for thousands of years. The ancient Phoenicians, Syrians, Egyptians, Greeks, Romans, Arabs and Chinese had battled the waves and winds of the Arabian Sea, or struggled across harsh deserts, marshes and mountains, to trade for spices with the dark-skinned people of India's Malabar Coast. Along that lush and verdant tropical shoreline and on the hills behind it, spices grew in profusion. The turmeric plant, with large, shining leaves obscuring its yellow flower spikes, and the pointed, bamboo-like shoots of ginger, pushed their fat rhizomes deep into the rich earth. Cardamom shrubs, towering over a man's head, thrust their spears of leaves and yellow-and-blue flowers towards the sun. Pepper vines tangled and wound their way around the jungle trees, brightening the dark foliage with clusters of orange-and-scarlet berries. Cinnamon trees from Sri Lanka and their Chinese cousins, cassia plants, peeled off their aromatic bark in curled quills. Nutmeg trees drooped under the weight of their luscious fruit, hanging like peaches from the smooth branches, each perfumed kernel swaddled in layers of lacy red mace. The nutmegs had emigrated to the Malabar Coast from the Moluccas, probably on the heaving decks of Arab *dhows*, in company with clove trees. The cloves now added their rosy pink flowers to the rainbows of light and their scent to the pot-pourri of spices. Seamen swore that a blind man could steer a vessel right to the coast when the breezes blew offshore.

As the traders took away, so they gave. The Arabs brought fenugreek to India – a small, pea-like plant that was mostly used for fodder until its pleasant-tasting seeds were discovered. They also introduced cumin and mustard. Coriander was contributed either by the Arabs or the Chinese. The saffron crocus came from the Mediterranean as well and transplanted healthily to the vales of Kashmir. Later still, the Portuguese introduced from the tropical islands of the Caribbean what was to become a dominant spice in Indian food, hot chilli peppers. These latecomers adapted like a weed to the Indian soil, flourishing under all but the most adverse conditions and stamping the cuisines with a hallmark of fire. The flow of traders continued. The Dutch, French and, finally, the English, followed the

Portuguese, like treasure hunters drawn to the lodestar of spices. The English prevailed. The trade was theirs.

Three hundred years ago, the English were a nation of farmers. The upper classes were gentlemen farmers – that is, they played at farming and somebody else did the work. The sons of the landed gentry were educated to the best of their parents' resources. The eldest sons administered their own, inherited lands; the younger sons became very good as administrators over someone else's terrain. India was the perfect test-bed for the latest theories of the English technocracy and, because of (and sometimes in spite of) these innovations in agriculture and irrigation, the precious resource of spices increased in size and value. After the British had finally left India, the spice production continued to expand until the subcontinent became one of the largest exporters of spice in the modern world. During the period between 1961 and 1970, India spiced the world with 150 million pounds of pepper and 100 million pounds of pungent chilli peppers. The exports of the sweeter spices were nearly as impressive: 32·5 million pounds of cloves; 30 million pounds of cinnamon and cassia; 22 million pounds of ginger; 12·5 million pounds of nutmeg and mace; 5·5 million pounds of cardamom. And all this after satisfying the spice requirements of a combined population (India and Pakistan) of nearly 840 million people! The mind and stomach reel.

During their long association with India, the British Raj must have sampled many of the diverse and fascinating local dishes, but the culinary legacy they took from India and thrust upon an unsuspecting world was ... curry powder! Many theories and vignettes arose round the terms

"curry" and "curry powder." The most likely explanation of curry is that it was an English corruption of the Tamil word for sauce, *karhi*. Subsequently it was used as a convenient catch-all for all Indian foods cooked in sauces – the Raj were inattentive to the finer points of Indian cooking, both with their palates and their selectivity.

As for curry powder (which some still think to be a single spice): probably an Englishman observed his kitchen *masalchi* grinding whole spices in preparation for his *tiffin*. Prior to his return to England, he undoubtedly ordered his cook to compose a mixture of those spices and to list the contents. The blend was then taken home and used in stews, subsequently termed curries. This scenario could have been repeated many times before the British finally quit the subcontinent. The unfortunate result was a "one-note," badly cooked dish, thickened with flour and sworn as the real thing by too many "old *kohais*." They tossed in further spoons of cayenne and insisted that the more the dish seared the mouth, the more authentic it was. By the late 1860s there were several versions of curry powder circulating in both England and America.

Charles Ranhofer, chef of Delmonico's from 1862 to 1894, says in his culinary tome, *The Epicurean*:

Curry, the best comes from India. An imitation curry is made of one ounce of coriander seeds, two ounces of cayenne, a quarter ounce of cardamom seeds, one ounce salt, two ounces of turmeric, one ounce ginger, half an ounce of mace and a third of an ounce of saffron.

The redoubtable Mrs Isabella Beeton, in *Beeton's Book of Household Management*, 1861, gives this:

Indian Curry Powder, founded on Dr Kitchener's Recipe. $\frac{1}{4}$ lb of coriander seed, $\frac{1}{4}$ lb of turmeric, 2 oz cinnamon seed, $\frac{1}{2}$ oz of cayenne, 1 oz of mustard, 1 oz of ground ginger, $\frac{1}{2}$ oz of allspice, 2 oz of fenugreek seed.
Mode. – Put all the ingredients in a cool oven, where they should remain one night; then pound them in a mortar, rub them through a sieve, and mix thoroughly together; keep the powder in a bottle, from which the air should be completely excluded.
Note. – We have given this recipe for curry powder, as some persons prefer to make it at home; but that purchased at any reputable shop is, generally speaking, far superior, and, taking all things into consideration, frequently more economical.

Unfortunately she was far from correct about the superiority of flavour of commercial curry powder over home-made, and "taking all things into consideration," while store-bought could be cheaper, the Victorians had not grasped the key to Indian cooking, namely that the spices are freshly ground and individually mixed according to the composition of the individual dish.

Even royal circles were not immune to the plague of "curry." When Charles Elmé Francatelli was chief cook and *maître d'hôtel* to Queen Victoria, he prepared curries for the royal household – a hopeful note. But the hope

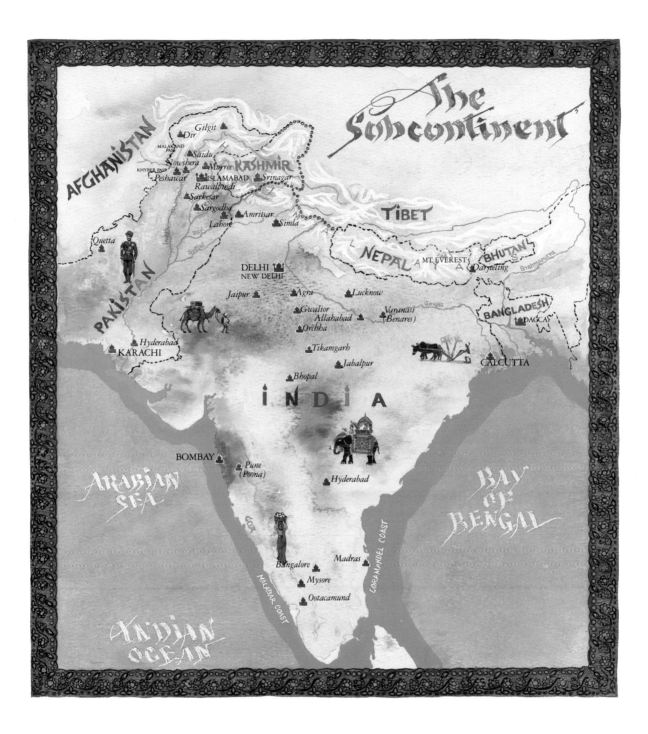

Jennifer Breman

The Frontier Express

Jennifer Brennan.   After Jackal Hunting

Jennifer Brennan

The camel Caravans from the Mountains.

Jennifer Brennan.

Bazaar – Punjab

Jennifer Brennan.

Murree Hills

Jenifer Brennan.   Tea in the Garden.

Jennifer Brennan.

The Residence at Night

founders in a bog of thickening as we look at an excerpt from his recipe for "Indian Curry Sauce" in his book, *The Modern Cook* (1846), for it uses:

... two tablespoons of Cook's or Bruce's meat curry paste, a tablespoon of curry powder, and as much *roux* or flour as may be required to thicken the quantity of sauce needed.

But Queen Victoria won in the end – as Empress of India it is appropriate that she should – for in 1887 an Indian, Abdul Karim, was appointed groom of the

chamber and cooked authentic Indian meals for the monarch, as well as teaching her a few words of Hindustani.

Two other transmogrified concoctions polluted the tables of the British: bottled mango chutney and vinegary pickles of a virulent yellow. The chutney was attributed mostly to the efforts of a Major Grey; the pickles were anonymous – a well-deserved fate. They were both probably concocted by a clever "box-*wallah*," or English merchant, who, knowing his countrymen's penchant for pickles and preserves, cooked up the creations and commercialized them. Whatever their origin, they obscured the many delicious Indian chutneys, both cooked and uncooked, which subtly counterbalance and complement true Indian food. Well, at least these badly transplanted hybrids boosted the Indian spice trade. But sadly, by their insistence on instant, bottled nostalgia, the British Raj bedevilled the reputation of Indian food in the eyes of the rest of the world for a long time.

Following is an account of the principal spices of India. These aromatics are the signatures of her many cuisines, as well as the substances that have shaped the history of the world and brightened its food. I have included strange trivia, odd historical facts, medicinal attributes and, for the curious, some of the nutritional values of these spices. Dip into the lore as you will, and the spices on your kitchen shelves will take on new dimensions.

Asafoetida (Ferula asafoetida) *Hing*

Asafoetida is relatively unknown to the West, so a nutritional breakdown of the spice is unavailable at this time. It is a member of the *Umbelliferae* family, which includes parsley and the wild cow parsley, and resembles the latter, although its stems are thick and ribbed like angelica. Asafoetida is 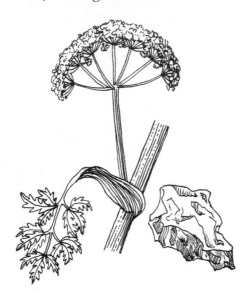 native to Afghanistan and eastern Iran but is now grown in India as well, since it is eaten mostly in southern India. The Afghans cook the whole plant as a vegetable, but its principal product is the sap or resin which is used as a spice. The stems are cut close to the root in early summer and the milky sap flows and sets into a reddish-brown resin which is sold in lumps or ground into a powder. Both the plant and its resin have a fetid smell, hence the name, but, oddly enough, when the spice is fried in oil, it mellows and produces a pleasant oniony taste. However, the bad name and smell linger on – in medieval times it was called "devil's dung."

The Romans were partial to asafoetida, calling it *laser, laseratum* or *laserpitium*. Apicius used asafoetida, in quantity. He wrote of dissolving it in lukewarm, moderately acid broth, or in a mixture of broth seasoned with pepper, parsley, dry mint, honey and vinegar. He also included the spice in a mixture of pepper, spikenard, ginger and parsley to flavour roast lamb. He reported that the Romans added *laser* to a sauce for boar, together with pepper, lovage, origany (*sic*), celery seed, cumin, fennel seed, rue, broth, wine and raisin sauce, and that it provided the necessary accent to a dish of snails. *Laser* was so expensive and prized that Apicius wrote a prescription for making it go further – much in the same way that we extend vanilla pods with sugar. He advised: "... to extend laser, put an ounce of it in a large glass vessel and add 20 pine nuts, taking them out and crushing them when the flavour is required."

In India today asafoetida-flavoured oil is used in vegetarian cuisines, particularly those of the Hindu brahmins and Jains, whose religions forbid them to eat onions. Since the cooked spice provides a taste of onion, it is never used in recipes together with onions. It is an ingredient in many lentil dishes and is also mixed in vegetarian kebabs by the Kashmiri brahmins.

Capsicum or chilli peppers (Capsicum frutescens) *Mirchi*

First, the composition of these hot little devils of the plant world:

> One teaspoon of dried, ground red peppers, or 1·8 grams in weight, contains 6 calories, 1·029 grams of carbohydrates, 0·22 grams of protein, 0·45 grams of fibre, and a total of 0·31 grams of fat. It contains no cholesterol. Additional benefits are a high 749 IU (International Units) of vitamin A, 0·006 milligrams of vitamin B_1, 0·017 milligrams of vitamin B_2, 0·157 milligrams of niacin, 1·38 milligrams of vitamin C. Peppers are rich in salts and minerals: 1 milligram of sodium, 5 milligrams of phosphorus, 0·36 milligrams of potassium, 3 milligrams of calcium, 0·14 milligrams of iron, 3 milligrams of magnesium and 0·05 milligrams of zinc.

Not a bad reward for searing one's palate!

Capsicums are prized for their pungency or bite; although this may seem strange to those accustomed to bland food. Paprika (*Capsicum annuum*) is the mild cousin of hot peppers and is valued mainly for the red tint it gives to dishes. The burning sensation of hot peppers is caused by a substance called *capsaicin* which is concentrated in the membranes and seeds. If you wish to tame the bite of chillies, merely remove those parts of the pepper. *Oleoresin* gives them their scarlet colour when they are fully ripe.

The capsicum grew naturally in Central and South America and in the West Indies, and the indigenous Indians knew all about it. The Olmecs raised chilli peppers before the time of the Toltecs, and the Mayans in Guatemala dosed themselves with chillies when they had stomach aches or intestinal upsets – a definite case of fighting fire with fire. The Aztecs apparently regarded the plant as one of their most important herbs, but its use in their rituals is not recorded.

From ancient times, chillies were reputed to have qualities as a stimulant, digestive, tonic and disinfectant. They were used as a remedy for chills, fevers and indigestion, and were also set alight to smoulder and fumigate rooms. Their property of raising the body temperature, thereby causing perspiration, was well known in the tropics and was finally discovered by Europeans, who spent much of their time sweating profusely and fanning themselves after a spicy lunch. As perspiration, in turn, lowers the body temperature, chillies were especially useful to break fevers. As a digestant, chillies stimulate the saliva and gastric juices – obvious to anyone who eats them. Their juices were even used in folk-medicine in a poultice as a counter-irritant for rheumatism and arthritis, but one would imagine that the resultant blisters would make the ailment preferable.

A Peter Martyr wrote in September 1493 that Christopher Columbus had brought to Spain "peppers more pungent than that from Caucasus." The first Spanish to try the new import probably thought the long sea voyage had affected Columbus's sanity. But those whose palates were accustomed to the sting of peppercorns, ginger or mustard must have welcomed the addition to their diet with alacrity, for by 1548 peppers were being cultivated in Europe and England. The Portuguese introduced them to India. Vasco de Gama may even have carried them as cargo as early as 1498, and by 1560 they were happily transplanted and flourishing in the subcontinent.

Today India is the world's largest exporter and within that country more of the hot little devils are consumed than any other spice. They are the sole ingredient of Indian chilli powder (*lal mirchi*), which is not to be confused with the *chile* powder mix of Mexico and the south-western United States.

Cardamom (Elettaria cardamomum) *Elaichi*

One teaspoon of ground cardamom is 2 grams in weight. It contains 6 calories, 1·37 grams of carbohydrates, 0·21 grams of protein, 0·23 grams of fibre, 0·13 grams of fat. It has no cholesterol. Vitamins and minerals include: 0·004 milligrams of vitamin B_1, 0·004 milligrams of vitamin B_2, 0·022 milligrams of niacin, a trace of sodium, 4 milligrams of phosphorus, 22 milligrams of potassium, 8 milligrams of calcium, 0·28 milligrams of iron, 5 milligrams of magnesium and 0·15 milligrams of zinc.

Cardamom belongs to the ginger family, although the plant is taller than most gingers, growing to a luxuriant eighteen feet in the hilly, evergreen forests of southern India and Sri Lanka. The leaves are large and spear-shaped and flower stems, as tall as a three-year-old child, grow from its base. The fruits – oval capsules divided into three cells with each containing as many as twenty black seeds – are harvested when they are nearly ripe and are then dried in the sun until they are a pale green colour. About 5 percent of the production is bleached white and fumed with hydrogen peroxide or burning sulphur, and 10 percent of the pods are shucked for their seeds. The seeds alone are expensive to buy because 10 pounds of pods yield only about 6 ounces of seeds. Cardamom oil is also extracted from the seeds for use in the perfume industry.

Indians love to use cardamom as a breath sweetener and the seeds are chewed after meals as a digestive. They are an ingredient of *paan*. But the first recorded use of the spice was in the fourth century BC in India, when Ayurvedic medicine recommended it as a cure for urinary

29

problems and also to aid weight loss. About the same time, the Greeks were trading in the spice.

Cardamom is extremely popular in the Arab world, where it is infused with green coffee beans to make an intensely aromatic brew. This coffee is drunk at all times of the day in Saudi Arabia – a somewhat puzzling oddity until one finds that the Arabs value it for cooling properties and believe it to be an aphrodisiac. Perhaps the Arab belief is just part of a successful Indian marketing campaign, for more than 2,500 tons of cardamom are exported annually!

Cinnamon (*True*) (Cinnamomum zeylanicum) *Dalchini Cassia* (Cinnamomum cassia) *Dalchini*

Cinnamon and cassia have approximately the same structure of nutrients, the difference being in the amount of essential oil (cinnamic aldehyde) that they contain. Cassia has more: 1 percent to about 4·5 percent, and cinnamon between 0·5 percent and 1·5 percent. One teaspoon of either spice (ground) weighs 2·3 grams, has 6 calories and no cholesterol. It also contains 1·84 grams of carbohydrates, 0·09 grams of protein, 0·56 grams of fibre, 0·07 grams of fat. Its vitamin content is: 6 IU of vitamin A, 0·002 milligrams of vitamin B_1, 0·003 milligrams of vitamin B_2, 0·03 milligrams of niacin, 0·65 milligrams of vitamin C, 1 milligram of sodium, 1 milligram of phosphorus, 11 milligrams of potassium, a high calcium content at 28 milligrams, 0·88 milligrams of iron, 1 milligram of magnesium, 0·5 milligrams of selenium and 0·05 milligrams of zinc.

Both cinnamon and cassia are among the oldest spices known to man, but there has always been confusion about which spice is which. True cinnamon has tightly rolled quills or tubes which are thinner than those of cassia. It is also sweeter and more delicate than cassia and is more expensive. The cinnamon tree itself is smaller than the cassia plant and is native to Sri Lanka, but also grows in the Seychelles, Madagascar, the West Indies and in southern India. Cassia, or false cinnamon, has looser, coarser quills and is stronger and more pungent. The ground spice is reddish-brown. Cassia originated in China and was taken from there to Burma, Vietnam, Malaysia, Indonesia and southern India.

To look at the historical confusion between the spices, Galen, a Greek physician and author in the second century AD, pointed out:

The finest cassia differs so little from the lowest-quality cinnamon, that the first may be substituted for the second, provided a double weight is used.

Medicinally, cinnamon is known as a stimulant and digestive, while cassia is merely used for indigestion. Herbal remedies indicate half a teaspoon of cinnamon to be brewed in a cup of water for an upset stomach, and many people also put the spice into hot milk when they have a cold or influenza. Cinnamon leaves are believed to have curative properties in India. Called *tejpat*, they are used to cure colic and diarrhoea. The leaves have value in the West also, as a constituent used in the perfume industry.

Apart from its use as a spice for apple pie and on sugared toast, cinnamon is also used in pickles, chutneys, sweets and beverages. In India it is an important ingredient in the sweet spice mix, *garam masala* (see page 293), and the quills are cooked together with other whole spices in rice pilaffs. As a child in India, I recollect that whenever I was snuffling with an incipient cold, the bottle of cinnamon-and-quinine mixture would be brought out and I would be soundly dosed with the dreadful-tasting potion. Appropriately enough, the bottle came sheathed in a funereal black, tubular carton. Perhaps that is why, to this day, any cinnamon-flavoured sweets remind me of it. (I'll take lemon drops, please.)

Cloves (Syzygium aromaticum *also* Eugenia caryophyllata) *Laung*

One teaspoon of ground cloves weighs 2·1 grams and contains 7 calories. It also has 1·29 grams of carbohydrates, 0·13 grams of protein, 0·2 of fibre, 0·42 grams of fat and no cholesterol. There are also 11 IU of vitamin A, 0·002 milligrams of vitamin B_1, 0·006 milligrams of vitamin B_2, 0·031 milligrams of niacin, 1·7 milligrams of vitamin C, 5 milligrams of sodium, 2 milligrams of phosphorus, 23 milligrams of potassium, 14 milligrams of calcium, 0·18 milligrams of iron, 6 milligrams of magnesium and 0·02 of zinc.

The Romans called the clove *clavus*, which means a "nail" in Latin. Drive tidy little rows of cloves into an orange to make a pomander and they look just like nail heads. In fact, many kinds of fruit may be studded with these scented tacks, for their aromas or flavours blend like a two-note chime. Clove trees originally grew in abundance in the Moluccas, or Spice Islands, and when they flowered the dark and sober trees were covered in tiny rose-red blossoms. During the monsoon season, when gales stripped the branches of their tight red buds, which withered on the earth beneath, the natives discovered that these immature flower "nails" had a wonderfully sweet and poignant aroma. Soon, nobody waited for the winds to blow. The buds were hand-picked and dried in the sun.

First the Portuguese and then the Dutch controlled the cultivation of cloves in the Spice Islands. The Dutch imposed discipline ruthlessly to protect their trade. They decreed that cloves could be grown only on the island of Amboina and that all clove trees on the other islands must be

destroyed. The Moluccans were greatly distressed because they planted a clove tree to mark the birth of a child and believed that if the tree died, so would the child.

In 1770 a daring Frenchman, Pierre Poivre (he of the "peck of pickled peppers"), smuggled out clove saplings to Mauritius, where they thrived. Recently, owing to a blight on the African trees, India has become a large producer and exporter.

Cloves are rich in essential oils, the principal being eugenol, which is used in soaps, perfumes, toothpastes, mouthwash, the manufacture of artificial vanilla and in medicines. Nowadays, half of the world's production of cloves is sent back to its birthplace, Indonesia, where it is used in the ubiquitous clove cigarettes. India incorporates cloves in *paan*, the after-dinner digestive, using a clove to fasten the leaf wrapper. Cloves are also used in rice pilaffs and in *garam masala*.

Coriander (Coriandrum sativum) *Dhania*

One teaspoon of ground coriander seed weighs 1·8 grams and contains 5 calories. It also contains 0·99 grams of carbohydrates, 0·22 grams of protein, 0·52 grams of fibre, 0·32 of total fat, no cholesterol. There are 0·004 milligrams of vitamin B_1, 0·005 milligrams of vitamin B_2, 0·038 milligrams of niacin, 1 milligram of sodium, 7 milligrams of phosphorus, 23 milligrams of potassium, 13 milligrams of calcium, 0·29 milligrams of iron, 6 milligrams of magnesium and 0·08 milligrams of zinc.

Coriander seed belongs to a small leafy plant, resembling the flat-leafed Italian parsley, which, in Mexico and the south-western United States, is

also known as *cilantro*. Another name for it is Chinese parsley. One of the oldest herbs known in cooking, it grows wild in south-eastern Europe and has been cultivated in India, China and Egypt for thousands of years. The leaves, stems and unripe seeds have a rather pungent smell and taste. The ripe seeds are globular and ribbed and, when dried to a light brown, are aromatic and sweet with a taste that is at once slightly bitter and pleasant.

The name coriander is from the Greek word *koris*, meaning "bug," probably referring to the smell of the leaves. In Europe it was called "dizzycorn," a reference to the effect on the animals that ate it, for the seeds are slightly narcotic if eaten in large quantities. They must also have had some reputation as an aphrodisiac for they were used in love potions of the Middle Ages and the herb was written about as such in *The Thousand and One Nights*. The French placed emphasis on the coriander seed's perfume for it was made into a liqueur called *eau-de-carnes* in Paris in the seventeenth century. This liquid was not only taken as a tonic but was also used as a perfumed toilet water.

In India, coriander is used medicinally as a tonic, a digestive, a cough medicine and also to give taste to and modify other medicinal mixtures. It is also one of the principal spices in seasoning mixtures of Indian meat and fish dishes.

Cumin (Cuminum cyminum) *Jeera*

One teaspoon of ground cumin weighs 2·1 grams and contains 8 calories. It measures out at 0·93 grams of carbohydrates, 0·37 grams of protein, 0·22 of fibre, 0·47 of total fat, no cholesterol. It has 27 IU of vitamin A, 0·013 milligrams of vitamin B_1, 0·007 milligrams of vitamin B_2, 0·096 of niacin, 0·16 of vitamin C, 4 milligrams of sodium, 10 milligrams of phosphorus, 38 milligrams of potassium, 20 milligrams of calcium, 1·39 milligrams of iron and 1 milligram of zinc.

To the ancient Greeks, the definition of a miser was someone who divided everything, even cumin seeds – no mean feat because of their tiny size. The Greeks crossed the Mediterranean to Egypt for their cumin, for the spice is indigenous to the Land of the Nile. Well-preserved seeds have been found in the tombs of the Pharaohs, and the spice is mentioned in the *Ebers Papyrus*. Pliny talks about cumin and it is written about in both the Old and New Testaments. In Isaiah 28:27 there is an admonition about appropriateness: "For the fitches are not threshed with a threshing instrument, neither is the cartwheel turned upon the cummin; but the fitches are beaten out with a staff and the cummin with a rod." Matthew recorded Jesus reproving the scribes and Pharisees in 23:23: "... for ye pay tithe of mint and anise and cummin" – while they neglected the virtues of justice, mercy and faith. The Celts of the first century BC, on the west coast of France, were fond of fish and baked it with cumin. The spice was extensively used in Norman monasteries around AD 719, and in medieval times, cumin was reputed to keep lovers faithful.

Cumin seeds are pale brown when dried, and sharp-ended, similar to fennel, aniseed and caraway. Their taste, however, is warm, slightly bitter and very identifiable. Cumin is used frequently in Moroccan food and enlivens the mixtures of ground beef and lamb which are rolled and deep-fried into the *kibbeh* of the Arab world. Mexicans spice their *chorizos* (sausages) and *chile* mixtures with it.

In India cumin is used equally as a medicine and as a spice for food. As a medicine it is employed as a stimulant and a remedy for internal upsets, stomach cramps and colic. In Indian cooking, the seed is used in meat dishes, particularly with ground beef and lamb. Cumin seeds are lightly roasted and then ground for some versions of *garam masala* spice mix. In coastal Goa freshly caught fish are spiced with a paste of ground cumin, chillies, turmeric, coconut and coriander before being fried. Indian cooking also uses black cumin, or *kali jeera* (*Bunium persicum*), the seeds of which are smaller and sweeter than cumin and also more expensive. Black cumin is mostly cultivated in Iran and in the Vale of Kashmir, but it grows wild in the Middle East.

Fennel (Foeniculum vulgare) *Saunf or Sonf*

One teaspoon of the ground seed weighs 2 grams and counts for 7 calories. Fennel rates 1·05 grams of carbohydrates, 0·32 grams of proteins, 0·31 grams of fibre and 0·3 of fat, with no cholesterol. It has 3 IU of vitamin A, 0·008 milligrams of vitamin B_1, 0·007 milligrams of vitamin B_2, 0·121 milligrams of niacin, 2 milligrams of sodium, 10 milligrams of potassium, a high 24 milligrams of calcium, 0·37 milligrams of iron, 8 milligrams of magnesium and 0·07 of zinc.

The Greeks used fennel for slimming and some herbalists still recommend it for weight loss. The Romans ate it as a vegetable, and as *finocchio* the plant is still very popular in Italian cuisine. It tastes a little like celery after cooking.

Both the plant and the seeds of fennel have large medicinal values. It is used as a stimulant and digestive, as well as for coughs, ear aches, toothaches, asthma and rheumatism. Fennel leaves were employed as a poultice for inflamed or swollen eyes and their juice for eyewash. The plant sounds like a cure-all and, indeed, Pliny recommended its use for twenty-two separate ailments. He also watched snakes eating fennel after sloughing their skins and thought that it was probably to restore their eyesight. Oddly enough, both the Hindus and the Chinese use fennel as an antidote for snakebite, so there seems to be a definite connection in folk medicine, although it is difficult to tell where. Indian women also take fennel to stimulate breast-feeding.

In the eleventh century, a large English household consumed eleven pounds of fennel seed a month. Fennel was mentioned by Chaucer in a fourteenth-century manuscript. "Fennel in potage and in mete is good to done whane yu schalt ete." In the Middle Ages the spice made unsavoury food palatable. It also played a part in magic, being hung above doorways to ward off the evil eye, and cow's udders were smeared with fennel paste so their milk would not be bewitched. King Edward I's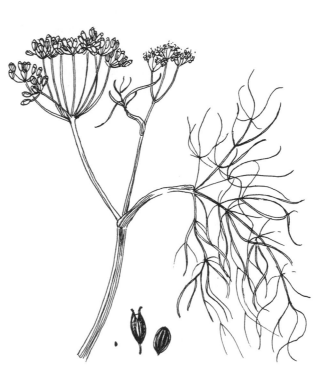
household accounts mentioned fennel and the Saxons termed it one of their nine sacred herbs, giving it the power to ward off disease. It is still used as an ingredient in "gripe water" to prevent colic in babies, and as a tisane for mild sedation to induce sleep, made by infusing a teaspoon of the seeds in a cup of boiling water.

With all its medicinal uses, one can expect that, no matter how it tasted, fennel would be eaten anyway. But both the herb and its seeds have a sweet, mellow taste, reminiscent of aniseed. Fennel complements rich meats such as pork and ham, and fish such as mackerel, salmon and trout. The leaves blend well with other salad greens and the seeds are used in breads and cakes. Dried fennel stalks make a good bed under roast chicken or lamb. Fennel seeds are rich in an essential oil called anethole, which flavours pickles, liqueurs, cough drops and medicines, and scents soaps, perfumes and perfumed products. In India fennel seed is incorporated into spice mixes and is often cooked with fish. The seeds are also dry-roasted and used in *paan*.

Fenugreek (Trigonella foenum-graecum) *Methi*

One teaspoon of fenugreek seed weighs 3·7 grams and contains 12 calories. It is rich in proteins, minerals and vitamins, and is often used as a diet supplement. Fenugreek contains 2·16 grams of carbohydrates, 0·85 grams of protein, 0·37 grams of fibre and 0·24 grams of total fat, but no cholesterol. It has 0·012 milligrams of vitamin B_1, 0·014 milligrams of vitamin B_2, 2·11 milligrams of folic acid, 0·061 milligrams of niacin, 0·11 milligrams of vitamin C, 2 milligrams of sodium, 11 milligrams of phosphorus, 28 milligrams of potassium, 6 milligrams of calcium, 1·24 milligrams of iron, 7 milligrams of magnesium and 0·09 milligrams of zinc.

The botanical name for fenugreek comes from the Latin generic *trigonella*, meaning little triangle, which refers to the shape of the flowers, and *foenum-graecum*, meaning Greek hay, because this member of the bean family was a fodder plant for the Greeks before the Romans assimilated it. Its uses are all-embracing for the seed is both a spice and a food. The plant is food for animals, and fenugreek has medicinal values as well.

The seeds, which swell and produce a sticky jelly after soaking, were used for mouth ulcers, blistered lips and stomach ailments. In India today, they are still taken as a digestive and to stimulate lactation in both humans and animals. They are also ground for a spice or sprouted for use in salads. The leaves are utilized in Indian cooking and are also dried as a herb.

Fenugreek is one of the oldest plants known to be cultivated. Papyri from the tombs in Egypt report its use as medicine and, interestingly, it was one of the compounds used in the Egyptian sacred incense, called *kuphi*, for fumigation and embalming. The origins of fenugreek lie somewhere in the eastern Mediterranean area. In the second century BC, the Romans ordered it to be used as a fodder for cattle, as did the Emperor Charlemagne in Europe, in AD 812.

In the Middle Ages, fenugreek was touted as a cure for baldness and continues to be used as a conditioning powder to produce a glossy coat on horses. In Indonesia it is incorporated in a hair tonic. There is a basis for this application, since fenugreek is rich in folic acid (far higher per comparable weight than dried yeast or liver), which is essential for the formation of red blood cells and nucleic acid. Recent studies indicate fenugreek seed to contain a steroidal substance called *diosgenin*, which is a starter in the partial synthesis of sex hormones and oral contraceptives. In spite of all this promise, the principal uses of the seed in the West are still in the production of chutney, commercial curry powders and as the main flavouring ingredient in artificial maple syrup.

Ginger (Zingiber officinale) *Adrak (Dried ginger is Sunt)*

One teaspoon of dried, ground ginger weighs 1·8 grams and has 6 calories. It also contains 1·27 grams of carbohydrates, 0·16 grams of protein, 0·11 grams of fibre, and 0·11 grams of total fat with no cholesterol. In addition, ginger has 3 IU of vitamin A, 0·001 milligrams of vitamin B_1, 0·003 milligrams of vitamin B_2, 0·093 milligrams of niacin, 1 milligram of sodium, 3 milligrams of phosphorus, 0·24 milligrams of potassium, 2 milligrams of calcium, 0·21 milligrams of iron, 0·3 milligrams of magnesium, 0·01 milligrams of copper and 0·08 milligrams of zinc. Fresh ginger root is very high in vitamin C.

Ginger grows wild in the damp forests of South-east Asia, but India is the world's largest producer. The fat, knobbed rhizome or swollen root of the edible ginger plant is sold fresh, dried, ground or preserved in most countries and is an essential part of oriental cookery. Ginger is the spice most closely associated with maintaining good health and keeping warm. It has been cultivated since ancient times by the Chinese and Indians and has long been used in medicine by both countries. It is frequently mentioned in Sanskrit literature, Chinese medical books, the Koran and the Talmud. Confucius wrote about the plant in his *Analects*.

The Latin name *Zingiber* comes from the Sanskrit *singabela*, or horn-shaped, because the roots slightly resemble deers' antlers. The Greek physician, Dioscorides, wrote in *De Materia Medica* that ginger was an antidote to poison, a digestive, and warmed the stomach.

In the seventeenth century a preparation of aromatic herbs, ginger wine and other ingredients, known as Doctor Steven's Water, was commonly found in most English medicine chests. Under the old theory of "look-alike" sympathetic medicine, both the Chinese and the English believed ginger to be an aphrodisiac. As such, it was much beloved of Henry VIII, who probably turned in desperation to anything that would bolster his flagging sexual powers and give him the heir to the throne he wanted so badly. Perhaps if ginger had worked the sexual miracles claimed for it, two unfortunate English queens would not have lost their heads.

Ginger roots were taken to the West Indies by the Spanish and were grown in, and then exported from, Jamaica, Santo Domingo and Barbados. Mrs Beeton told her readers that the best preserved ginger came from Jamaica, which, in a roundabout way, it probably did.

In China and South-east Asia, the young tubers of ginger, pinkish-yellow and delicate in taste, are dug up in the spring and pickled in brine or preserved in syrup, as well as being used in drinks, marinades and desserts. The roots left in the ground become fibrous, strong and pungent, with a brown, shiny skin. These roots of old ginger store well and are used throughout the remainder of the year. It was roots such as these that Chinese sailors carried on their ships, to be eaten as a protection against scurvy. The mature ginger root is also dried and packaged whole (it must be soaked in water before use), or ground into a powder.

Ginger is cooked with fish in both China and India, to remove the fishy smell. In Indian cookery the fresh ginger root is often ground together with garlic and onions into a wet paste, which is then fried before the dry, powdered spices are added. The resultant purée forms a delicious and aromatic base and thickener for many gravied meat, fish and vegetable dishes.

Nutmeg and Mace (Myristica fragrans) Jaiphal, Javriti

One teaspoon of ground nutmeg weighs 2·2 grams (ground mace, 1·7 grams), has 12 (8) calories, 1·08 (0·86) grams of carbohydrates, 0·13 (0·11) grams of protein, 0·09 (0·08) of fibre, 0·8 (0·55) grams of total fat and neither substance contains cholesterol. Nutmeg has 2 IU of vitamin A (mace has 14 IU), 0·008 (0·005) milligrams of vitamin B_1, 0·001 (0·008) milligrams of vitamin B_2, 0·029 (0·023) milligrams of niacin, a trace (1 milligram) of sodium, 5 (2) milligrams of phosphorus, 8 (8) milligrams of potassium, 4 (4) milligrams of calcium, 0·07 (0·24) milligrams of iron, 0·4 (3) milligrams of magnesium, 0·4 (0) milligrams of selenium and 0·05 (0·04) of zinc.

The fruit of the nutmeg tree looks like a large apricot or peach with a pale yellow skin, shading to deep yellow. Inside, the glossy brown seed or nutmeg is enclosed in a bright red fleshy-and-lacy wrapping, which is mace. The scarlet shade of the mace is testimony that the wrapper is very rich in

vitamin A, while the nutmeg contains very little. In harvesting, the nuts and their mace wrapping are removed from the fruit and the mace carefully eased from the nutmeg and stretched flat. Both are dried in the sun, whereupon the nutmeg kernel is then broken from its hard shell. During the drying process the mace becomes brittle, changes from red to a yellowish-brown and acquires its strong aroma.

Like the clove, the nutmeg tree is indigenous to the Moluccas in the East Indies, now Indonesia. It was known to Hindu doctors of antiquity, appearing in Vedic medical texts as a cure for headaches, fevers, intestinal upsets and halitosis. Arab traders first took the spice to the eastern Mediterranean and by the twelfth century it was familiar to Europe. Nutmeg was included in the spices burned to fumigate the smelly streets of Rome prior to the coronation of the Emperor Henry VI. In fourteenth-century England, mace was so costly that a pound was valued at three sheep.

The Portuguese were the first to capture the nutmeg and mace trade. At that time, mace was regarded as more valuable than nutmeg, for its taste was more pronounced. It remained costly until the seventeenth century, when the increased use of sugar obviated the need for strong spices. When the Dutch took the spice trade from the Portuguese, the administration in Holland was unaware that both spices came from the same source and, as mace was much in demand, ordered the planters to reduce the number of nutmeg trees and grow more mace trees!

The British took the Spice Islands away from the Dutch in 1796, spreading the cultivation of the trees to Penang and Singapore and, later, to the

West Indies. It is conceivable that the Spanish may have made an abortive attempt to secure some of the trade, for a jingle of that time went:

> I had a little nut tree and nothing would it bear,
> But a silver nutmeg and a golden pear;
> The King of Spain's daughter came to visit me,
> All for the sake of my little nut tree.

(It can be surmised that the "golden pear" referred to the colour and size of the nutmeg fruit.)

The nutmeg was recommended by Arab physicians for kidney and stomach disorders and was thought (again) to be an aphrodisiac. In the sixteenth and seventeenth centuries the Europeans employed the spices as a panacea but nowadays, apart from their role in food preparation, nutmeg and mace are used only for stomach upsets and nausea. Both spices are rich in essential oils, but the oils contain about 4 percent of myristicin, which is poisonous in large amounts and can cause fatty degeneration of the liver; they are used with caution. Commercially the spices are used in baked goods, confectionery, sauces and toothpastes, and give their aroma to cosmetics and perfumes.

Pepper (Piper nigrum) *Kali mirchi*

One teaspoon of ground peppercorns weighs 2·1 grams and contains 5 calories. It also has 1·36 grams of carbohydrates, 0·23 grams of protein, 0·28 grams of fibre, 0·07 of fat and no cholesterol. Vitamins and minerals measure: 4 IU of vitamin A, 0·002 milligrams of vitamin B_1, 0·005 milligrams of vitamin B_2, 0·024 milligrams of niacin, 1 milligram of sodium, 4 milligrams of phosphorus, 26 milligrams of potassium, 9 milligrams of calcium, 0·61 milligrams of iron, 4 milligrams of magnesium, 0·012 milligrams of copper, 0·02 milligrams of selenium and 0·03 milligrams of zinc.

Pepper, the world's most widely used spice, comes from the berries (peppercorns) of a climbing, evergreen vine which is indigenous to the Malabar Coast of south-west India. Also named as peppers are: the capsicum or chilli pepper, Jamaican pepper or allspice, melegueta pepper or "grains of paradise" from West Africa, cubeb pepper, the "long peppers" of South-east Asia and the Szechwan pepper (the dried flower buds from a tree in China). These other substitutes for true pepper have caused much confusion

over the years, since all produce an aromatic, stinging or hot taste and fulfil a similar function in seasoning. Indeed, there is some evidence that the "long peppers" of South-east Asia (pendant strings of berries) were known to the ancient Mediterranean world long before our present-day pepper. But the *Piper nigrum* vine is now considered the only true pepper.

The vine produces black, white and green peppercorns. Black peppercorns are the whole berries which are picked unripe and left in the sun until the skins are black and dried up. Black peppercorns have a beautiful perfumed aroma and taste, as well as the characteristic pungency and bite of pepper. White peppercorns are the ripe berries from the vine, which are picked when the skins have turned scarlet. They are then soaked and rubbed to remove the skins. The inner seeds are dried in the sun until they are bleached white. White pepper is used in pale-coloured dishes where specks of black would spoil the effect, or where a milder taste is desired. Green peppercorns are the whole, immature berries that are picked and then pickled in brine or freeze-dried while still fresh. They have neither the intensity nor the pungency of black or white peppercorns.

While we are looking at the descriptions of varieties of peppercorns currently available, there are also the pink peppercorns which have been in recent vogue. They are the berries of a tree grown in Mauritius and the Reunion Islands by the French, and are mostly available in freeze-dried form. They are similar in size and shape to true pepper and are very aromatic, but the seed inside is smaller and they lack the pungency of *Piper nigrum*.

Of the varieties of true pepper on the market, the "Telicherry" peppercorn of Malabar is considered the finest, followed by "Malabar" pepper. Peppercorns also come from Lampong in Sumatra, Muntok in Banka, Indonesia (mostly white pepper), Sarawak in Borneo, Ponape in the Pacific, and from Brazil.

The search for pepper was really the main impetus that led to the discovery of the East and West Indies and the New World, so it can truly be termed a spice that altered the history of the world.

Medically, pepper has value as a stimulant and digestive and has been used frequently as a cure for cholera, diarrhoea and arthritis, but its use as medicine is completely overshadowed by its usefulness and popularity as a universal seasoning.

Saffron (Crocus sativus) *Kesar*

One teaspoon of saffron weighs 7 grams but has only 2 calories. It contains 0·46 grams of carbohydrates, 0·08 grams of protein, 0·03 grams of fibre and 0·04 grams of fat. No cholesterol. Strangely, it is not a source of vitamins except a little vitamin B_2 or riboflavin, but it does contain 1 milligram of sodium, 2 milligrams of phosphorus, 12 milligrams of potassium, 1 milligram of calcium and 0·08 milligrams of iron.

Saffron is indigenous to southern Europe and to the eastern Mediterranean countries. Indeed, its name derives from the Arabic *za'faran*, meaning yellow. The dried stigmas, or female part of the saffron crocus, constitute the spice but as some 70 to 80,000 flowers, yielding about 210,000 stigmas, make up 1 pound of saffron – and each stigma must be hand-picked – it is the world's most costly spice. Spanish saffron from the

45

Valencia area is considered the finest, although Greece, Iran and Kashmir also produce the spice. Saffron has traditionally been used as a dye, a spice and a medicine. The bright orange comes from a pigment called *crocin*, which is extremely concentrated, with an ability to tint up to 150,000 times its volume of water. In ancient times, women used saffron to make hair turn fairer and it is still employed in India for printing caste marks on the forehead.

The Romans bathed in saffron-tinted water and used saffron-scented oils for massage. They undoubtedly introduced the plant to England and for a long time Saffron Walden in Essex was the heart of a saffron-growing industry.

Because saffron has always been costly, it was frequently adulterated with other substances. Pliny warned about the dangers of adulteration and, during the Middle Ages, in Germany, tamperers of the spice were burnt alive. Even today there are no bargains in saffron. If it is cheap to buy, it is not saffron, for it holds its price even in the countries that produce it.

Medical folklore attributes miraculous cures to saffron. John Gerard wrote in *The Herbal*, around 1597: "For those at death's doore and almost past breathing, saffron bringeth breath again." A certain J. F. Hertodt of Germany so loved the spice that in 1670 he wrote a weighty tome about it, called *Crocologia*, in which he vowed saffron would cure all from toothache to the plague. More reliably, saffron has been used as a digestive and stimulant. It is still used in Asia as a tonic. But saffron's chief use today is in tinting and flavouring food. Subtlety is the key to its use because, apart from the expense, too liberal a hand with the spice results in food tasting as if a medicine cabinet has been emptied over it.

Turmeric (Curcuma Longa) *Huldi*

One teaspoon of dried, ground turmeric weighs 2·2 grams and yields 8 calories. It also contains 1·43 grams of carbohydrates, 0·17 grams of protein, 0·15 grams of fibre, 0·22 grams of fat and no cholesterol. Vitamins and minerals in 1 teaspoon measure: 0·003 milligrams of vitamin B_1, 0·005 milligrams of vitamin B_2, 0·113 milligrams of niacin, 0·57 milligrams of vitamin C, 1 milligram of sodium, 6 milligrams of phosphorus, a high 56 milligrams of potassium, 4 milligrams of calcium, 0·91 milligrams of iron, 4 milligrams of magnesium and 1 milligram of zinc.

Since time immemorial, turmeric has been grown in China, India, Java and Peru. The plant, a member of the ginger family, has rhizomes or underground stems which look like fat fingers. Under their brown skin they are bright orange. Like ginger, the plant is propagated from these fingers. The mature rhizomes are dug up, boiled and then peeled, after which they are dried and ground to a yellow powder. The yellow pigment is called *curcumin* and since ancient times has been employed as a dye for cloth in Asia, particularly for the yellow robes of Buddhist monks. The plant is also used in medicine and cosmetics, but its chief use is culinary. In truth, turmeric was traditionally used as a cheaper substitute for saffron in food, although the taste is very different — warm and pleasant, with a hint of bitterness. It is still used in this capacity in India. In South-east Asia turmeric plays a part in many folk rituals and customs. The Indonesians use turmeric water like a cologne. The spice also dyes the arms of the bride and bridegroom at a traditional wedding, and yellow rice is also part of the ritual. The Malays believe turmeric offers protection against evil spirits and rub it on the stomachs of women who have given birth and on the umbilical cord of the baby. In India it is used by women to discourage facial hair.

Medicinally, turmeric is believed to be good for the liver and digestion. Possibly this originated as "sympathetic" medicine for the yellow, jaundiced tinge that liver ailments give to the skin. Externally, the Indians make turmeric into an ointment for skin sores and take it internally as a treatment for ulcers. It is also drunk as a cold cure, being dissolved in hot milk, sweetened with sugar.

2

KIPPERS AND KEDGEREE
FOR BURRA HAZRI

•

Breakfasts large and small

In the hush of the cool, dim dawn when the shades begin to retreat
And the jackal bolts to his lair at the sound of your horse's feet;
When the great kite preens his wings and calls to his mate in the tree
And the lilac opens her buds ere the sun shall be up to see;
When the trailing rosebush thrills with the sparrow's pent-up strife,
Oh! a ride in an Indian dawn, there's no such pleasure in life.

  Rudyard Kipling, "A Morning Ride, October–November 1882," *Early Verse*

Those early-morning rides, when the air was still and cool and the plains
stretched to the horizon in blue and dun infinity, were the chief pleasure
and recreation of the British Raj. A hard canter across the *maidan*; the
horse's breath in regular snorts; the chink of the harness; the smell of the
smoke from the morning cooking-fires in the village; the clear notes of the
reveille bugle from the distant parade ground; the sleepy chatter of the
sparrows; the soft greetings from the workers on their way to the fields; a
sense of all being well in God's world – these were the small things that
restored a feeling of calm and order into the souls of overworked civil
administrators and hard-pressed military alike. And if you had partied too
hard the night before, the ride blew away the sticky cobwebs of sleep and

---

1. Crawford market, Bombay; 2. Hunting group, 1890; 3. The lawn, Nowshera, 1936; 4. Khyber
caravan at the entrance to the Khyber Pass; 5. Berenice ready for tennis, Sargodha, 1927; 6. Chicken
man on the road, Kashmir; 7. Misty dawn at Ootacamund; 8. The Remount Depot, Sargodha; 9.
At the Afghanistan border.

dispelled the incipient hangover, and you returned to the house refreshed and ravenous for breakfast.

The British in India worked hard and played hard and rising before dawn was customary and sensible in a country where the sun already baked the earth and grilled its inhabitants before ten o'clock in the morning.

Chota hazri – a pot of tea, milk and sugar, brought to your bedroom on a tray complete with lace-edged traycloth by a sleepy bearer long before dawn – started the day. Yule and Burnell record in *Hobson-Jobson* that, back in 1866, Waring wrote of that "break fast": "It is commonly known in India by the Hindustani name of *chota-hazri* and in our English colonies as 'Early Tea' ..."

At 7 a.m. you rode, and rode hard, so by the time the exercise was over and everyone had assembled in the dining-room or on the veranda, duly bathed and changed, appetites had achieved a fine edge. The meagre continental breakfast of today would have been greeted with a snort of contempt. Something satisfyingly solid was needed to fortify the head of the household before he departed for the office or the parade ground, and for the ladies of the family before they embarked on several energetic games of tennis or a long trip to the native bazaar, or even a prolonged session of household accounts with the *khansamer* and a protracted negotiation with the local tailor, the *durzi*.

Of course, breakfasts in the last thirty years of the British tenure in India were not nearly as substantial as those of the preceding century. In 1856 a typical breakfast at Government House in Calcutta included fish, meat, eggs, fresh fruit, dessert and hot chocolate to drink. But Charlotte Canning, the wife of the governor-general at that time, would have developed quite an appetite by breakfast time, as she began her daily schedule well before daybreak, often making official visits to schools and orphanages as well as her regular sketching expeditions and rides before breakfast.

Steel and Gardiner made a plea for more refined breakfasts in their comprehensive compendium on the British household and cuisine in India, *The Complete Indian Housekeeper and Cook*, written in 1893:

Breakfasts in India are for the most part horrible meals, being hybrids between the English and French fashions. Then the ordinary Indian cook has not an idea for breakfast beyond chops, steaks, fried fish, and quail; a *menu* rendered still less inviting by the poor quality of both fish and meat. Tea made and poured out by a *khitmutgar* [*sic*] at a side table, toast and butter coming when the meal is half finished, and the laying of the table for lunch while the breakfast-eaters are still seated, combine to make new-comers open their eyes at Indian barbarities.

Of course, at Government House, a succession of formidable first ladies, who trained their servants with iron authority, ensured that breakfast at the highest levels operated smoothly. In John Bradley's *Lady Curzon's India*, Lady Curzon wrote of breakfast at Government House in Barrackpore, outside Calcutta, 1900:

... quite a different lot wait on you at breakfast and there is a waiter for every person at table. The result is that the waiting is *admirably* done – and they all glide about in red livery & bare feet ...

But later, on an official visit to the Nizam of Hyderabad, there was a chaotic and somewhat bizarre breakfast given for the governor and his lady at the minister's house. Lady Curzon wrote:

One hundred and forty people sat down, as all the English residents in Hyderabad and Secunderabad had been asked. We began with Mulligatawny soup, had fourteen courses, and ended with ice-cream. The Nizam ate it all – I mean his share – but George and I wanted tea and bacon and eggs!

In the midst of all that bounty you hear Lady Curzon's plea for the simplicity of bacon and eggs. By the turn of the century, the British predilection for hearty breakfasts of between ten and twenty courses was already on the wane.

While our family's breakfasts were simple, we always had freshly made yoghurt (*dhai*) on the table. Poured into little pottery containers before it set, it was silky and deliciously tangy under its wrinkled crust of cream. I also remember piles of hot *chapattis*, wrapped in a linen cloth, to be eaten with freshly churned butter and whisky marmalade. White damask or linen cloths always covered our table and the china was English – white, with a navy-blue band edged with gold. It's funny how the small details stick in the memory across the years.

The normal routine of breakfast was broken on weekends during the cold weather (November to March) on the plains. That was the hunting season. *Chota hazri*, augmented by a few thin fingers of buttered toast, began the day well before dawn, and nothing else was eaten until the large, traditional hunt breakfast after the event.

There were well-known hunts and meets all over India: Delhi, Calcutta, Ootacamund. My family hunted with the Peshawar Vale Hunt (starring the viceroy when he visited the area), and in Lahore as well as Sargodha.

In Sargodha the Remount Depot organized the hunt and supplied the horses, usually spirited young four-year-olds. The master of the hunt was the Remount Officer, who was also head of the depot and an army colonel. Between ten and twenty riders would make up the hunt and the *sowars* would join in the sport because they had trained the horses. Women were included in the sport, and my mother and my aunt, both accomplished and spirited horsewomen – referred to as "those Whitburn sisters!" – hunted frequently, together with the other unmarried daughters of the depot and a sprinkling of married women.

Sometimes there were visiting females. Iris Portal, an acquaintance of our family, wrote of the "Fishing Fleet females":

They rode anything with four legs and fell into every river and had to be pulled out and, generally speaking, added an enormous amount of sparkle to our lives.

The hunt began at 5 a.m. and lasted for four or five hours. What classic style was lost owing to local circumstances was certainly made up for by enthusiasm. Jackals, familiarly termed "jack," were hunted instead of foxes, but the hounds were English, imported or bred from English stock. They would "put up" a jackal and if that one were lost they would sniff out another. The night dew, which held the scent of the jackal, only lay on the ground in the cool, dark pre-dawn. So the scent went off the ground as soon as the sun was up and radiating heat. This brought the hunt to an abrupt end if there was no prior kill.

Instead of the rolling, green fields of England, the territory of the hunt consisted of desert scrub and fields of wheat and sugar-cane. The boundaries of the fields were marked by deep irrigation ditches, called *nullahs*, bordered by paths. The riders always tried to keep to the perimeters of the fields but, when they became infected by the excitement of the chase, they crashed right through the middle. However, the farmers were compensated handsomely for the damage.

At the close of the season, when the encroaching hot weather left no dew upon the ground, the die-hard

members of the depot would organize a "drag" instead. A *sowar* would ride out ahead of the pack, trailing behind his horse a canvas bag rubbed with animal grease, bouncing on the end of a rope. The scent attracted the hounds. No "kill' and no "brush" for the victor, but the hunt breakfast, hearty and traditional, still awaited the riders.

These breakfasts were frequently laid out on trestle tables on the lawns of the club and attended by bearers and *khitmagars* in spanking white uniforms. The boards groaned under hams, mixed grills, eggs, tumbled fish kedgerees, platters of tropical fruits, breads and, of course, the traditional hunt cup to sluice away the disappointments of the unlucky riders and toast the victorious. Starring dishes from some of those celebratory breakfasts follow in this chapter, together with more modest repasts for quieter *hazris*.

Devilled eggs

•

Devils – the culinary variety – date well back into the eighteenth century of British eating. To try for a definition of these piquant dishes is a difficult task, for their ingredients were varied and up to the whim of the cook. To my mind, they are "twice-spiced" concoctions. The basic meat, fish or eggs (often leftovers) were cooked with proprietary sauces or chutneys and often mustard for good measure, in addition to liberal sprinklings of cayenne, black pepper, or other spices that looked promising or came first to hand groping in the spice cabinet. So spices were already part of the bottled ingredients that went into the *mélange*, as well as being added anew while the dark-hued, aromatic mixture was bubbling on the stove.

This conspicuous consumption of spices catered to the Georgian, Victorian and Edwardian gentry's lust for the piquant and tangy (and they possessed the deep pockets that could afford the indulgence), but there was also a practical side. It seems that "devils" were most efficient in helping a delicate constitution recover from the after-effects of an over-indulgence of drink. In short, they were splendid for hangovers.

And how those British in India drank! Their tippling was well documented. Harriet Tytler (*An Englishwoman in India*, ed. Anthony Sattin) wrote in the 1830s of the first-class passengers to India on the P & O liners:

Wine of the very best was provided *ad lib.* at meals. There was such a waste in everything. I have seen stewards pouring good whisky into blacking bottles to clean the boots with. Champagne flowed like water on Thursdays and Sundays at dinner.

In Ann Morrow's *Highness: the Maharajas of India*, the Maharawal of Dungarpur remarked: "When there was a viceregal ball or banquet we used to get roaring tight."

From the same book we hear Kate Strachey, wife of Sir John, Lieutenant-Governor of Allahabad, commenting disapprovingly on the alcoholic consumption of the Prince of Wales during his visit to India: "... between seventy and eighty dozen of champagne in a fortnight and fourteen dozen of soda water a day."

But not everyone had the robust constitution of the British. Lord Curzon informed his wife (*Lady Curzon's India*, ed. John Bradley):

The Rana of Dholpur is dying at Pelitis Villa at Mashobra. I expect he will die tonight – acute pneumonia following upon hard drinking: one of the more drastic consequences of English tastes, habits and sports upon an undisciplined native mind.

Perhaps the unfortunate Rana had not discovered the recuperative powers of a "devil" as part of a necessary "morning-after" breakfast. Here is one of those that helped the British Raj "pull themselves together."

Serves 4

4 eggs, hard-boiled and shelled	half a small onion, peeled and finely chopped
1 tablespoon/$\frac{1}{2}$ oz butter	1 teaspoon powdered mustard
$\frac{1}{3}$ teaspoon freshly ground black pepper	1 tablespoon Worcestershire sauce
$\frac{1}{2}$ teaspoon salt	4 fl oz chicken stock
$\frac{1}{2}$ teaspoon cayenne	

1 Cut the eggs in half round their equator; then slice a little off each end so they stand up nicely.

2 Slip the yolks out into a bowl and mash them with half the butter, all of the pepper, half the salt and all of the cayenne. Fill the eggs with the yolk paste – pipe it if you like – and stand them in a heated dish.

3 Heat the remaining butter in a small pan over medium heat. Fry the

onion, stirring, until it is soft and slightly darkened, then add the remaining ingredients, including the reserved salt.

4   Stir the sauce for 3 minutes and pour it over the eggs. Bring the dish directly to the table.

Notes: Some retired Indian Army colonels liked to add a tablespoon of sieved, sweet mango chutney to the sauce while it was hot. Reprobate "box *wallahs*" substituted ½ teaspoon of curry powder for the cayenne, under the principle of "the more the merrier," but I think the devil stands on its own regenerative merits without further complications.

Spiced scramble in fried-bread cups

•

I have been passionate about fried bread ever since I was a child. Perhaps lustful is a better word. Those crisp, golden slices, redolent of the bacon drippings in which they have been fried, are the perfect counterpoint to the creaminess of scrambled eggs. Toast collapses into a soggy mattress if it is left under them for more than thirty seconds.

In celebration of one of Britain's least-known culinary back-room joys, here is an elegant modification on the traditional platters of scrambled eggs, garnished with snippets of fried bread, which were served at formal breakfasts in both India and England.

Serves 6

vegetable oil for deep-frying, plus 4 oz bacon drippings

6 slices day-old white bread, crusts removed

12 eggs

4 fl oz cream

½ teaspoon salt

1 level teaspoon curry powder

¼ teaspoon ground cardamom

2 tablespoons/1 oz unsalted butter

3 tablespoons finely chopped chives

4 oz smoked salmon, cut into 1-inch squares

2 oz salmon roe

parsley for garnish

1   Heat the oil and bacon drippings in a large saucepan or deep-fryer to just over 350°F (180°C).

2   Arrange a slice of bread in a small (approximately 4-inch), handled mesh strainer and force it down with the back of a ladle to form a cup shape.

3   When the oil has stabilized at temperature, immerse the strainer/bread/ladle arrangement in the oil, keeping slight pressure on the ladle against the strainer. Fry the bread until it is golden-brown and crisp, about 2 minutes.

4   Invert the contents of the strainer on to paper towels to drain and, while the bread is still warm and pliable, indent the curvature of its base so that the cup will sit upright when turned over and filled.

5   Repeat the process (Steps 2, 3 and 4) with all 6 slices and keep them warm in a low oven for use in Step 8.

6   Break the eggs into a large mixing bowl. Add the cream, salt, curry powder and cardamom. Beat them with a wire whisk until they are well blended and slightly frothy.

7   Place a non-stick saucepan over medium-low heat and melt the butter. Pour in the eggs and cook the mixture, stirring patiently with a wooden spoon, until it thickens into a creamy, custard-like consistency. Continue to stir, lifting the pan off the heat from time to time and scraping the sides and bottom until the eggs coagulate into large, soft, creamy curds. At this point, remove the pan from the heat and stir in the chives.

8   Remove the fried-bread cups from the oven and layer a few pieces of smoked salmon into the bottom of each. Ladle the eggs in to fill each cup. Spoon 1 teaspoon of salmon roe on to the middle of each, garnish with parsley and serve immediately.

Notes: You may serve the cups all at once on a bed of parsley on a large platter, or individually, garnished with sprigs of parsley. An interesting substitute for the salmon roe would be an equivalent amount of braised asparagus tips.

Drappit eggs with herbs

•

In some ways, the Scots were the backbone of the British in India. What is it about Scotland that compels its sons to wander the far corners of the earth? Perhaps a desire to warm bones chilled by the damp mists of the Highlands, or maybe a ceaseless urge towards adventure. The engineers in the grimy boiler rooms of the smoky rust-buckets of ships that ploughed through the Indian Ocean; the hardy foot-soldiers who scrambled over the barren rocks of the North-west Frontier; the doctors who ministered to shattered bodies in the erratic glare of kerosene lanterns behind the lines – so many of them were phlegmatic Scotsmen.

This recipe dates from the eighteenth or nineteenth century, probably written down by a homesick Scottish lass who set up housekeeping in a bare bungalow in the civil lines of an Indian garrison town.

Incidentally, "drappit" eggs are poached eggs, for they are "drapped" into the water, and "herbs" is a broad term for all manner of greens.

Serves 6

1 lb spinach, well washed	$\frac{1}{2}$ teaspoon ground white pepper
1 head of iceberg lettuce, washed and separated into leaves	$\frac{1}{2}$ teaspoon salt
3 tablespoons/1$\frac{1}{2}$ oz unsalted butter	1 teaspoon grated nutmeg
2 tablespoons chopped fresh chervil (optional)	$\frac{1}{4}$ teaspoon *garam masala* (sweet spice mix, p. 293)
8 sprigs of parsley, chopped	4 fl oz cream
	vinegar
	6 eggs

1   Wilt the spinach and lettuce for 2 minutes in a large sieve over a pan of boiling water. Drain and chop finely.

2   Melt the butter in a large saucepan over moderate heat and toss the greens, adding the chervil and parsley. Season with the salt, pepper, nutmeg and *garam masala*. Pour in the cream and stir well. Scrape the mixture into a heated oven-proof dish and keep it warm in a low oven.

3   Acidulate some water with a teaspoon or so of vinegar and poach the

eggs. When the eggs are firm, drain them and trim the whites into circles. Make 6 indentations in the greens and slide an egg into each. Brown for a minute under strong heat and serve at once.

Notes: Drappit eggs can be garnished with a *coulis* of peeled, seeded and chopped tomatoes to give good contrast.

Devilled shrimp

•

Here is another of those spicy "devils," this one from the oven rather than the stove top. The recipe is an adaptation from one in an old recipe book from India, published in 1894. Called the *Memsahib's Book of Cookery*, the author, male or female, hides behind the initials "A. C. S." – a common practice in the days before writers of cookbooks shed their anonymity and owned up to any cookery blunders they may have initiated!

There is an appealing simplicity to the dish and, while it was not intended for a *burra hazri*, it could be the perfect component of a brunch.

Serves 4

1 lb after shelling, cleaned shrimp	½ teaspoon cayenne
2 tablespoons/1 oz unsalted butter, melted	½ teaspoon anchovy paste
the juice of 1 lemon or lime	3 eggs, beaten
1 tablespoon Worcestershire sauce	3 slices of day-old bread, crusts removed, finely crumbled

1　Preheat the oven to 450°F (230°C, Gas Mark 8).
2　Mix all the ingredients (except the breadcrumbs) in a large bowl; then transfer to a greased, shallow baking dish. Sprinkle the breadcrumbs over the top.
3　Bake until the mixture puffs up and the crumb topping is a light golden-brown. Serve immediately.

Notes: For a more extravagant dish, substitute lobster or crabmeat for the shrimp. If you want to be economical, use a firm white fish, such as haddock or cod, cooking it briefly first and breaking it into small chunks. Try blanched almond halves over the top before baking, instead of breadcrumbs, and garnish with fried sprigs of parsley.

Indian masala omelette

•

By the by, an omelette is never cooked to such perfection anywhere as by an Indian cook.

Harriet Tytler, *An Englishwoman in India*, ed. Anthony Sattin

My mother owns a venerable cookbook. It is not one of your weighty, self-important tomes, but a small, slim volume called *Indian Dishes for English Tables*. The author hides behind the pen name of "*Ketab*," originating from an Indian term which really has to do with household accounts, and the cover bears an illustration of a white-bearded *khitmagar* with turban and cummerbund, bearing a tray with whisky, water and glasses for the nightly ritual of a *chota peg*. As a child I thought the ancient bearer was named Ketab and that he was, surprisingly, the author. Illumination came gradually.

This masala (spiced) omelette, the stuff of which good breakfasts are made, is from that book.

Serves 3

6 eggs, separated
½ teaspoon salt
2 tablespoons finely
  chopped onion
1 small green chilli, finely
  chopped
1 tablespoon finely
  chopped parsley

½ teaspoon good brand
  curry powder
1 tablespoon *ghee*
  (clarified butter)
parsley sprigs for garnish

1   Beat the egg whites to a very firm snow.
2   Beat the yokes in a basin, together with the salt, onion, chilli, parsley and curry seasoning, until the mixture lightens.

3 Fold the yolk mixture smoothly into the whites.

4 Melt the *ghee* in an omelette pan over moderate heat. Pour a third of the mixture into the pan but do not stir it. Reduce the heat slightly and let the omelette set; then fold it over with a broad-bladed knife or spatula and slip it on to a heated dish. Repeat for the other 2 omelettes. Garnish with parsley and serve immediately.

Notes: To save time, chop the onion, chilli and parsley simultaneously – they are ending up in the same bed. For a more substantial dish you may incorporate, as a filling, a little finely chopped cold meat, or a leftover fish curry.

Bacon and coriander pancakes

•

It was a brave *khansamer* who first used coriander as a chopped herb in these pancakes. Possibly, he could find no parsley so substituted the closest-looking herb. I can picture the scene at the breakfast table:

THE MEMSAHIB: "I must ask the cook where he bought this parsley. It tastes quite strange."

THE SAHIB (buried behind *The Times of India*): "Yes, m'dear."

THE MEMSAHIB: "Charles! Did you hear what I said?"

THE SAHIB: "Hrmmph! Yes, m'dear, quite."

THE MEMSAHIB: "Maybe it's the bacon; but it's tinned, so it should be all right. Unlike these local pigs. You never know how they've been raised."

THE SAHIB (finally putting down the paper as something catches his attention): "Did you say pig, m'dear? Old Carruthers has asked me to go pig-sticking on Wednesday. I say, old dear, these are frightfully good pancakes!"

THE MEMSAHIB: (sighs).

Serves 8

12 slices bacon	2 tablespoons finely
4 oz/1 scant cup flour	chopped coriander
2 eggs, beaten	leaves
8 fl oz milk	4 oz mango chutney

1   Dice the bacon finely and set it aside.

2   Sift the flour into a bowl and make a well in the middle. Stir in the eggs and half the milk and beat until the batter is smooth. Gradually beat in the remaining milk; then stir in the chopped coriander.

3   Fry a heaped tablespoon of bacon in a small pan until it is crisp. Pour enough batter for one pancake over the bacon and fry until the underside is light brown. Turn it over and fry the other side. Turn the pancake out on to a clean tea towel and fold the towel over it to keep it warm.

4   Repeat Step 3 until all the pancakes are cooked.

5   Spoon the mango chutney into a small saucepan, finely chopping any pieces of mango. Thin the chutney slightly with a tablespoon of water. Warm and use as a sauce.

6   Roll up the pancakes and place them on a heated platter. Drizzle the mango chutney across the top and keep the dish in a very low oven until breakfast is served.

Notes: If you are not serving eggs in any other style at breakfast, these pancakes are delicious rolled up around soft scrambled eggs, sprinkled lightly with a little curry powder.

A kedgeree by many other a name . . .

Kedgeree or kitcherie is an old Anglo-Indian dish. The word derives from the Hindi *khichri* which, in turn, stems from the Sanskrit *k'ysara*. The growth of the name is as lengthy as the transitions through which the venerable dish has gone. Originally, *khichri* was a mess of rice cooked with butter and lentils, sometimes with a little spice added to it and topped with shredded fried onions.

A reference to the dish in AD 1340 says: The munj [*moong* or mung bean] is boiled with rice, and then buttered and eaten. This is what they call *Kishri*, and on this dish they breakfast every day.

Ibn Batuta

In 1443:

The elephants of the palace are fed upon *kitchri*.

Abdurrazzak, *India in XVth Cent.*, 27

Both the above excerpts are from *Hobson-Jobson*, by Colonel Henry Yule and A. C. Burnell.

Colonel Kenney-Herbert defined both the augmented Indian and Anglo-Indian versions very well in his *Wyvern's Indian Cookery Book*, written in India in 1869:

Kegeree (khichri) of the English type is composed of boiled rice, chopped hard-boiled egg, cold minced fish, and a lump of fresh butter: these are all tossed together in the *sauté*-pan, flavoured with pepper, salt, and any minced garden herb such as cress, parsley, or marjoram, and served in a hot dish.

The Indian *Khichri* of fish is made like the foregoing with the addition of just enough turmeric powder to turn the rice a pale yellow colour, and instead of garden herbs the garnish is composed of thin *julienne*-like strips of chilli, thin slices of green ginger, crisply fried onions, etc.

Kedgeree is sometimes referred to as "breakfast rice" by the Indians. This is probably where "fusion" came out of "confusion," for it is totally unclear whether they term it thus because of the long-standing custom of the British in making the dish part of their large breakfasts, or because, in certain parts of the subcontinent, Indians have truly preferred their own indigenous version as a breakfast dish. Sufficient to say that the original Indian *khichri* contained no fish. It was, and is, a dish of pulses and rice, butter, spices and onions.

It is entirely possible that the *sahibs*, with their predilection for smoked fish at breakfast, and particularly their beloved kippers – brought out on slow ships from England at enormous expense – insisted that the cooks incorporate it into the *khichri*. Whatever the moment or method of birth, we are the benefactors, for a kedgeree, tumbled with chunks of smoked or fresh fish, gilded with crumbled or sliced egg yolks and blessed with a benediction of crisp-fried onions and pungent parsley, has to be one of the nicest ways to break a fast.

Masala khichri

•

Although there are as many versions of this dish as there are cooks in India, I have chosen this old recipe over those that merely toss precooked rice and lentils together. Be careful of the type of lentils you use as not all of them take the same length of time to cook. Nor, indeed, do all of them arrive at the desired state of readiness at the same time as the rice. (Hence the many recipes that specify that both be cooked separately before combining.) This recipe calls for yellow lentils, known as *toor dhal*. They are not to be confused with yellow split peas which are made from *channa dhal*, a different pulse.

Serves 6

8 oz/1 cup long-grain rice
4 oz/½ cup *toor dhal*
   (yellow lentils, p. 115)
½-inch slice of ginger root,
   peeled and chopped
1 green chilli, chopped
1 clove of garlic, smashed,
   peeled and chopped
4 tablespoons *ghee*
   (clarified butter)

2 medium onions, peeled
   and slivered
2-inch stick of cinnamon
3 whole cloves
1 teaspoon salt (or to taste)
½ teaspoon ground
   turmeric

1   Preheat the oven to 375°F (190°C, Gas Mark 4).

2   Wash and drain the rice and lentils. Spread them out together on a flat oven-proof dish or tray and roast them in the oven for 10 minutes.

3   Meanwhile, pound the ginger, chilli and garlic into a paste in a mortar, or use a food processor. Set it aside.

4   Melt the *ghee* in a large saucepan and fry the onions over moderate heat until they are brown and crisp. Remove half the onions, draining them over the pan, and place them on a paper towel. Reserve.

5   Add the reserved spice paste, cinnamon stick and cloves to the pan and stir. Pour in the rice and lentils and fry them, stirring, for 3 minutes.

6   Pour in 1 pint of hot water and add the salt and turmeric. Cover the pan. Bring to a boil then reduce the heat and let it simmer for 15 minutes,

or until the rice and lentils are cooked but still whole and separate.

7   Pick out the cinnamon stick and cloves, which will be lying on top of the grains, then turn the *khichri* out on to a flat, heated dish and sprinkle the reserved fried onions over the top. The *khichri* can be kept warm in the oven until it is served.

Notes: This dish may also be garnished with slivers of green chillies, fine julienne strips of ginger root and slices of hard-boiled egg.

Khuni khichri

•

Here is a family recipe for a different Indian *khichri*, spicier and more substantial than the previous dish, for it includes potatoes. The quantity of ingredients make it suitable for a breakfast or brunch buffet for a large group.

Serves 8–10

1 heaped tablespoon coriander seeds

1 3-inch stick of cinnamon

$\frac{1}{4}$ teaspoon cardamom seeds

2 red chillies

1 bay leaf

1 tablespoon ground turmeric

1 teaspoon cayenne

$\frac{1}{2}$ teaspoon ground aniseed

16 tablespoons *ghee* (clarified butter)

2 large onions, peeled and slivered

2 medium potatoes, peeled and cut into 1-inch cubes

1lb/2 cups long-grain rice

1 lb/2 cups *moong dhal* (mung bean lentils, p. 115)

1 teaspoon salt

2 tablespoons vegetable oil

$\frac{1}{2}$ oz blanched almonds

1   Pound the coriander, cinnamon stick, cardamom seeds, chillies and bay leaf until they are cracked and broken up. (They will release their essential oils more efficiently.)

2   Add them, together with the remaining spices, to 3 pints of water in a

64

small saucepan. Bring to a boil and simmer for 10 minutes. Strain the liquid through a muslin and reserve.

3   Melt half the *ghee* in a pan and sauté half the onions and all the potatoes until they are lightly browned. Set the pan and its contents aside.

4   In a large saucepan, melt the remaining *ghee* and fry the rice and *moong dhal*, stirring constantly, for 2 minutes. Pour in the spiced water from Step 2 and add the contents of the pan from Step 3. Add the salt. Cover the pan and bring it to a boil; then let it simmer for 15 minutes or until the moisture is absorbed and the grains, pulses and vegetables are cooked and tender.

5   While the *khichri* is cooking, heat the oil in the pan. (You need not wash it after its previous use as the residual *ghee* will add to the taste.) Slowly fry the remaining onion slivers over low heat until they are brown and crisp. Drain them on paper towels. Put the almonds into the same pan and sauté them briefly until they turn golden. Drain them on paper towels.

6   Uncover the *khichri* and fluff it with a fork to let the steam escape. Turn it on to a heated platter and scatter the fried onions and almonds over the top. The *khichri* may be kept in a warm oven until you are ready to serve.

Notes: Such vegetables as cauliflowers or peas or cubes of aubergine/eggplant may be included as well as or instead of the potatoes.

Kedgeree of smoked haddock

•

This dish, far simpler than the foregoing, carries with it fond memories of my childhood breakfasts. Our sense of taste is so closely allied with our sense of smell, and one mouthful takes me back to Ootacamund in the Nilgiris: valleys full of arum lilies, wood-smoke stealing up the steep hillsides, and a steaming dish of haddock kedgeree on the snowy-white breakfast tablecloth.

Serves 4

½ lb smoked haddock
4 tablespoons/2 oz
    unsalted butter
1 lb/2⅓ cups cooked long-
    grain rice
2 hard-boiled eggs,
    shelled and chopped

3 sprigs of parsley, finely
    chopped
a pinch of nutmeg
½ teaspoon salt
¼ teaspoon ground white
    pepper
1 tablespoon herb vinegar

1   Poach the haddock in a little water until the fish flakes easily with a fork. Drain, remove any skin and bones and flake the flesh into a bowl.
2   Melt the butter in a medium pan over moderate heat and sauté the rice until it is warmed through. Add it to the haddock.
3   Add all the remaining ingredients, stirring lightly to combine everything; then turn the kedgeree out on to a heated platter. The kedgeree may be kept in a low oven for 5–10 minutes before serving.

Notes: Kippers or any other smoked fish may be substituted for the haddock. The kedgeree can also be surrounded by a ring of thickly cut, lightly grilled slices of tomato.

Baluchi carpet-wallah kebabs

•

In the spring, when the thaw began, and at the beginning of each cool season, the camel caravans, or *kafilas*, came down from the hills of the Frontier to the Frontier Province and to the plains of the Punjab. The tinkling bells of the camels' harnesses woke us at dawn. Long lines of humped beasts, tied head to tail, swayed slowly down the mountain road, groaning and grunting with expressions of scorn and disdain on their faces.

The women and children of the tribes rode on the camels, flanked by boxes, bundles and bales of household goods and merchandise, even chickens, squawking and flapping as their rough wooden cages bumped up and down.

The women were clad in loose-fitting shirts over voluminous skirts or trousers. Some wore dresses with heavy bands of embroidery and ornamentation at neck and wrists. Their heads were modestly covered by huge shawls. Some wore chains of silver coins across their foreheads.

The tribesmen walked alongside the camels, accompanied by sheepdogs – ferocious animals that stood guard when the tents were pitched for the night. The men were tall and strong, often fair of complexion and greyeyed. The faces of the elders were bronzed from the wind and sun and wrinkled like the skins of Caucasian walnuts. Hawk noses and luxuriant beards added to the impression of unyielding toughness, even cruelty. Bright waistcoats topped baggy black or white trousers. Faded jackets or shawls protected them from the biting winds of the summits and their heads were wrapped in floppy turbans, often with a loose end swathed round their chins.

These *powinders* or nomads knew no traditional borders, and no invading or occupying army – not even that of Alexander the Great, the mythic Iskander of tribal fame – had ever stopped their seasonal migrations.

Among their boxes and bales were carpets to be sold in the bazaars, and soon after the arrival of the caravans the carpet-*wallah* would appear at our gates. Squatting on our veranda, he would flick his wrists with the skill of a magician and the rugs would unroll before our marvelling eyes. And, oh! What beautiful rugs and carpets they were! Aqcha and Baluchi, Andkhoy, Mauri and Daulatabad. Karakul and Khandahari wool from sturdy mountain sheep, and camel hair, finely knotted by hand and dyed in deep, bright shades of maroon, scarlet, indigo, black and regal blue. Decisions! Decisions! For such low prices, months and years of the painstaking handiwork of families and tribes would become ours; priceless heirlooms for the future, fifty years on, long after the Raj had gone home.

This recipe, whose marinade betrays a Turkish or Persian origin, was probably passed on to our cook by one such nomad, having been carried in tribal memory from beyond the far mountains. Serve it with plain or *pilaff* rice for a hunt breakfast, a brunch, or some stellar morning occasion.

Serves 6

For the marinade
3 cloves
1 large onion, peeled and chopped
2 tablespoons chopped parsley
the juice of 2 lemons
1 tablespoon olive oil
1 teaspoon salt
½ teaspoon freshly ground black pepper
¼ teaspoon ground ginger

½ teaspoon ground turmeric
½ teaspoon ground cumin
½ teaspoon paprika

2 lb boned leg of lamb, cut into 12 chunks
9 lamb's kidneys, washed, cleaned and halved
6 tablespoons/3 oz butter, melted

1   Combine all the marinade ingredients in a large bowl and add the lamb and kidneys, stirring well to ensure they are coated thoroughly. Marinate overnight.

2   Preheat the grill or broiler or light your barbecue. Thread the lamb and kidneys alternately on skewers, 2 chunks of lamb to 3 kidney halves on

68

each. Baste them with the melted butter.

3   Cook the loaded skewers over or under fierce heat, basting with any remaining butter and the leftover marinade. The meats should be dark brown and crusty on the outside, but tender and juicy within. Serve at once.

Notes: To extend the meats further, alternate them between chunks of tomato, onion and/or mushroom halves. These additions should not be marinaded, merely basted.

Nowshera fishcakes

•

How we love our fishcakes! They are the humble and unchanging companions from the tables of our childhood, still constant when we desire them in our adult life. No poems of celebration are dedicated to them; no paeans of praise. Indeed, it is rather *infra dig.* to say that one even *eats* them let alone *enjoys* them. Of course, we are not discussing the solid roundels of potato and fish – curling stones composed largely of the former, together with a few anonymous, white whiskers of the latter. They deserve their blankets of tomato ketchup as a shroud and sousings of Worcestershire sauce as heavy rains on their grave. We're talking about the honest, home-made fishcake; cooked fish that we know was bought just before cooking. Its tender flakes have been lovingly combined with eggs and, maybe, garden herbs or freshly crushed spices, then breadcrumbed or dusted with flour before being fried to crisp perfection.

That is how our *khansamer* made fishcakes, in the whitewashed kitchen outside our Nowshera bungalow, in the North-west Frontier Province of what was then India. My mother probably gave him the recipe from her beloved little cookery book by "Ketab," *Indian Dishes for English Tables.* The recipe gives the instructions perfectly, so why gild the lily? Here it is, quoted verbatim:

Take any remains of boiled or fried fish, free it carefully of all bones, skin, fat, and, if fried fish, of the egg and bread-crumbs. Put the fish in a mortar, and pound it with salt, pepper, cayenne pepper, or a chopped green chilli, and anchovy sauce to taste; add a small piece of butter, and when well mixed, beat up one or two eggs, according to the quantity of the fish, and work into the mixture lightly.

Make up the fish in round flat cakes about half an inch thick, dredge them with a very little flour, and fry them in boiling ghee to a nice brown colour. Have some nice pieces of parsley well washed and perfectly dry. When the fish cakes are all fried, fry the parsley in the same ghee till crisp, and garnish the dish with it.

Clam and bacon koftas with apricot sauce

•

This is an unabashed update of an eighty-year-old recipe which featured only bacon. But clams and bacon partner happily and the tangy apricot sauce makes a lively companion.

Serves 6–8

18 small, fresh clams or 8 oz drained, tinned clam meat, or mussels
6 oz bacon (pieces and ends are fine)
½ small onion, peeled and finely chopped
3 medium potatoes, cooked and mashed
1½ tablespoons finely chopped parsley
1 teaspoon Worcestershire sauce
salt and pepper to taste
2 eggs

2 tablespoons breadcrumbs
3 tablespoons finely chopped walnuts
vegetable oil for deep-frying
6 oz dried apricots, soaked for 30 minutes
2 tablespoons sugar
⅓ teaspoon *garam masala* (sweet spice mix, p. 293)
2 tablespoons plain yoghurt

1   Steam and open the clams (if using fresh molluscs). Finely chop the clam meat and put it in a bowl.

2   Chop the bacon finely. Combine with the clams and add the onion, mashed potato and parsley. Season with the Worcestershire sauce, salt and pepper. Beat one of the eggs and mix it in thoroughly. Chill the mixture for 1 hour so that it becomes solid enough to be formed into *koftas* (balls).

3   Beat the remaining egg and pour it into a saucer. Mix the breadcrumbs and walnuts together in another saucer. Roll the clam and bacon mixture

into walnut-sized *koftas*. (If the *koftas* have softened after rolling, chill them again until they are firm.)

4   Heat the oil to 350°F (180°C). Dip the *koftas* into the beaten egg and then into the crumb/nut mixture and fry them, 3 at a time, until the coating is golden-brown. Drain them on paper towels and keep them in a low oven.

5   Simmer the apricots in just enough water to cover them until they are soft. Stir in the sugar until it is dissolved. Place the apricots in a blender, together with the liquid, and add the *garam masala* and yoghurt. Blend everything to a purée. Serve the clam and bacon *koftas* accompanied by the sauce in a sauceboat or bowl.

Chapattis with butter and marmalade

•

In other books that I have written, I have touched upon the memory I have of my grandmother rolling out *chapattis* in India. The picture is vivid in my mind although I cannot remember if she was in the outside kitchen or in the house (which was a more proper place for a *burra memsahib* to be). And why she should be performing this mundane task I don't know, for there were plenty of servants. Perhaps she merely found it soothing and relaxing, which it is. But my taste-buds are permanently imprinted with the texture and flavour of the puffy, hot *chapattis*, folded over creamy white butter, freshly churned from buffalo milk, the butter melting into liquid richness on the tongue. The crowning touch was her home-made marmalade spread on top. I could have died and gone to heaven and found the angels eating the same food!

Serves 6 (2 for each person)

1 lb/4 cups wholewheat flour (*atta*)	Granny Whitburn's Scottish whisky marmalade (p. 72–4)
a little plain/all-purpose flour	
unsalted butter	

1   Sift the flour into a large bowl. Make a hole in the middle and add enough cold water to make a stiff dough. Knead it thoroughly for 5 minutes,

if necessary adding a little more water to make the dough pliable but not sticky. Cover the bowl with a damp cloth and leave for 2–3 hours.

2   Knead the dough briefly after it has rested then break it into pieces, each the size of a small egg. Roll each into a ball and flatten it slightly. Dust your board and rolling pin lightly with flour and roll out each ball very thinly into rounds the size of a small plate.

3   Heat a griddle until it is very hot (when a drop of water will bounce off violently); then place a *chapatti* on it for about 15 seconds. Turn it over and cook until brown freckles appear on the surface. Turn it over again and press it gently with a spatula around the perimeter until the *chapatti* puffs up. Remove it to a dish and wrap it in a cloth to keep it warm. Repeat with the remaining *chapattis*.

4   Spread the *chapattis* lavishly with butter, top with marmalade and fold each over in half. Keep them wrapped in the cloth and serve immediately while they are warm.

Notes: You may butter each *chapatti* as soon as it is made and stack them in the cloth. Of course, they will be a little buttery on both sides, but that is what napkins are for. Serve the marmalade at the table. Lemon curd (cheese) is another preserve that goes splendidly with *chapattis*.

Granny Whitburn's Scottish whisky marmalade

•

Some experts say that the orange originally grew in southern China or South-east Asia, some 20 million years ago. Well, a great deal of centuries, and fruit, later, it was found growing in the valley of the Indus River in India, some 300 years before the birth of Christ. Then the Arabs, it appears, loaded orange saplings on their *dhows* and lugged them home to the eastern Mediterranean and to northern Africa, whence the Moors, thirsting for their early-morning orange juice, propagated the orange in Spain to sustain them on their conquests. Hence Valencia and Seville oranges.

Of course, the Crusaders had a nodding acquaintance with the fruit, when they weren't too busy spearing Saracens, but the orange did not appear in England until about 100 years later. We wouldn't recognize it today. It was a sour, coarse little fruit and it was squeezed for its juice which became an addition to, or substitute for, vinegar. So when some

European goodwyves began boiling up fruit with sugar into some form of preserves, it never occurred to them to use the orange. The quince was their choice. It set well and was readily available. It was known as a *marmelo*, from the Latin word, *melimelon*. (Of course, the Romans borrowed the word from the Greeks, for the first half means honey in Greek, and the latter half means apple.) Therefore the sugar messes that were boiled up from the quince were called marmalades.

Of course in time the British brought the art of marmalade-making out to India. The ever-resourceful housewives, lacking their beloved Seville oranges, used the local fruits. In our family, marmalade-making came quite naturally. In fact, word was whispered about that the Scots had invented marmalade anyway. Whether they did or not, this recipe from my grandmother blends oranges and whisky together in a quite delightful way. Of course, it graced her breakfast table in India.

Quantity: about 7 lb

2¼ lb Seville oranges
1 lemon
4 lb/8 cups sugar

3 tablespoons Scotch
whisky

1   Wash and dry the fruit. Peel the zest from the lemon and reserve the

peel for some other use. (Dry it on a low setting in a microwave and then keep it in a jar.)

2   Cut the lemon in half and squeeze the juice into a large non-stick or enamel saucepan. Peel the oranges and cut the peel into chunky slices. Put the orange seeds into a bag and add them as well. Pour in water to cover the fruit by 2 inches. Bring to a boil and turn the heat down. Simmer the mixture gently for 3 hours. (This releases the pectin that will set the marmalade.)

3   Remove the bag of seeds and squeeze it over the pan. Discard. Add the sugar and stir the mixture gently over the heat until the sugar is dissolved.

4   Bring the marmalade to a rolling boil; reduce the heat and, stirring frequently, let it simmer for about $1\frac{1}{2}$ hours until it becomes dark and thick. Turn it up to a fast boil to let it set.

5   Remove it from the heat and add the whisky. Return it to the heat and stir gently for 1 minute.

6   Leave the marmalade to cool for 15 minutes. When a skin forms on top, stir it in and then ladle the marmalade into warm, sterilized pots. Cover, seal and label.

Notes: The white pith or *albedo* of citrus fruits and their juice contains the pectin. The peel and pith are both the main source of vitamin C, but, since the vitamin is destroyed by cooking, they only provide the essential oils which contain the flavour.

Nimboo curd

•

As a child, I was quite sure that the old nursery rhyme telling what little girls were made of should have been amended to include lemons, sugar, butter and eggs – the heavenly quartet that makes lemon curd. And my mother's confection, tangy, creamy and golden, was, and is, one of the finest curds to come out of a kitchen.

In my memory, however, it is the lime that is inextricably linked with the start of the hot weather on the plains of India. So here are limes instead of lemons in a cool curd. Serve it for breakfast on sunny summer mornings and move the meal to the patio.

Quantity: 1¾ lb

grated rind and juice of 6
   large limes
1 lb/2 cups sugar

½ lb unsalted butter
4 eggs, lightly beaten

1   Put the lime juice and rind into a double boiler or a heat-proof bowl fitted over a pan of simmering water. Add the sugar and butter, the latter cut into small pieces.

2   Stir or whisk until the sugar has dissolved; then gradually beat in the eggs.

3   To avoid curdling, cook slowly over *low* heat, stirring continuously with a wooden spoon, until the mixture thickens and will coat the back of the spoon.

4   Pour the curd into warm, sterilized jars, cover and seal. The curd should keep for 3–4 months in a refrigerator or a cool larder.

Sooji

•

I almost hesitate to add this to the compendium of breakfast dishes, it is so simple. But simple is often best, and *sooji* is a direct connection to memories of childhood breakfasts in India. I have never even seen a recipe for it, but it comes closest to a hot cream of wheat cereal. There is a big difference, however. Toasting the grains gives a delicious, nutty flavour. Try it for breakfast on a cold winter morning, the kind of weather that used to ice the cream which rose to the top of the old-fashioned milk bottles on the front step.

Serves 1

½ cup semolina
a pinch of salt

1–2 tablespoons coarse,
   brown sugar
1 tablespoon cream

1   Pour the semolina grains into a heavy saucepan and place it over medium heat, shaking it to agitate the grains until they toast a pale brown. Watch

carefully because the grains will darken quickly once they start to colour.

2   Immediately after the grains have darkened, pour in some water and add the salt. Reduce the heat to medium-low and stir the cereal with a wooden spoon until it thickens to the consistency of porridge.

3   Transfer the *sooji* at once to a cereal bowl and drench the top with brown sugar. Place a generous dollop of cream on top and eat, just as the cream and brown sugar begin to melt and run over the surface.

Notes: Another more utilitarian version is to place a knob of butter on top of the sugared cereal and pour milk into the bowl.

Ham, lord of the breakfast sideboard

•

The cooked ham was the splendid standby of the house-party breakfast in India, elevating all the surrounding dishes, hiding under their silver covers, to the level of its own importance. In fact, this lordly hunk of delicate pink meat was indispensable to the tables of the British, appearing in different guises for breakfast, *tiffin* and dinner. At breakfast, gammon was generally served cold, pristine and free from all fol-de-rols and garnishes save for a light coat of breadcrumbs. The guests carved it according to their appetites and skills, the greedy or clumsy cutting it into fat, uneven slices. The experts brandished the knife to the flourish of unseen trumpets, proceeding to "neaten off the ham" in a subtle message of reproach to their predecessors before producing marvellously thin slices.

Quantity: depends on the size of the ham

1 uncooked ham (5 lb or more)

1 pint chablis or similar white wine

1 large onion, peeled and stuck with 6 cloves

1 large carrot, scrubbed

2 stalks of celery, cleaned and cut in two

a bouquet of thyme, rosemary and a bay leaf

3–6 black peppercorns

$\frac{1}{2}$–1 cup fine breadcrumbs

1   If the ham is a brined variety, place it in a large container and pour on a quart of lukewarm water for each 1 lb of ham. Soak it for 12 hours or overnight. If the ham has been dry-cured, reduce the soaking time to 6 hours.

2   Pour off the soaking water and place the ham, skin-side down, on a trivet in a large saucepan or pot. Pour over the wine and add enough water to immerse the ham. Bring to a boil and skim the surface.

3   Reduce the heat to a simmer and add the remaining ingredients to the pan, with the exception of the breadcrumbs. Simmer the ham for 20 minutes for each 1 lb of weight. (If the ham is over 10 lb, add another 5 minutes per 1 lb. If over 12 lb, add another 15 minutes per 1 lb to the boiling time.)

4   Meanwhile, heat the oven to 350°F (180°C, Gas Mark 4) and pour the breadcrumbs on to a baking tray. Bake them in the oven until they are a light golden-brown; then remove immediately and let them cool.

5   When the ham is tender, remove it from the saucepan and let it cool until you can handle it. Gently peel off the skin. Do not cut or pare away the skin with a knife, as when the skin is pulled the resulting roughened surface helps the breadcrumbs adhere better. (You may let the ham cool down partially in its own liquid before performing this step. The flavour will be better, but it does not keep as well.)

6   Press the breadcrumbs firmly on to the surface of the fat and let the ham sit in a cool place or larder before serving.

3

A PROPER TIFFIN

•

Everyday lunch at the house

"Here we eat," he said resolutely, as the Kamboh, blue-robed and smiling, hove in sight, a basket in one hand and the child in the other.

"Fall to, Holy Ones!" he cried from fifty yards. (They were by the shoal under the first bridge span, out of sight of hungry priests.) "Rice and good curry, cakes all warm and well scented with *hing* (asafoetida), curds and sugar . . ."

Rudyard Kipling, Kim (1901)

Reader! I, as well as Pliny, had an uncle, an East Indian Uncle . . . everybody has an Indian Uncle . . . He is not always so orientally rich as he is reputed; but he is always orientally munificent. Call upon him at any hour from two till five, he insists on your taking *tiffin*; and such a *tiffin*! The English corresponding term is luncheon: but how meagre a shadow is the European meal to its glowing Asiatic cousin.

De Quincey, Casuistry of Roman Meals (1832),
from Yule and Burnell, Hobson-Jobson

Tiffin, the midday meal, was a welcome break in the long Indian day; the pause for sustenance and prelude to a siesta. Noël Coward wrote: "Mad dogs and Englishmen go out in the mid-day sun," but, in truth, they fled to the club for pre-prandial gimlets or pink gins, to the mess if they were bachelors, or home to their bungalows, waiting wives and *tiffin*.

---

1. Sweetmeat seller, Kulu; 2. Village shops, Tangmarg, Kashmir; 3. Water carrier, *c*.1916; 4. The Whitburn sisters and Sir Albion Bannerjee; 5. Lunch at Judge Purbi's. His wife dressed the female guests in her saris; 6. Three tribesmen from the border, 1927; 7. Tiffin carriers, Bombay; 8. Village bazaar, Anantagiri; 9. Miss Prentice and Mr Prentice, 1908.

The repast was simple or relatively so in comparison to the formal, multi-course dinners of the evening. *Tiffin* was a domestic meal, a chance for husbands and wives to eat together if they wished. However, children were seldom present at the table, eating their *tiffin* under the watchful eyes of nannies or *ayahs* in the nursery. They may have breakfasted with their parents but they would not be admitted to the adult world again until teatime or just before dinner.

If guests were invited for the meal, then *tiffin* would be formalized into luncheon. The exception to that being the relaxed Sunday curry *tiffins*; jovial occasions with much gin, beer and merriment, where the "done thing" was to eat until you were uncomfortably full, and then fall asleep on the nearest bed or couch for a nap if you didn't make it home. Certain unwritten rules applied to *tiffin*. Salads were commonly served, particularly in the hot weather, and curry was a common occurrence. Our family ate it about three times a week. *Tiffin* was a meal for certain preferences and family choices; unpretentious dishes that often had their beginnings in the many counties and shires of the British Isles. The remains of the large roast from dinner the night before often appeared on the sideboard, flanked by dishes of home-made pickles and relishes. Many other leftovers appeared under pastry crusts or minced into cutlets and meatballs. "Eshepherd's pie" was the dish that every *khansamer* could produce at the drop of a *topee*. Fruit fools, jellies and ice-creams brought the meal to a close.

Naturally, the *tiffins* of the twentieth-century British were much lighter than those of the preceding centuries. The eighteenth-century meals reflected the custom of dining in the middle of the day while eating merely a light supper at night – a custom which was already dying out back home in England among the aristocracy, though still pursued by the middle and lower classes. Even so, not all the British in India had the means to indulge in such extravagance. Pat Barr's *The Memsahibs* tells that one Sarah Terry, wife of a struggling English merchant in Bombay in 1844, had: ". . . sometimes just marrow-bone soup" at *tiffin* and ". . . for family dinners, curry and rice for ever."

In 1853, the journal *The Family Friend* advised wives that luncheon should be taken about five hours after breakfast, ". . . to allay the cravings of nature, but not entirely to destroy the appetite." And Mrs Isabella Beeton decreed in *The Book of Household Management*, 1861, that the "solidity" of luncheon "must of course in some degree be proportionate to the time it is intended to enable you to wait for your dinner and the amount of exercise you take in the meantime."

Very little physical exercise was taken by Englishwomen in India in the eighteenth and nineteenth centuries. In the home, servants catered to every whim, while outdoors they rode in carriages (*tongas*, which were two-wheeled, and four-wheeled *gharries*) or in covered litters (*doolies*) or rickshaws. The typical routine of a *memsahib* in a small town or cantonment in the late nineteenth century was stultifying as well as sedentary. They rose at dawn and those who rode horses would take a gentle ride, side-saddle, for an hour before breakfast. After that meal, they bathed and dressed to receive visitors or went visiting themselves. Social gossip profitably used

up the four hours until *tiffin*. This was followed by a siesta, then an inspection of the garden, or some such small task, until it was time to bathe again, dress once more and promenade near the bandstand on the mall, or on the parade ground. This would be followed by a supper party and some home-made entertainment, such as a piano recital, poetry readings or charades, until bedtime.

It was not until the twentieth century that sports played a prominent part in women's lives in India. By then, of course, they had shed the corsets, stays and heavy petticoats which had hampered their movements. The fashionable, slender silhouettes of the 1920s, lighter, supple fabrics and shorter skirt lengths were far more conducive to riding and playing tennis. By then, too, a rash of cookery writers had published books in India wherein they urged that lighter meals be eaten; a diet far more suited to the Indian climate.

The recipes in this chapter reflect that trend to lightness in *tiffins* of the twentieth century.

Spiced tomato soup with saffron cream

•

Our *khansamer* made a very good tomato soup: thick, rich and with a subtle hint of spice. As a child, I was oblivious to the spicing, merely acknowledging that it "tasted nice," but I was enchanted by the textural counterpoint of crisp, fried croutons with the silky-smooth soup. I have taken the recipe a step further with the visual fillip of a swirl of saffron-scented cream.

Serves 6

3 lb ripe tomatoes

3 tablespoons/1½ oz
    unsalted butter

1 large onion, peeled and
    chopped

2 cloves of garlic,
    smashed, peeled and
    chopped

1-inch piece of fresh
    ginger root, peeled and
    finely chopped

2 green chillies, seeded
    and chopped

1 teaspoon salt

½ teaspoon ground cumin

1 tablespoon honey

1 pint chicken stock

freshly ground black
    pepper to taste

½ teaspoon, or a fat pinch of
    saffron strands

2 tablespoons hot milk

10 fl oz heavy cream

¼ teaspoon ground
    cardamom (optional)

3 slices of stale white
    bread, crusts removed

butter, oil or bacon fat

sprigs of mint

1   Peel the tomatoes by immersing them briefly in boiling water. Remove the skins and discard. Chop the tomatoes finely and set them aside.

2   Heat the butter in a large saucepan and sauté the onion until it becomes limp, then add the garlic and ginger and cook over low heat for 5 minutes, stirring frequently. Add the tomatoes and chillies and season with the salt, cumin and honey. Let the mixture simmer for 30 minutes, stirring from time to time.

3   Place a large sieve over a bowl and pour the contents of the pan into the sieve, stroking the mixture through the mesh with the back of a wooden spoon. Rinse out the saucepan and return it to the heat. Pour in the sieved

tomato and add the chicken stock. Cook gently until the soup is the texture of cream. Season with pepper and set the soup aside to keep warm.

4   Soak the saffron strands in the hot milk until they have yielded their colour and flavour. Place the cream in a bowl and blend in the saffron liquid.

5   Dice the slices of bread. Heat the butter, oil or bacon fat in a pan and fry the croutons until golden and crisp. Drain them on paper towels.

6   Divide the soup among 6 soup bowls and swirl in the saffron cream in a spiral. Sprinkle lightly with cardamom if desired, and decorate each with a sprig of mint. Pile the croutons into a bowl and serve separately.

Notes: Mint cream is a pleasant alternative to saffron. Stir 2 tablespoons of puréed mint leaves into the cream, together with a pinch of salt, and swirl the soup with pale green instead of yellow.

Cool green almond and watercress soup

•

For the heavens are red hot iron and the earth is burning brass,
And the river glares in the sun like a torrent of molten glass,
And the quivering heat haze rises, the pitiless sunlight glows
Till my cart reins blister my fingers as my spectacles blisters my nose.

Rudyard Kipling, "Dear Auntie, Your Parboiled Nephew,"
verse-letter to Edith Macdonald, 12 June 1883,
Early Verse by Rudyard Kipling

One cannot out-Kipling the arch-chronicler and poet on descriptions of India during the hot season. My sentiments lie with Emily Eden, who, in 1836, wrote: "It is so very HOT, I do not know how to spell it large enough!"

My memories paint everything behind a shimmering curtain of heat waves, like a theatrical backdrop seen through a muslin scrim; the sky a steely blue or pewter, the landscape overlaid with choking clouds of dust, dun-coloured and suffering. Every living thing seemed desiccated by the giant fireball that rode daily in total command of the heavens.

The British, in those days before air-conditioning, made every conceivable effort to appear cool or to further the illusion of coolness. The rooms in the bungalows lay sweltering in the climate, but the green-painted *chicks*, or wooden-slatted blinds, hanging from the arches of the verandas to shade the tall windows, gave an undersea, cool green tint to the white-washed walls. The sweeper half-heartedly dashed water over the blinds so that any stray puff of hot wind would drop a degree or two from the evaporating moisture before entering the house. The occupants of the bungalows lay motionless on the rough, white sheets of their beds, their forms outlined in a pool of perspiration. The *punkahs* disturbed the hot, stale air with no relief. There was no movement in the household until the sun mercifully began to sink below the horizon.

I remember my mother's rooms as green, and now I know why. It was her favourite colour and it gave the beds and chairs and cushions the illusion of English countryside and of more temperate summers.

This soup furthers the effect. Its cool green is the perfect antidote to the baking days of high summer.

Serves 6

1 pint chicken stock	6 fl oz milk
4 spring onions/scallions, chopped	2 tablespoons ground almonds
2 bunches of watercress, washed and chopped, 6 large leaves reserved for garnish	$\frac{1}{2}$ teaspoon salt, or to taste
	$\frac{1}{4}$ teaspoon white pepper, or to taste
	4 fl oz cream

1 Heat the chicken stock and bring to a boil. Add the onions and watercress and reduce the heat to a simmer.

2 Stir enough of the milk into the ground almonds so that a liquid paste results. Scrape the mixture into the remainder of the milk and then add it to the soup. Stir until the soup thickens a little then set it aside to cool.

3 Purée the soup in batches in a blender, adding the salt and pepper. Taste the result and adjust the seasoning if necessary. Remember that more seasoning is needed when a soup is chilled.

4 Refrigerate the soup until you are ready to serve, then divide it among 6 soup plates. Swirl a little cream into each and garnish with the reserved leaves of watercress.

Notes: A cup of green peas may be added at the same time as the watercress. Spinach can be substituted for watercress for another variation but it will taste quite different and not so tangy.

Mulligatawny soup

•

One of my special soups. When I wrote an earlier cookbook, *The Cuisines of Asia*, I could not resist including it, and although I knew that one day I would write a book about cooking in India, the lure of mulligatawny was too strong to wait. But no story about the British in India would be complete or truly authentic without the appearance of this dish, so beloved of the Raj. And the recipe below is more true to its polyglot ancestry than the recipe in the earlier book.

What polyglot ancestry? It started with the Tamils in the south of India. The name proclaims it – *molagu*, meaning pepper in Tamil, and *tunni*, meaning water. The brahmin yogis of the south, who were strict vegetarians, drank this "pepper water" and it was adopted by the poor, who could always afford a few chillies. They added some salty dried fish to make it more substantial, and a little tamarind juice to counteract the fish. From there on, its history is a little muddled. Somewhere along the line, the Anglo-Indians (in this case, those with one British and one Indian parent) adopted the soup and even added a little chicken – which would have horrified the brahmins. The British Raj appropriated it or rather their cooks did, and it began to show up on lunch tables throughout the British areas of the subcontinent, particularly in Madras. The redoubtable Colonel Henry Yule and his associate, A. C. Burnell, gathered up a delightful little ditty which they put into their hefty tome of Anglo-Indian words, *Hobson-Jobson*, under the heading of *Mulligatawny*:

> 1794–
> In vain our hard fate we repine;
> In vain our fortune we rail;
> On *Mullaghee-tawny* we dine,
> Or *Congee*, in Bangalore Jail.

Well, I lived in Bangalore as a child, and loved it, *and* ate mulligatawny soup with some regularity, but not, I'm glad to say, in Bangalore jail. Here is a close approximation to the soup I consumed at the West End Hotel in Bangalore.

Serves 6

2 cloves of garlic, smashed, peeled and finely chopped

1-inch piece of fresh ginger root, peeled and finely chopped

1 teaspoon cayenne

1 teaspoon ground turmeric

1 teaspoon ground coriander

1 teaspoon ground cumin

1 bay leaf, broken into fragments

1 tablespoon vegetable oil

2 tablespoons *ghee* (clarified butter)

1 large onion, peeled and finely chopped

the meat from 4 boned and skinned chicken thighs, diced, with the bones reserved

6 fl oz coconut milk

1 quart chicken stock

6 tablespoons lentils (*toor*, *arhad* or *masoor dhal*, p. 115)

1 teaspoon tamarind concentrate or 2 tablespoons tamarind pulp, dissolved in 4 tablespoons boiling water, strained

3 tablespoons rice

$\frac{1}{2}$ teaspoon *garam masala* (sweet spice mix, p. 293)

coriander leaves for garnish

1   Place the first 8 ingredients, including the vegetable oil, in a food processor or grinder and process or grind into a paste.

2   Place the *ghee* in a large saucepan and fry the onion, stirring, over moderate heat until it is golden, then add the spice purée from the processor and continue to fry and stir for 3 minutes, until the spices are well cooked and mellowed.

3   Add the chicken meat and the bones and stir for 1 more minute. Then pour in the coconut milk and let the mixture simmer, uncovered, for 5 minutes.

4   Pour in the chicken stock and add the *dhal*; stir and cover the pan. Bring barely to a boil, reduce the heat and let the soup simmer for 30 minutes, or until the *dhal* has totally disintegrated and the onion is soft enough to squash against the side of the pan. Fifteen minutes before the end of the cooking, add the rice.

5   Strain out the meat and rice on to a plate and discard the bones. Purée the soup in batches in a blender and then return it to the pan over heat. Stir in the tamarind until it has dissolved, bring the soup just to the point of boiling again.

6   Turn off the heat and pour the soup into a tureen or into individual soup bowls. Sprinkle with *garam masala* and garnish with coriander leaves.

Notes: There are as many ways to make this soup as there are people to drink it. Lamb stock can be substituted for chicken, or the soup may be made entirely in vegetarian style by using water as the cooking liquid, omitting the meat and, perhaps, frying a few almonds and peanuts in the spice paste instead. Additional onions can be crisp-fried in butter and used for garnish. The soup may also be enriched by chopped celery, carrots and tomato purée being added with the stock.

Tamarind is available in various forms from Asian foodstores.

Cucumber raita salad mould

•

It is always fun to experiment with a traditional recipe and transpose it to another category and setting. The classic Indian *raita* which, in fact, acts as a salad in a curry lunch situation and, not so incidentally, cools the palate heated by fiery peppers, moves here into the chilled salad setting. Try serving this dish with cold chicken breasts which you have masked with a creamy curried mayonnaise. A perfect light luncheon for high summer.

Serves 6

2 tablespoons gelatine	12 oz natural yoghurt
1 teaspoon grated onion	4 fl oz cream
2 teaspoons salt	1 bunch of mint leaves
1 teaspoon ground cumin	4 tablespoons walnut
½ teaspoon freshly ground black pepper	halves
1 small cucumber, pared, seeded and chopped (about 1 cup)	1 tablespoon salad oil
	1 head of lettuce, washed and separated into leaves

1　Dissolve the gelatine in 3 tablespoons of hot water in a large bowl. Stir in the grated onion, salt, cumin, black pepper and cucumber and blend together.

2　Add the yoghurt and cream and mix well. Chop approximately 2 tablespoons of the mint leaves and stir them in, reserving the remainder.

3　Oil a decorative ring mould and spoon in the mixture, tapping the side of the mould to settle the contents and remove air bubbles. Chill in the refrigerator for approximately 4 hours.

4　Arrange the lettuce leaves on a large platter. Invert the mould over the platter, tapping it sharply to turn out the contents. Scatter the reserved mint leaves and walnuts around the mould, decorating the top with a few as well. Serve immediately.

Notes: If the mould does not slip out easily, place a cloth, wrung out in hot water, briefly over the top, then try again.

Marinated paneer and wilted spinach salad

•

Here is another cross-over fusion; an updating of the traditional Indian *saag paneer*. This dish transforms it into a wilted spinach salad but with a hint of the original spicing.

Serves 6–8

3 tablespoons salad oil
the juice of 1 lime
½ teaspoon curry powder
¼ teaspoon salt (if the
　cheese is unsalted)
1 tablespoon finely
　chopped mint leaves
½ lb *paneer* (Indian curd
　cheese, see p. 172–3),
　into ½-inch cubes
2 tablespoons vegetable
　oil
1 teaspoon cumin seeds,

toasted to a light brown
　then slightly crushed
¼ teaspoon cayenne
½ teaspoon ground
　coriander
1-inch piece of fresh
　ginger root, peeled and
　finely chopped
1 lb spinach leaves, well
　washed then drained
2 tablespoons toasted
　sesame seeds

1   Combine the 3 tablespoons of oil, lime juice, curry powder and salt in a bowl and stir in the mint. Add the cubes of *paneer* and toss them gently until they are coated with the marinade. Let them marinate for about 2 hours.

2   Five minutes before you are ready to serve, heat the vegetable oil in a wok over medium heat and add the cumin seeds, red pepper and coriander. Stir quickly until the spices just begin to darken then add the ginger. Stir for 30 seconds. Add the spinach in large handfuls, tossing and stirring until all the leaves are coated with spices and oil and begin to wilt.

3   Transfer the spinach to a salad bowl and, draining the *paneer* cheese from Step 1, scatter the cubes over the spinach. Sprinkle the salad with the toasted sesame seeds and serve immediately.

Notes: You may substitute a good local farmer's cheese for the *paneer* or it can be home-made by turning 1 quart of whole-cream milk to curds with the juice of half a lemon. Add a pinch of salt and hang the curds in a muslin bag over the sink to drain. The longer it hangs, the firmer the cheese will be. When the cheese is almost dry, it can be pressed into a block by placing it on a plate, with another plate on top, weighted down by a heavy object. Press for 4 hours then refrigerate.

Finely chopped spring onions/scallions can also be added to the wok at the same time as the ginger. This should be a separate course for a luncheon.

Parsee patia

•

The old tale goes that when a boat-load of Parsees – the Zoroastrian Persians who fled from the invasion of Islam – arrived at the shores of Gujarat in AD 745, they sent emissaries to the King of Surat requesting permission to land and settle in the country. The emissaries returned bearing a full glass of milk, to indicate that the land was rich but already thickly populated. Legend has it that the Parsee captain added a teaspoon of sugar to the milk and sent it back to the king, indicating that the new arrivals would add sweetness to the land. Some die-hards insisted that he dropped a coin into the milk to underscore the prosperity that they would contribute.

Well, it is already the stuff of legends that the Parsees became one of India's most influential and wealthy minorities, contributing shipping magnates, bankers and business tycoons to society, particularly in Bombay where they became established in the 1670s. Air India was originally founded by the Parsee Tata dynasty, who also built the Taj Mahal hotel. Another Parsee, Dorabji Rustomji, helped establish the original racecourse at Byculla.

This recipe, as rich and luxurious as the lavish Parsee wedding banquets, was given to my aunt, Lady Macfarquhar, by Dolly Khan, one of her oldest friends and also a Parsee.

Serves 6–8

6 red chillies, chopped
2 green chillies, chopped
1 head of garlic, smashed and peeled
1 teaspoon cumin seeds
8 fl oz vegetable oil
3 lb onions, peeled and finely chopped
1 teaspoon ground turmeric

1 teaspoon ground coriander
1 teaspoon cayenne
1 teaspoon salt
6 tablespoons tamarind pulp
1 tablespoon sugar
3 lb (shelled and cleaned) prawns/shrimp

1   Grind the chillies, garlic and cumin to a paste, gradually adding half a cup of water. Set aside.
2   Heat the oil in a heavy saucepan over medium heat and fry the onions, stirring constantly, until they become light gold. Add the spice paste from the previous step and fry until it bubbles; then add the turmeric, coriander and cayenne and fry for 1 more minute, still stirring.
3   Add the salt, tamarind pulp, sugar and 4 fl oz of water and cook for 10 minutes, stirring from time to time, until the mixture becomes a thick, rich, mellow sauce.
4   Add the shellfish and cook for 2 minutes. Turn off the heat and let the *patia* sit for at least 30 minutes, so that the shellfish absorb the spices.
5   Reheat just before serving.

Notes: This dish is rich, hot and spicy so a little goes a long way. Serve it with lashings of plain rice and a green vegetable, such as spinach or broccoli.

Tamarind is available in various forms from Asian foodstores.

Machi kebabs

•

In the North-west Frontier Provinces, kebabs or kababs were more commonly eaten than curries. Meat was more plentiful and dishes were drier than in central and southern India. I have fond memories of the kebabs which the *khansamer* made when we lived in Rawalpindi. The smell of roasting meat with an overtone of charcoal floated on the air in the bazaars and hung around the outside kitchens in the compounds of the houses.

The stove in the outside kitchen was simplicity itself. In the corner of the mud-floored kitchen, a rectangular box would be constructed, walled with earth. The top would be covered in pieces of iron grating which lay over the glowing charcoal inside. The *dekshis* and *chattis* were balanced on this grating and it was also used for kebabs, which were placed directly on the metal. The cook would fan the glowing coals with a palm-leaf fan and clouds of smoke fled out of the open door, often accompanied by the sound of coughing.

Sometimes, instead of lamb or chicken kebabs, we would have fish. Chunks of white fish, long-marinated in curds and spices, were threaded on skewers and barbecued. They were accompanied by stacks of freshly made *chapattis* which were served hot and wrapped in a cloth.

Tamatar bhugia is a great foil to the taste and texture of the fish and a recipe for it follows this one.

Serves 6

8 oz plain yoghurt
2 tablespoons *gram* or
  chick-pea flour (*besan*)
  (all-purpose flour may
  be substituted)
3 cloves of garlic,
  smashed, peeled and
  finely chopped
2 teaspoons ground
  coriander
1 teaspoon ground cumin
1 teaspoon ground
  turmeric
½ teaspoon cayenne

½ teaspoon *garam masala*
  (sweet spice mix,
  p. 293)
½ teaspoon salt
the juice of 1 lemon
2 lb firm white fish fillets,
  as fresh as possible, cut
  into 1-inch cubes or
  approximate pieces
mint leaves
lemon wedges

1 Preheat a charcoal grill or broiler.
2 Place the yoghurt in a large, shallow bowl and stir in all the rest of the ingredients except the fish. Make sure that the mixture is well blended.
3 Add the fish, stirring gently to coat the pieces, and set it aside to marinate at room temperature for 30 minutes.
4 Drain the pieces of fish and thread them on metal skewers, 4 or 5 to a skewer, reserving the marinade. (This is a messy procedure so carry it out over the marinade bowl.) Arrange the skewers over the grill or place them on a rack over a foil-lined baking pan and grill or broil for 10 minutes, turning them occasionally and basting them with the marinade. Let the marinade dry and become crusty over the fish before basting each time.
5 Slide the cubes off the skewers on to a warm serving dish, garnish with mint and lemon wedges and serve immediately, accompanied by a stack of *chapattis* and (possibly) the following tomato recipe.

Tamatar bhugia

•

In northern India and Pakistan, the local tomatoes are often pear-shaped and very similar to Italian tomatoes. If you can find fresh Italian tomatoes in your greengrocer, by all means use them. If you cannot, then use ordinary fresh tomatoes. This dish just does not taste as well when made with tinned tomatoes, so please don't be tempted to take a short cut.

Serves 6

2 fl oz vegetable oil
1 teaspoon cumin seeds
1 large onion, peeled and finely chopped
5 cloves of garlic, smashed, peeled and chopped
1 teaspoon *garam masala* (sweet spice mix, p. 293)
1-inch piece of fresh ginger root, peeled, thinly sliced and cut into shreds

2 small green chillies, seeded and cut into julienne strips
8 large tomatoes, scalded and skinned, cut into 1-inch chunks
1 teaspoon salt
2 heaped teaspoons brown sugar
1 tablespoon unsweetened desiccated coconut
2 tablespoons chopped fresh coriander leaves

1 Heat the oil in a wok or large saucepan over medium heat and fry the cumin seeds briefly until they are lightly browned. Add the onion and garlic and fry, stirring, until the onion is soft.

2 Stir in the *garam masala* and add the ginger and chilli strips. Continue to fry and stir the mixture for 2 minutes.

3 Now add the tomatoes, salt and sugar and bring the mixture to a boil. Sprinkle in the desiccated coconut and stir. Cover the saucepan and reduce the heat to low. Simmer the dish for 10 minutes, lifting the cover and stirring from time to time. The finished dish should have a little gravy but should not be soup-like, and the tomato pieces should still be discernible.

4 Transfer it to a serving dish and sprinkle with coriander leaves.

Notes: This dish has many uses and guises. It can be cooked until the tomatoes disintegrate and it concentrates into a purée. In this form you can substitute it for tomato sauce in many dishes, giving them a different and unique Indian flavour. As an alternative try making meatballs, flavoured with a teaspoon each of ground cumin and ground coriander, fried and then simmered in this sauce.

Eshepherd's pie

•

I mentioned earlier that this old English recipe was the standby of all Indian cooks. Its made-in-advance qualities appealed to them, particularly when they had spent longer than they should in the bazaar. I can't exactly blame them. I always found the Indian bazaars to be the most fascinating and stimulating places imaginable.

One bazaar in the Punjab I particularly remember, although I now cannot tell you which city it was in. There was a large square lined with wholesale and retail grocers and grain merchants. Heaps of grains, *dhals*, *gur* (Indian coarse brown sugar, also known as *jaggery*) and rice lay on mats outside the open shop fronts. In the middle of the square was a spreading banyan tree, in the shade of which sat women selling vegetables from reed baskets. Bargaining was traditional, but there was very little profit margin.

Then there was the main street of the market. Fruit shops with pyramids of gold and green mangoes and hands of bananas – not just yellow, but pink and green – soft-drink shops with large glass tanks of juice all hues of the rainbow, and bottles of fizzy pop in brilliant pinks and virulent greens. Most were sickly sweet.

The cookshops followed, full of aromas that tantalized, and you could quite spoil your appetite for dinner while munching on potato chips, stuffed *naan* bread, fried mixtures of *gram* and spices, kebabs sizzling over charcoal, kidneys, liver, spiced crisp potatoes and innumerable other snacks. After them, a row of shops selling sweetmeats: pyramids of glistening *jaggery* toffee, *gurpapedi*; pale-green pistachio *barfi* or fudge; soft and chewy *halvas* in Bombay or Karachi style – carrot, banana or cashew-nut; big bowls of sweetmeats in syrup – *gulab jamun, rasagullas*; and *naruel pantua* – coconut crescents in pink, white and green. My special treats were the *jellabies*, fragile towers of crisp, golden batter spirals. When you bit into them, rose-scented syrup was released in a rush to seduce your taste-buds. When he wasn't selling to customers, the shopkeeper's hands were always in motion, waving a large reed fan to keep the flies at bay.

The general merchandise shops didn't appeal to me. I was too young to be interested in buttons, thread, mirrors, Pears and Vinolia soaps, combs, highly scented hair oils, socks and razors. But I was fascinated by the *pansari* shops, which sold intriguing potions and herbal medicines. They also displayed little bottles of sweet-smelling essences and extracts, rose and *kewra* waters, spices, and all kinds of aromatic things in little jars and boxes. My English nanny always sniffed in disapproval and pulled me away. I think she suspected they were selling aphrodisiacs and love potions . . . and they probably were.

But the cook has overstayed his time in the bazaar. Hailing a *tonga*, he puts all his packages inside, hauling his bulk up after them, and clip-clops *juldi-juldi* (quickly-quickly) back to the kitchen of the bungalow in the British cantonment. The eshepherd's pie awaits its finishing touches for the *memsahib*'s *tiffin*.

Here is a new twist on the old friend.

Serves 6

2 tablespoons vegetable oil	$\frac{1}{2}$ teaspoon salt
1 large onion, peeled and diced	28-oz tin Italian tomatoes, chopped, with their juice
1 large red bell pepper, seeds and membranes removed, diced	12 black olives, pitted and chopped
1 clove of garlic, smashed, peeled and finely chopped	the grated rind of half a lemon
1 lb lean ground beef	4 large potatoes, peeled and cubed
1 teaspoon ground cumin	2 tablespoons/1 oz unsalted butter
$\frac{1}{2}$ teaspoon ground ginger	4 fl oz milk
$\frac{1}{2}$ teaspoon ground cinnamon	1 teaspoon salt
$\frac{1}{2}$ teaspoon cayenne	$\frac{1}{4}$ teaspoon ground white pepper
$\frac{1}{4}$ teaspoon freshly ground black pepper	1 large egg, beaten
	1 tablespoon sesame seeds

1   In a large, heavy saucepan or flame-proof casserole, heat half the oil and sauté the onion and pepper over moderate heat until soft (about 5 minutes). Drain and remove to a plate. Set aside.

2   Add the remaining oil to the pan and briefly sauté the garlic. Crumble in the beef and turn the heat up a little. Stir for a minute then add the spices and salt. Cook for a further 2 minutes, still stirring, then add the tomatoes with their juice. Stir for another 5 minutes until the mixture thickens, then add the olives, lemon rind, and reserved onion and pepper from Step 1. Simmer for a further 3 minutes. (The recipe can be prepared to this point up to a day ahead. Cover and refrigerate. Bring back to room temperature before continuing.)

3   Preheat the oven to 375°F (190°C, Gas Mark 5). Drop the potatoes into a saucepan of boiling water and cook for about 15 minutes. Drain them and leave in the pan. Add the butter, milk, and salt and pepper. Mash and beat them until fluffy. Beat in the egg until well blended.

4   Turn the beef mixture into an oven-proof casserole and spread the potato mixture over the top. Swirl it decoratively or score it with the tines of a fork. Sprinkle sesame seeds over the top and bake in the oven for 30 minutes or until the top is golden brown. Let it rest for 10 minutes before serving.

Notes: This dish may also be made with ground lamb. Please use fresh meat, not leftovers. The *khansamer* sometimes made it with cooked meat but it was a poor substitute.

Madras Club quoorma

•

A good recipe travels well. A great recipe travels in time in addition to distance, appealing to so many cooks that it becomes part of many culinary repertoires. It is the substance of domestic lore passed from mother to daughter, or through a family of professional chefs or *khansamers*. Old soldiers fade away. Old recipes are merely translated, transformed and, sometimes, transmogrified; taking on new leases of life and vogue in the process.

The *korma* is actually the Indian name for the technique of braising meat. It originated in the lavish Mogul cuisine wherein lamb or chicken was braised in velvety, spiced sauces, enriched with ground nuts, cream and butter. While *kormas* are rich, they are also mild, containing little or no cayenne or chillies. Travelling in the kitchens of the conquering Mogul emperors, the *korma* gradually spread from the north-west of India into much of the rest of the country.

This particular recipe found its way into the kitchens of the renowned Madras Club where, around 1830, it was referred to by the British as "quoorma." Here is a transformation of that recipe. Serve it with a fragrant rice *pilaff* for a formal luncheon.

Serves 6

3 lb lean, boneless lamb, cut from the leg

1½-inch piece of fresh ginger root, peeled and finely chopped

1½ teaspoons salt

10 tablespoons/5 oz unsalted butter

3 large onions, peeled and sliced into rings

3 cloves of garlic, smashed, peeled and finely chopped

1½ teaspoons coriander seeds

1½ teaspoons black peppercorns

6 whole cardamom pods

6 whole cloves

6 oz/1 cup ground almonds

6 fl oz cream

2 teaspoons ground turmeric

1½ teaspoons sugar

the juice of 2 small limes

1 Cut the lamb into 1½-inch cubes and pat them dry with paper towels. Place them in a large mixing bowl with the ginger and salt and toss well.

2 Melt the butter in a large non-stick saucepan and put in the onions and garlic. Fry them slowly over low heat, stirring occasionally to prevent the garlic from sticking to the bottom of the pan, until the onions are limp and very soft.

3 While the onions and garlic are frying, place the coriander seeds, peppercorns, cardamom pods and cloves in a spice grinder or mortar and grind or pound them to a fine powder. Stir the spice powder into the onion mixture and cook it, stirring, for 5 minutes.

4 Turn the heat up to moderate and add the lamb mixture from Step 1, scraping in all the ginger and salt remaining in the bowl. Fry the meat, stirring and turning it until it is nicely browned. Remove the pan from the fire.

5 Place the almonds in a 1-quart measuring jug or heat-proof bowl and

pour in $\frac{1}{4}$ cup of boiling water, stirring to bring out the essential oil and its aroma. Work in the cream, turmeric and sugar.

6   Replace the saucepan on the heat and wait until the oil begins to sizzle again; then stir in the almond cream mixture. Turn the heat as low as possible and stir the lamb well until it is coated with the sauce. Let the meat simmer for about 30 minutes, stirring from time to time to prevent it sticking. The rich gravy should reduce to the consistency of thick cream and should thoroughly coat the lamb. (The length of time that the *quoorma* takes to reach this stage will depend on the diameter and depth of your pan and the amount of moisture in the lamb, so there will be variations in the cooking period.)

7   Transfer the *quoorma* to a serving dish and sprinkle it with lime juice. The dish may be kept warm in a low oven for a short while before serving, but do not let the gravy dry out.

Notes: I discovered a useful note from my grandmother amid a collection of jottings and handwritten recipes. She urges the inclusion of bones in the meat-cooking process: "If you use lamb in a recipe, you can use filet and 1 lb neck for the bones which makes it richer." The proportion was about 1 lb of bones to 3 lb of meat. After the meat bones have given off their taste, they are of course removed prior to serving.

Saag ghosh

•

One of the perennial problems with which the Indian *khansamer* had to deal was the toughness of meat. It was the exception rather than the rule to find a tender cut and, consequently, the low, dull thud of a pestle or the flat of a cleaver hitting flesh was the normal sound issuing from the outside kitchen as he placed the offending piece of meat on a low, solid, three-legged stool and beat it into submission. "Lamb" was too often old sheep and "mutton" was probably goat. So dishes that relied on long simmering were often part of his repertoire and, indeed, a mainstay in traditional Indian menus.

This lamb and spinach dish originated as one of these slow-cooked specialities but today, with the tender and prime meat we have available, the cooking time can be considerably shortened. The brown rice recipe that follows this yields a deliciously aromatic accompaniment.

Serves 4

3 tablespoons *ghee*
(clarified butter)

2 large onions, peeled,
finely chopped and
squeezed dry in paper
towels

5 cloves of garlic,
smashed, peeled and
finely chopped

½ tablespoon ground
cumin

½ tablespoon ground
coriander

1 teaspoon cayenne

1 teaspoon salt

2 lb lamb, fat and fell
trimmed, cut into
1-inch cubes

1 lb spinach, washed well
and chopped finely

6 medium tomatoes,
blanched in boiling
water, skins removed,
finely chopped

1   In a large, heavy saucepan, melt the *ghee* over medium-low heat and fry the onions, stirring constantly, until they become golden brown. Add the garlic and continue to fry, still stirring, for a further minute.

2   Stir in the spices and salt and continue to fry the mixture for 2 more minutes, scraping the pan to prevent the spices from sticking to the bottom. Add the lamb and brown it on all sides.

3   Stir in the spinach and tomatoes, cover the pan and simmer until the meat is tender and the spinach and tomatoes are reduced to a rough purée (approximately 45 minutes). Check the pan from time to time and stir the contents. If the gravy appears to be drying up, add a couple of tablespoons of water. The finished dish should have a little thick, rich gravy.

4   Transfer the contents of the pan to an oven-proof serving dish and keep it warm until serving time in a low oven.

Notes: The finished dish can be sprinkled with lightly browned pine nuts. Some cooks alter the gravy by adding ¼ cup of finely chopped coriander leaves along with the spinach.

Brown rice

•

The title of this dish refers to the look of the finished product and not to the variety of rice. Please use the normal long-grain variety.

Serves 4–6

8 oz/1 heaped cup long-grain rice, washed well and drained

3 tablespoons *ghee* (clarified butter)

3 medium onions, peeled, finely chopped and squeezed dry in paper towels

5 whole cloves

6 whole cardamom pods, crushed

2-inch stick of cinnamon

1 teaspoon salt

½ teaspoon freshly ground black pepper

2 teaspoons sugar

the grated zest of ½ an orange

1   Place the rice in a rice-cooker or heavy saucepan.

2   Melt the *ghee* in a frying pan over medium heat and fry the onions, stirring, until they are just browned.

3   Add the cloves, cardamom and cinnamon and continue frying and stirring for 1 more minute. (The onions should be crisp and brown but not burnt.)

4   Empty the onions and spices into the pan containing the rice. Add the salt and stir well.

5   Cook according to the rice-cooker instructions or cover the rice mixture with cold water to the depth of 1¼ inches above the surface of the rice and bring to a boil. Cover, reduce the heat and simmer and cook until the rice is tender and all the liquid evaporated (approximately 30 minutes).

6   When the rice is cooked, uncover, add the pepper, sugar and orange peel and stir, allowing the steam to escape. Transfer to a serving platter.

Sind Club ham in gin

•

Good ham was not often to be found in India. When it was, its habitat (off the hoof) was in the provisioners in the larger cities rather than in the remote countryside. It was not that pigs were not to be found – indeed, pigsticking was a popular sport, and wild pig roamed the *dak* jungle, or low, bushy scrub, frequently devastating the crops of the villagers – it was that the eating of pork was the preserve of the White Man, the Raj, for the meat was considered unclean by the majority of religions in India.

The pig, as a game animal, was given a respect not accorded his domestic brethren. The wild variety is wily and uncertain, with a propensity to use his sharp tusks with speed and indiscrimination. So great was his number in the jungles of the north that he often caused a disruption in the orderly programmes of the *shikars* for larger game. (*Shikar* is the term for a shoot or hunt and a *shikari* is a hunter.) One such occasion relates to a tale of my grandfather. The beaters had swept through the jungle once and there was a lull in activity. The members of the shoot had stepped down from their *machans* (concealed, often raised, structures, from which one shot game) for a smoking break when there was a rustle in the foliage and out dashed a baby pig. He swerved to an uncertain stop right in front of my grandfather. My grandsire looked at the little piglet, milk was still in drops around its snout. He said, very softly, "Run away, you little b—— or I'll shoot you!" The animal uttered a small squeal and dashed back into the jungle. The shoot continued.

As to pigsticking in the *dak* jungle, the pigstickers' song goes:

> Over the valley, over the level,
> Through the *dak* jungle, ride like the devil!

Serves 6–8

5 lb smoked ham	4 slices white bread, finely
1 large onion, peeled	crumbled
12 cloves	parsley for garnish
8 fl oz gin	

1   Place the ham in a large bowl and cover with cold water. Soak for 3 hours, then drain.

2　Place the ham in a large saucepan together with the onion, cloves and gin. Add enough cold water to cover the ham to a depth of 1 inch above its surface. Cover the pan and bring to a boil over medium-low heat. Simmer for approximately 2 hours. Let the ham cool to lukewarm in its liquid.

3　Meanwhile preheat the oven to 400°F (200°C, Gas Mark 6). Drain the ham from its liquid and strip off the skin. (Tear it by hand, do not pare it away or the breadcrumbs will not adhere.)

4　Sprinkle the breadcrumbs over the surface, pressing them in gently, then place the ham in the oven to brown the bread coating lightly. Send it to the table garnished with parsley.

Notes: The Sind Club served the ham with new potatoes and spinach. Another popular way to serve the ham for special occasions was to boil it, cut it into pieces and fry them in butter. After the frying, they were then marinated in champagne before serving!

Aam murghi Bombay

•

Oh, the mangoes of India! Sonnets should be written to them, *haiku* praising their beauty. Many years ago I saw a coffee-table book, full of exquisite, hand-painted illustrations, devoted entirely to all the varieties of mangoes in India. I know there were well over 100 different species.

Debate has always raged hotly over the subcontinent as to which region boasts the best mangoes. Any consensus reached says it's Bombay. There it is sworn that the only way to eat these prize specimens is naked and in the bath. Come to think of it, that *is* probably the best dress, or undress, for the task of eating a mango. "Mango showers" are the rains that "set" the fruit on the branches after the trees have blossomed. I always thought they named your ablutions after you had eaten the fruit.

This mango chicken dish is for the season when the imported mangoes are at their best in your greengrocer. Smell the stem end. If it is delicately scented, buy the fruit. If it has no smell or an odour of turpentine, wait until the next shipment. One last comment: this dish can be sanely, safely and soberly eaten with your clothes on. Pity!

Serves 6

3 tablespoons *ghee*
(clarified butter)
3 lb chicken pieces,
skinned
2 large onions, peeled and
sliced
2 cloves of garlic,
smashed, peeled and
finely chopped
3 large, ripe mangoes,
peeled and the flesh
roughly chopped
(reserve half of one

mango, sliced
crosswise, for garnish)
$\frac{1}{4}$ teaspoon ground nutmeg
$\frac{1}{4}$ teaspoon freshly ground
black pepper
1 teaspoon salt
$\frac{1}{2}$ teaspoon turmeric
the zest of half a lemon,
cut into strips
8 fl oz chicken stock
the juice of 1 lemon
8 fl oz cream

1　Heat the *ghee* in a large saucepan over a moderately high setting and sauté the pieces of chicken, stirring and turning, until they are lightly browned. Remove them, draining them over the pan, and set them aside.

2　Turn the heat down and, in the same pan and butter oil, fry the onions and garlic, stirring until the onions are soft and limp. Put in the chopped mangoes and season with the nutmeg, black pepper, salt, turmeric. Add the strips of lemon zest. Stir for 2 minutes then return the chicken to the pan and pour in the chicken stock.

3　Cover the pan and simmer over low heat for 45 minutes, or until the chicken is tender. Remove the chicken to a heat-proof casserole and keep it warm in a low oven.

4　Reduce the mango gravy in the pan by half, then stir in the lemon juice and the cream. Cook it, stirring, for another 5 minutes, but do not let it come to a boil.

5　Pour the gravy into a blender or force it through a sieve. Pour it over the chicken pieces in the casserole. Place the reserved slices of mango decoratively on top and let the dish stay in the oven for a further 10 to 15 minutes before serving.

Notes: Serve the mango chicken with *pilaff*-style rice and semi-ripe banana halves, sautéed in a little butter or *ghee*. Fried cashew-nuts may also be sprinkled over the top of the finished dish.

The British Army in India: bugles and barracks

Cooking and housekeeping in the Army have now reached such a high standard of proficiency that they are not comparable with the methods existing twenty years ago. This is primarily due to the following factors: That well-cooked food, clean and comfortable surroundings and a quick and effective service, with all meals served on hot plates, all combine to make the soldier contented and keep him in good health whilst in training at home and abroad during peace, and fit him to stand the rigours and hardships of war.

Manual of Military Cooking and Dietary, 1933, published by His Majesty's Stationery Office

The plan for invasion involved living off the land, but there was little to live off, and the camels carrying the supplies suffered badly on the stony paths; baggage was discarded, and troops were reduced to eating sheepskin cooked in blood, while officers, who still had their personal baggage animals, were enjoying cold meats, game, cheese, port, wine, and whisky.

Robert Wilkinson-Latham, First Afghan War, December 1838, *North-West Frontier, 1837–1947*

My father commented at the close of the Burma Campaign, World War II:

I wish never to see a piece of bully beef again.

There was no doubt that the British soldier in India had life very hard for many, many years. While, between hostilities, the officers lived in some degree of civilization and – for those whose personal fortunes or lenient bank managers permitted – luxury, the rank and file led mostly tough and wretched existences until the twentieth century. When they were allowed to marry and when they were lucky enough to acquire a bride from England, for the most part their new wives put up with dreary, often squalid and frequently dangerous lives. Even so, the married-quarters roll, which authorized a soldier to have his wife with him and house her in married quarters, was a list of achievement and status among the other ranks.

Pat Barr writes in *The Memsahibs*:

"The Lines" – what untold misery was contained for so many in those two little words. Each company of each regiment had its own lines – rows of brick and plaster barracks for the English soldiery, huts for the native infantry. Commonly, the quarters were overcrowded, sparsely furnished and poorly ventilated ... If it was that bad for the men, what must it have been like for the wretched English women, the lowest in rank and least remembered of all the "mems," who chose, or were obliged, to accompany their menfolk for the ten-year stint on the hot hell of the Indian plains? Officers and travellers glimpsed them – jolting along in bullock carts from one barracks to another.

What a contrast with the idealized officer's wife spoken about in *Letters from India* by Lady Wilson, Rawalpindi, 1896:

The one I perhaps especially appreciate is Mrs L., the wife of the Colonel of the 4th Dragoon Guards. Before we knew her we often used to see her in our evening walk, in her lovely garden, under her archways of roses, or moving about in her wilderness of flowers, herself the "fairest of them all." Now I know her in her own home, where everything speaks of her love of beauty and her personal charm. There she is amongst her books and her pictures, devoting her life to her husband and children, a living refutation of the wholesale assertion that every woman in India is a gadabout and a butterfly.

Such was the social and economic gap between the families of officers and those of the corporals and sergeants. Even if the lives of the latter were not as squalid as that of the ordinary soldier, money was sparse and their domestic arrangements frugal. But the British Army itself cannot wholly be blamed for these social inequities; it merely mirrored the gap in living standards and prosperity within British society at large during that era.

Honey/lime spiced grilled chicken

•

Here is a slightly different slant on the usual Indian grilled chicken. Serve it for *tiffin* accompanied by a fresh green salad and *chapattis* or plain rice.

Serves 4

2 whole chicken breasts, boned, skinned and halved

the juice of 2–3 limes (depending on their size)

3 cloves of garlic, smashed, peeled and chopped

$\frac{1}{2}$ teaspoon *garam masala* (sweet spice mix, p. 293)

½ teaspoon freshly ground
black pepper
¼ teaspoon cayenne
1 tablespoon honey

3 tablespoons *ghee*
(clarified butter), or
unsalted butter

1   Place the prepared chicken breasts in a shallow dish. Combine the lime juice and garlic and pour over them. Combine the spices and sprinkle them over the chicken. Cover the dish and let the chicken marinate for at least 45 minutes, turning the breasts over 2 or 3 times.

2   Preheat your grill or broiler.

3   Drain the chicken and cook it over or under a fierce heat for about 5–10 minutes, turning it frequently. Transfer the cooked chicken to a serving dish.

4   In a small saucepan, gently heat the honey and *ghee* together. Drizzle it over the chicken and serve immediately.

Notes: This dish is also delightful for picnics. In that setting, do not glaze with the honey/butter mixture, but let it soften at room temperature, stir and put it in a small container for dipping.

Pathan chicken pilaff

•

The North-West Frontier, or the "Grim" as it was called by generations of British soldiers, stretched along the borders of Afghanistan and included Little Pamir, Chitral, Kohistan, Bajaur, Khyber, Tirah, Waziristan and Baluchistan. Though it once belonged to Afghanistan, the tribal territory was inhabited mainly by Pathans, one of the fiercest warrior tribes on earth . . .

Robert Wilkinson-Latham, *North-West Frontier 1837–1947*

The Afghan is a Pathan merely because he inhabits a Pathan country, and has to a great extent mixed with its people and adopted their language.

Bellew, *Races of Afghanistan*,
from Yule and Burnell, *Hobson-Jobson*

The little towns and villages scattered over the slate rock and scrubland of the arid North-west Frontier were, and are, poor and primitive. The villagers were isolated in their mud or brick huts behind earth and stone walls, tending small herds of lean and scraggy goats for subsistence. A state of perpetual feud existed between the tribal villages. Raids were continual, so the settlements were heavily guarded. The smallest slight, even imaginary, was considered an insult by the proud, fierce and hot-tempered peoples of the Frontier, and was avenged in blood. This was the tradition that had

ruled the area since the time of Genghis Khan and even before. The only links between the tenth-century existence of the tribespeople and the nineteenth- and twentieth-century world of the British Raj were the roads that the British built. The roads were considered neutral ground by the Pathans — a sort of No-Man's-Land of macadam — and in the late 1920s these roads were partly under my father's jurisdiction, for he was a junior officer in the Royal Engineers at that time and his job was to tour and inspect them. Wherever he went the people received him with warm hospitality, but it was an edgy and uncertain part of his work, like walking through a political minefield.

Peshawar, where I first lived as an infant, was the headquarters for the Frontier, and the main road which ran west out of the city was the only route into Afghanistan from the Frontier Province and the Punjab. That road went up into the mountains through the Khyber Pass. So the towns and cantonments in which the British lived were fortified and garrisoned by soldiers. In Nowshera, where we subsequently lived, the tribes had been known to sweep down from the hills and abduct people, or mount a full attack, depending on their mood. The military were always on alert to take part in campaigns against rampaging tribesmen and the civilians were forbidden to go beyond the barbed-wire perimeters of Nowshera. Unrest was part of our lives.

But the Pathans were also loyal and faithful, one-on-one; capable of generosity, gentleness and deep attachment. When you had "eaten of their salt" they became as brothers. Before my father and mother met, my father had a manservant, a Pathan named Umar Khan. He was devoted to my father and even helped him pass his exam for an interpretership in Pushtu (the Pathan language). Surprisingly (for Pathans hold women in low regard), when my parents met, Umar Khan liked my mother. After a two-year engagement (quite customary then) they married, and Umar Khan guarded her and accompanied her everywhere. My father, somewhat chagrined but also amused, swore he had gained a wife and lost a bearer. When Umar Khan was speaking about my mother to my father he referred to her as the *bul-bul*, meaning nightingale, because she was always singing.

It was Umar Khan who had commissioned the letter-writer to pen the ornate letter of congratulations to my parents in England upon my birth. Unfortunately, I never set eyes on him for he died of cancer before we returned to India. Even while seriously ill, he still had our welfare at heart for he charged his son, Farid, with the responsibility of taking over his job. Another Pathan, Mohammed, became the Number Two *khitmagar* and responsible for the nursery. As a small child, my memories were of these two hawk-like Pathans, with their fierce faces. But their aspect did not trouble me. I knew only their unfailing kindness and gentleness.

This Pathan dish is what they would have eaten when they were welcomed back to their villages. It was also prepared many times for my father during his tours around the North-west Frontier.

Serves 6

$1\frac{1}{2}$ lb/$3\frac{1}{2}$ cups long-grain
    rice, washed and
    drained
4 tablespoons *ghee*
    (clarified butter)
3 large onions, peeled and
    thinly sliced
1 $3\frac{1}{2}$-lb chicken, cleaned
    and skinned
1 teaspoon salt

$\frac{1}{2}$ teaspoon freshly ground
    black pepper
$\frac{1}{2}$ teaspoon ground
    cinnamon
$\frac{1}{2}$ teaspoon ground cloves
$\frac{1}{2}$ teaspoon ground cumin
$\frac{1}{2}$ teaspoon ground
    cardamom
4 tablespoons raisins

1 Bring 3 pints of water to a rolling boil in a large saucepan. Add the rice and parboil it for 3–4 minutes before draining it in a sieve. Set it aside.

2 Reserving 1 tablespoon of the *ghee*, place the rest in another large and heavy saucepan (with a tight-fitting lid) and melt it over moderate heat. Add the onions and fry them until they are quite a dark brown, stirring to prevent them from burning. Remove them from the pan with a slotted spoon and set them aside.

3 Put the chicken into the same pan and sauté it on all sides until it is nicely browned. Add $\frac{1}{2}$ pint of water and salt and pepper and bring it to a boil. Cover and simmer for 20–30 minutes, or until the chicken is just cooked.

4 Preheat the oven to 300°F (150°C, Gas Mark 2). Pour the chicken stock from the pan into a blender and add the onions from Step 2. Blend into a thick gravy.

5 Place the rice from Step 1 into a large casserole and sprinkle in the spices. (These four spices are known as *char masala* in Afghanistan.) Pour the onion gravy from the blender over the rice and mix it gently with a fork. Place the chicken on top. Cover the casserole and place it in the oven for 30 minutes.

6 While the *pilaff* is cooking, heat the *ghee*, which was reserved in Step 2, in a small pan and fry the raisins until they puff up like grapes. Set aside.

7 Warm a large serving platter. Remove the chicken carefully from the casserole and place it in the middle of the platter. Surround it with half the rice and place the remainder of the rice on top of the chicken so that it is buried. Sprinkle the raisins and butter oil from the last step over the top and serve.

Notes: Traditionally, the Pathans will cook the dish in a large, covered pan or *dekshi* on top of the stove, sealing the lid with a flour and water paste. Ovens are rare in small tribal villages.

Chicken stuffed with apricots

•

The Persians referred to apricots as "eggs of the sun" and the fruit became beloved of the Mogul emperors of India. *Zard alu*, or golden plums, as they were known in the north of the subcontinent, were grown in Kabul in Afghanistan and in the Vale of Kashmir, and their sweetness lent itself to preserves and chutneys. My memories are of golden pyramids of the fruit in the bazaars and shops of Rawalpindi and of munching the aromatic flesh until the juice ran down my chin. (I hasten to add that the fruit had first been taken home and thoroughly washed in "pinki-pani," a solution of potassium permanganate, as decreed by the rules of household hygiene – one never ate fruit unwashed.)

The combination of chicken and apricots is wonderful, and this recipe is a variation on a pet dish of a Kashmiri cook.

Serves 4

the boned meat from 1 skinned chicken thigh

1 egg

8 oz dried apricots, soaked in cold water for 1 hour, drained

1 2-inch piece of fresh ginger root, peeled and finely chopped

1 small green chilli, seeded

1 medium onion, peeled and coarsely chopped

$\frac{1}{4}$ teaspoon cardamom seeds

1 teaspoon cumin seeds

6 black peppercorns

1 teaspoon fennel seeds

4 large chicken breasts, boned and skinned

2 tablespoons *ghee* (clarified butter)

$\frac{1}{2}$ teaspoon *garam masala* (sweet spice mix, p. 293)

8 fl oz cream

salt to taste

2 tablespoons/1 oz unsalted butter

3 tablespoons slivered almonds

sprigs of mint

1   Grind the thigh meat to a paste in a food processor. Add the egg, *half* of the apricots, *half* a teaspoon of the ginger and the green chilli. Give the processor a few more turns then remove the stuffing mixture to a bowl and refrigerate. Wash the processor bowl and replace it.

2   Place the onion, cardamom, cumin, black pepper, fennel and the remaining ginger in the processor. Add 3 tablespoons of water and purée the mixture.

3   Pound the chicken breasts to the thickness of $\frac{1}{4}$ inch, using a meat mallet or rolling pin. Pat them dry with a paper towel. Divide the stuffing mixture from Step 1 into 4 equal portions and spread the breasts evenly, leaving a border. Roll up each chicken breast, enclosing the filling completely, and secure with toothpicks. Truss each with kitchen string and refrigerate.

4   Melt the *ghee* in a large saucepan over moderate heat and add *half* of the remaining apricots. Sauté them to a light golden brown (about 5 minutes). Reduce the heat to low, add the spice purée from Step 2 and cook for 5 minutes, stirring occasionally. Stir in the *garam masala* and 2 fl oz of water. Bring back to a gentle simmer.

5   Place the chicken rolls from Step 3 into the spiced gravy. Cover the pan and simmer for 20 minutes, turning them occasionally, until they are springy to the touch. Drain the rolls over the pan with a slotted spoon and set them on a plate until they are cool enough to handle; then remove the toothpicks and the string.

6   Pour the gravy and apricots remaining in the pan into the processor or a blender and reduce them to a purée. Return the liquid to the pan and reduce it to 1 cup. Lower the heat and stir in the cream. Let the mixture thicken to the consistency of custard. Add salt to taste. Place the chicken rolls in a heat-proof dish or fairly deep platter and pour the sauce over the top. Keep it warm in a low oven.

7   Melt the butter in a pan and sauté the almonds until they are golden. Drain them over the pan with a slotted spoon and place them on a paper towel. In the same butter, sauté the remaining apricots until they are heated through.

8   Place the sautéed apricots round the chicken and sauce and sprinkle the almonds from the last step over the top. Garnish with the sprigs of mint and serve.

Notes: Fresh apricots in season can be used for this dish, in which instance, of course, no soaking is required. Serve the chicken rolls with plain steamed rice to counteract the richness of the dish. Steamed asparagus or broccoli would make a good accompaniment.

Jhalfarajie

•

Another typical sight, one of greater interest to the menfolk, was the women walking at noon to the fields carrying victuals. They carried flat reed baskets on their heads with thick oven-baked unleavened bread wrapped in a napkin and some cooked vegetables. On the basket rested a small pitcher full of *lassi*, buttermilk. Tired and hungry, the man kept looking towards the village till he caught sight of his wife . . . He stopped work when she came near and walked to his well under a tree, leading the bullocks in front. He watered them and spread some straw before them and after a wash himself sat down to eat his meal. She sat in front of her man and helped him to the food, but never ate herself. He ate silently while she talked about the morning's happenings, the children, the neighbours, in restful small-talk. After she had seen him eat his fill she collected the food left over and started to walk back. There was no farewell but a simple "*Acha main chalni han* – right, I am going."

Prakash Tandon, *Punjabi Century 1857–1947*

Some of our servants, who were lucky enough to have their wives living with them in the compound or living near by, would have their wives bring the midday meal to them, but our *khansamer* was seldom a local man. I think that sometimes this lack of the amenities of home weighed heavily on his soul and I fancy that those were the times he paid less than his normal attention to that particular meal he prepared for us. Of course, it may be merely my romantic imagination – the meal of the homesick cook – for such dishes as *jalfaraizi*, or *jhalfarajie*, as it is termed in this old recipe, were an excellent way to use up last night's meat.

Serves 2–3

2 tablespoons *ghee* (clarified butter)

2 large onions, peeled and cut into slivers

2 teaspoons curry powder

1–2 green chillies, seeded and slivered

½ lb cold, cooked lamb or beef, sliced

½ teaspoon salt

1 Melt the *ghee* in a medium saucepan and fry the onions, stirring over moderate heat, until they are crisp and brown.

2 Add the curry powder, chilli strips, slices of meat and salt. Stir well to coat the meat, then add 2 tablespoons of hot water. Cook everything, stirring, until it becomes a rich, dark brown with a modicum of sauce. Serve hot as a side dish with a curry or on its own with steamed rice and mango chutney.

Dhal churchurree

•

For many of the British who lived in India, *dhal* (*dal*, *dol*, or *doll*) was almost inseparable from curry and rice. It was the necessary third that made the trio of everyday food. For the Indian, *dhal* was the protein substitute for meat, although he would not have put it that way, nor, indeed, thought much about it. It was the substance of the daily meal – the taste over the rice.

For those who are curious, the word *dhal* or *dal*, from the Hindi, does not mean pulses or legumes – although many categories of those are included under the all-embracing name. It actually derives from the ancient Sanskrit, *dal*, to divide or split, which is exactly the treatment that the lentils, peas or beans undergo. Hence it referred to dishes made from those crops.

Of the *dhals*, there are five in common use: *Toor dhal* (also known as *toovar* or *arhar*), a split yellow lentil, sometimes referred to as a "pigeon pea." It is widely used and is often found coated with oil to preserve its freshness. The oil must be washed off before cooking.

Arhad dhal (also known as *urad* and *urhad*), which is a small black bean (known in its whole form as *kali*, meaning black), is white when split and, besides making a very tasty series of dishes, is ground into a flour used to make *dosa* (pancakes) and *poppadams*, the crispy wafers often served with curried dishes.

Masoor dhal is a salmon-pink lentil that turns pale yellow when cooked. It produces a rather thin purée but compensates for that by taking very little time to cook.

Moong dhal is the split mung bean. Dull green when whole, it is yellow when skinned and split. This is the *dhal* most often used in kitcherie. The whole bean is called *sabat moong*.

Channa dhal is a large yellow split pea. It much resembles *toor* or the split yellow lentil, but is larger.

Besides these five, there is also the *kabuli channa* (also known as *safaid*), which is known to us as the chick pea or, in the Spanish-speaking world, as the *garbanzo*. *Kali channa* (meaning black), is the chick pea before skinning and, in this form, it is often cooked by itself or combined with the skinned chick pea.

Finally, discounting the lesser-known and -used beans and pulses, there is the green split pea, called *matar dhal*. It is often used as a substitute for *channa dhal*, and its flour is a substitute for *gram* flour (*besan*).

While most of these *dhals* have their individual uses in Indian cooking, the nice thing to know is that they are largely interchangeable. Some need to be pre-soaked (generally the larger ones) and some take longer to cook than others. This is something to remember if you try to do a dish of mixed grains, or combine them with rice. But here below, we are merely concerned with a nice, old-fashioned *dhal* dish; one that is comfortably basic and which has basically comforted generations of expatriate Britons at their *tiffins* in India.

Serves 4

2 tablespoons *ghee*
(clarified butter)
1 medium onion, peeled
and sliced into slivers,
patted dry with paper
towels
½ lb/1 cup *dhal* (lentils),
washed well and picked
over

1 teaspoon turmeric
1 teaspoon salt
1 teaspoon cayenne
2 bay leaves
1 green cooking apple
(optional), peeled,
cored, cut into ½-inch
pieces

1   Melt the *ghee* in a medium saucepan over moderate heat and fry the onion slivers until they are brown and crisp. Drain them from the oil with a slotted spoon and set them aside on paper towels.

2   Fry the lentils in the same *ghee* for 2 minutes, stirring slowly. Add the turmeric, salt, cayenne and bay leaves and sufficient hot water to cover the lentils. Cover the pan, bring to a boil, reduce the heat and let it simmer, adding hot water if necessary, until the lentils are quite tender. If you are adding the apple, do so while the lentils are cooked but not fully tender.

3   Draw the pan to one side and leave it for a few minutes with the cover on to let the contents dry. Remove the bay leaves, transfer the contents to a serving bowl and garnish the top with the fried onions.

Notes: Most *dhal* is adulterated with small pieces of stones, husks and other debris and should be placed on a tray and picked over by hand until the eye sees no further trace of foreign matter. This *dhal* dish is quite dry and any left over will thicken to a solid, particularly under refrigeration. It can be formed into small cakes and fried for snacks.

Bombay pudding

•

This was the version of an Indian semolina sweet produced by one of our cooks.

Serves 4–6

½ lb/2 cups semolina	the juice of 1 lemon
1 egg, beaten	a few cardamom pods,
3 tablespoons flour	crushed
4 tablespoons/2 oz butter	a small pinch of ground
½ lb/1 cup sugar	cloves

1 Roast the semolina in a heavy pan over moderate heat, shaking the pan slightly, until the grains are lightly browned. Transfer the semolina to another saucepan and add 1 pint of hot water. Bring it to a boil, stirring, and cook until the semolina is quite thick.

2 Turn the semolina on to a buttered plate, let it cool slightly and then shape and smooth it into a flat cake, about 1 inch in thickness. Refrigerate. When the cake is firm and cold, cut it into 8 segments.

3 Brush the segments with beaten egg and dredge them with flour.

4 Heat the butter in a pan and fry the segments until they look rich brown. Transfer them to a warm, oven-proof serving dish and place them in a low oven.

5 Combine the sugar, lemon juice, spices and 2 fl oz of water in a small saucepan and boil until it forms a thick syrup. Pour the syrup over the semolina slices and serve.

Notes: The semolina slices can be lightened by stirring in 2 beaten eggs just after the grain has thickened.

4

PICNICS AND SHIKARS

·

Meals and snacks for outdoor occasions

It is impossible for anyone living in a temperate climate to realize what it means to escape after months of sizzling temperature into clean, cool air in a dustless land of ice-cold cascades that splash down among ferns and moss-covered rocks; where there are steeply sloping hillsides covered with deodar pines and firs that shelter, here and there, little pools of blue harebells, small islands of creamy-coloured tulips streaked with carmine, deeper blue lagoons of violets, and a whole spangled galaxy of anemones, hollyhocks, primulas, and wild roses.

Mark Channing, Simla, 1934, *India Mosaic*

In a land of, at once, such beauty and such harsh aridity, it was no wonder that the British would escape to cooler climes at the first opportunity, for, apart from the welcome respite from the heat, the hills and mountains were lush and wooded and reminded the British of England. The romantic idea of a picnic in a silvan glade, so beloved of the European heart, clung on in the British soul, no doubt sustaining the conscientious servant of the British Empire through his travails in the deserts, dusty plains and steaming jungles of the subcontinent.

When thrown on their own resources for amusement, the *sahib* or *mem-sahib* invariably organized a picnic. Even on the plains, during the cold weather, the nearest clump of trees, orchard, or garden became the venue

---

1. Indian field baker, *c*.1897; 2. Sweetmakers celebrating the new Maharaja's reign, Rajputana; 3. Swimming from the houseboat, Kashmir; 4. An avenue of poplars near Tangmarg, Kashmir, 1936; 5. My mother out shooting with my grandfather, Sarkesar, *c*.1927; 6. The nannies and their charges picnic at Leopards Valley, Kashmir, 1936; 7. My nanny, Lillian Sargeant, picnicking with friends, Kilanmarg, Kashmir, 1936; 8. Hiking at the Frozen Lakes, Kashmir; 9. Picnic, family and friends, Kashmir.

for an al fresco meal. When my mother and her elder sister were in Sargodha, in the Punjab, picnics were one of the chief forms of social activity. They were mostly informal and spur-of-the-moment. The school-teacher, the lady doctor, young men from the Indian Civil Service or the police or the Remount Depot were invited. Everybody contributed something. It was a standing joke in our family that my aunt, after organizing the whole outing and delegating everyone's responsibilities, would always conclude with, "I'll bring the gramophone and records." Everyone would motor to the nearby countryside; to an orchard or to the grassy banks of the canals, which were lined with magnificent, shady Shisham trees. Wicker picnic baskets would be opened by the servants and a cloth spread on the grass and all the food would be unpacked. And what a spread! To satisfy appetites sharpened by swimming in the canals there would be cold ham or tongue, *naan* bread or *parathas*, "steamroller" chicken, potato cutlets or rissoles, sausages, spiced beef, lettuce, tomatoes and fruit, such as Alfonzo mangoes and *behr* (a small, red plum the size of an olive), for dessert. Thermos flasks of lemonade, iced beer and ginger beer were provided to quench the thirst.

Moonlight picnics on the canal were very popular, with swimming or dancing preceding or following. Near Sargodha the railway lines ran close to the canal for a portion of its length, separated only by the tree-lined road that bordered the water. My mother recalls one memorable picnic:

One of our regular picnic guests was with the railways and he and my sister organized a night picnic I shall never forget. He supplied an engine with two flatbeds, one of which was fitted out with *dhurries*, cushions and the gramophone and records. The other, nearest the engine, had the servants on it with the food and drinks. We chugged off up by the canal and stopped just by a bridge over the water. We all had our swimsuits on under our clothes and we dived and swam in the canal, some of us off the bridge. The moon wasn't shining on the water and it looked very murky to me so I decided to do a backward dive because I couldn't face diving forward. I had never attempted it before but fortunately I dived shallow so I wasn't hurt. We had a great evening; swam, danced, listened to music, ate, and then it was time to go home. Well, on the way there we were pushed by the engine but on the way back to the station, we were pulled. So, by the time we reached Sargodha all the soot from the engine had coated us and we were all totally blackened.

From Sargodha my family went to Kashmir for the summers. One either went through Lahore to Sialkot, then through the Jammu tunnel under the mountains to Kashmir, or to Rawalpindi, then up through Murree, at 7000 feet, then down again, along the Jhelum River to the Vale of Kashmir, surrounded by snowcapped mountains, to Srinagar. Here are some of my mother's recollections of Kashmir around 1928–30:

In Srinagar, everybody lived on houseboats. There were two hotels but nobody wanted to live there; it was much more fun on a houseboat. You'd book through an agent, or arrive and spend one night in a hotel, then haggle for a houseboat. They had from two to four bedrooms, a drawing room, a dining room, and a flat roof, on which we would sit out in the evenings and enjoy the view, or dive off into the Dal Lake. Behind the houseboat was a small, local boat, where the owner, the *mangi*, and his family lived. The front part of that boat was the kitchen where all the cooking for both boats was done, and your *ayah* or whatever servants you had with you, would live there. If you had a lot of servants, they'd have two of these boats tied on the back. Your *mangi*, who was also head boatman, and two or three servants, would pole the houseboat along wherever you wanted to go. When you found a place you liked, you'd stop and the *mangi* would arrange permission with the owner of the land and you'd tie your boat up. (Nowadays, the houseboats do not move but are at permanent moorings.) Then you had your *shikara*, a small, flat-bottomed boat, like a punt, in which you sat on cushions. And it had a top with curtains hanging down for privacy or shade. So off you'd go on outings and picnics.

The golfers used to go up to Gulmarg. Above Gulmarg was Mount Kilanmarg, 14,000 feet high, and it overlooked the Frozen Lakes. They were called that because, even in the height of summer, they were frozen. We used to picnic there. There were little horses you could ride along a track that wound a long way up the side of the mountain. The more energetic could hike up. Then we'd set up the picnic and eat large quantities of all sorts of food that had been prepared for us before we set out.

There was often the unexpected side to picnicking in India:

Luncheon & tea we had under an enormous banyan tree, and as huge kites swoop down and carry off all the food on your plate native servants stand about with great sticks wh. they wave at them.

Lady Curzon, Calcutta, January 1899, *Lady Curzon's India*, ed. John Bradley

For those who tired of the gentler pursuits of picnics, swimming and hikes, riding and rambles, there were the more manly and exciting sports: big-game hunting (*shikars*), shoots, and the dangerous and uncertain sport of pigsticking.

The maharajas loved and excelled in hunting and many were superb shots. One of their favourite forms of entertainment for important guests was to organize a hunt. Much has been written of these lavish and often incredible exercises. (Forms of conservation and wild-animal herding would often ensure that enormous quantities of game were confined to small areas so that every guest could bring home quantities of trophies. One guest remarked that it was like "shooting ducks in a barrel.")

My aunt, who was also a very good shot, recalled a tiger shoot organized by the Maharaja of Orcha:

It lasted for two days. We all sat down in *machans*. Rifles were used and the first shot got a trophy. Then we had a meal. The guests sat at round tables and were served with *thalis* (metal trays) with the food arranged in silver bowls. There were chicken and meat curries, birds and game, lentil dishes and hot *chapattis* and *parathas* passed around by the servants. Boiled rice was in the middle of each tray. After the meal, silver bowls of scented water were passed around for the guests to wash their hands.

In letters home, Lady Curzon captured the excitement and, sometimes, amusement that could be encountered on the hunt. These extracts from *Lady Curzon's India* were written in December 1899:

After breakfast we drove 3 miles further and then went over rough ground on elephants to a deep gully where the tiger drive was to be. There we got up into a castellated tower ... A tiger broke back and the beat began anew, and about 5 there was a crunching and a growl, and a flash of yellow dashed before us, and George fired and missed him: the fraction of a second, and as the tiger galloped past, George shot him in the back and Captain Baker-Carr fired, and all was over and the tiger *gone*! It was so sudden and thrilling that my eyes were falling out and my tongue tied ...

We rode (temperature 100) to our afternoon beat, and lost no time in being ready for tiger this time, so of course we had a long wait, but a funny one, as a big bear came bounding out of the jungle, and the first person he met was Captain Yarde-Buller on an elephant. The bear gave him one look and then dashed at a tree in which Captain Wigram sat on a branch. He "booed" at the bear, which sat down with surprise and then rushed to another tree in which Lord Suffolk sat. This was a third shock, so off he bounded only to meet *us* in our *machan*, and his surprise was so complete that he sat down spellbound! We were posted in a long line waiting for the tiger, so could see the bear's adventures, and were shaking with laughter. He bounded up a bank where he met Evey Pelley on an elephant, and this shock was too much, and he turned a back somersault, and then fled grunting back into the jungle. In a tiger beat no one shoots anything else, but we were all sad not to have got a nice black rug.

Of course, lunch was served al fresco at these affairs. But, when the shoots were less formal, food could be donated and eaten *en route*. My aunt recalled that when she went shooting and walked into the villages, the villagers would give them *chapattis* made with *gram* flour (*besan*). Sometimes the hunters brought snacks with them, such as apricots, peaches and hard-boiled eggs.

The picnic fare in this chapter reflects accurately the snacks and meals that were eaten in the open air – whatever the reason. It is mostly finger food and where it is not, remember that a picnic in the days of the Raj often included snow-white tablecloths, silver cutlery, crystal glasses and finger bowls! I am afraid that imagination will have to supply the many uniformed servants lurking discreetly behind the trees, ready to run forward at a moment's notice to serve more refreshments or pour out more champagne!

Chicken croquettes

•

Of course, these rather unusual croquettes are not only for picnics. They are ideal for a first course at dinner, served hot, or for a light luncheon.

Serves 4–6

1 lb chicken meat (from breast and thighs), cut into small pieces

2 slices white bread, finely crumbled

1 medium onion, peeled and finely chopped

½ teaspoon freshly ground coriander seeds

1 teaspoon grated orange zest

1 tablespoon finely chopped parsley

1 teaspoon salt

½ teaspoon freshly ground black pepper

2 eggs, separated

2 tablespoons flour

2 tablespoons *ghee* (clarified butter)

1   Place the chicken in a processor or mortar and process or pound to a paste.

2   Add the breadcrumbs, onion, coriander, orange, parsley and seasonings and process or pound until the onion is pulverized and everything is well mixed. Then work in the yolk of 1 egg and the white of both, beaten separately into a stiff snow.

3   Shape the mixture into croquettes as lightly as possible. (You may wish to chill the mixture first.) Then brush them with the remaining egg yolk and dredge them with flour.

4   Melt the *ghee* in a wok or pan over moderate heat and fry the croquettes until they are a medium brown. Drain them well on paper towels. Serve hot or cold.

Notes: If you care to, you may leave out the orange zest and add instead a generous pinch of curry powder to the mixture. Then serve the croquettes with a little melted mango chutney on the side.

Chingree samosas

•

It really did depend on where you were stationed as to whether your cook could make these. Before the days of air travel, it was extremely difficult to obtain really fresh shellfish, although boxes of seafood, packed in ice, used to be loaded on the Indian trains for shipment to the landlocked cities in India. It meant, really, that your cook had to have eagle eyes and a very good nose when he set out to buy seafood in the market. Of course, the coastal cities such as Calcutta, Bombay and Karachi had no difficulty in keeping in a supply of really fresh seafood. Even then, with the heat of a great deal of the year, they had to be purchased very early in the morning.

C. C. Lewis says in *Culinary Notes for Sind*, 1923:

Sind in general (and Karachi in particular) is particularly happy in its food supplies. Its fish cannot be excelled in the whole of India and its meat compares favourably with the home article. Its vegetables and fruit are by no means bad, and it is possible to avoid entirely tinned or bottled goods. But here we will at once say that we by no means share the not uncommon prejudice against the latter. Ten years ago there was always the risk of ptomaine poisoning but the War did much to improve the canning industry and the risk is negligible at the present day. Certain articles which can now be purchased in tins and bottles are so perfectly done that – granted a good cook – it is absolutely impossible to tell the difference between them and fresh. To mention a few at random we would say mushrooms, white currants, raspberries (the Café Grand, Karachi, have some very excellent raspberries in tins which have the great merit of each raspberry being whole), celery, larks in *foie gras* and strawberries in brandy. None of these can be produced fresh in Sind and therefore if one desires any of them to complete a recherché dinner, it is necessary to obtain them in tins or bottles. Any of the last mentioned items can be obtained from the Army and Navy Stores, London, or Harrods and if ordered direct, are very cheap even including freight and customs duty.

Serves 6

10 tablespoons *ghee* (clarified butter)	$\frac{1}{2}$ lb shrimp or prawns, shelled, cleaned and finely chopped
1 small onion, peeled and sliced thinly	$\frac{1}{2}$ teaspoon salt
2 teaspoons curry powder	$\frac{3}{4}$ lb/scant 3 cups self-raising flour

1   Melt 2 tablespoons of *ghee* in a saucepan. When it is up to heat, fry the sliced onion until it is a light brown; then stir in the curry powder and fry it with the onion, stirring to keep it from burning.

2   Add the shellfish and the salt and lower the heat. Keep stirring the mixture for 2 more minutes and then set the curry aside. (It may be made ahead and refrigerated.)

3   Make a shortcrust pastry with the flour, 4 tablespoons of the *ghee* and just enough water to make it adhere. Roll it out thinly and cut 4-inch circles from the dough. Fill each with a spoonful of curry and fold each over in half, moistening the edges to seal them. Repeat until all the puffs are made.

4   Heat the remaining 4 tablespoons of *ghee* in a wok over medium heat. When it is up to 325°F/170°C, place 2 *samosas* in and fry them to a light brown. They should puff up in the frying. Drain on paper towels and continue frying all the puffs, two at a time. Serve hot or cold.

Notes: These puffs or *samosas* may also be made with crab, lamb or chicken.

Steamroller chicken

•

The Qissa Khawani Bazaar in Peshawar was immortalized by Kipling as the Street of the Story-tellers. It is on the old Grand Trunk Road from the Khyber Pass into the city and was traditionally not only a market, but a refreshment stop for people, where they could buy food and drink and also listen to the dramatic stories of the professional story-tellers. The stories they told were ancient ones, handed down from one story-teller to another. According to tradition, a story-teller is not born, he is made, and with certain high qualifications. Mark Channing is more explicit in *India Mosaic*.

In addition to having read all the known books on love and heroism, the teller of stories must have suffered greatly for love, have lost his beloved, drunk much good wine, wept with many in their sorrow, have looked often upon death, and have learned much about birds and beasts. He must also be able to change himself into a beggar or a caliph in the twinkling of an eye.

The past is still vividly present in Qissa Khawani. Here fierce Afghanis, sullen refugees, taciturn tribesmen and villagers from all over the North-west Frontier gather to buy and sell and to exchange news. The streets are choked by dilapidated trucks, horse-drawn carriages and recalcitrant camels. Snake charmers with woven baskets full of coiled venom, medicine men with boxes of patent medicines, and conjurers vie for the attention of the passing crowd. Above all floats the sweet smoke from hookahs and the pungent, spicy smell of charcoal-broiled chicken and lamb.

Steamroller chicken is thus named because it looks as if the flattened halves have been run over by a heavy object. In fact they are split open with a heavy cleaver and beaten into submission. To achieve the necessary effect, halve a small chicken lengthwise, so that each half has a leg and a wing. Then place the halves between dry towels and whack them repeatedly with the flat of a heavy cleaver blade or with a rolling pin, until they flatten. There is nothing delicate about this lusty dish, but the fiery and earthy tribesmen of the Frontier are not delicate either!

Serves 4

For the marinade
1 medium onion, peeled and coarsely chopped
1-inch piece of fresh ginger root, peeled and chopped
3 tablespoons *ghee* (clarified butter)
1 tablespoon ground coriander
$1\frac{1}{2}$ teaspoons ground cumin
1 teaspoon ground turmeric
$\frac{1}{4}$ teaspoon ground cloves
$\frac{1}{4}$ teaspoon ground cinnamon
$\frac{1}{4}$ teaspoon ground cardamom

1 teaspoon cayenne
2 tablespoons chopped coriander leaves
2 cloves of garlic, smashed and peeled
the juice of 1 large lemon

2 $2\frac{1}{2}$-lb chickens, halved and flattened
the marinade from above
4 tablespoons *ghee* (clarified butter)
2 lemons, cut into wedges
2 tomatoes, cut into slices
1 large red onion, peeled and cut into rings

1   Place the onion and ginger into a processor and process for 1 minute, stopping from time to time to scrape down the sides of the processor with a spatula. Add the remaining marinade ingredients and process everything to a fine paste.

2   Place the flattened chicken halves in a large bowl and, using your hands, rub them over with half the marinade. Spoon the remainder of it over them and cover the bowl. Refrigerate for at least $2\frac{1}{2}$ hours, even overnight.

3   Preheat the grill or barbecue and set a rack close to the source of heat.

4   Remove the chicken halves from the marinade, scraping off the surplus

and reserving it. Place the chickens over or under the source of heat and cook for 10 minutes on the first side and 8 minutes on the second. (If using the more gentle heat of a barbecue, adjust this to 20 and 15 minutes.)

5   After the first 5 minutes, baste the chicken with the marinade, and, after allowing the marinade to dry on the surface, baste again.

6   When the chicken is just done, baste all surfaces with *ghee* and, moving the rack closer to the heat if possible, sear the chicken until the surface is crusty and a rich brown.

7   Place the chicken in a cloth for your picnic basket. Serve it accompanied by the lemon wedges to be squeezed over the top and with a salad of the tomatoes and onions.

Notes: *Naan* bread is the perfect accompaniment for this chicken and a recipe follows. Fresh mint chutney is also a good accompaniment. Alternatively, you may make a bed of the tomato and onion slices on a large platter, place the chicken halves on top and garnish them with lemon wedges and mint leaves.

Naan bread

•

Naan is the leavened bread of the north-west of the subcontinent. Its home can equally be said to be Afghanistan, Pakistan and the adjacent portion of India. In the days when I was in India, this could be translated into the North-west Frontier Province and the Punjab, as well as the land of the Pathans and Afghans. It is a delicious, puffy, crusty bread and the ingredients vary slightly from area to area. The Afghans' version uses wholewheat flour and a sourdough starter instead of yeast, called *khamir tursh*. In this respect, there is a slight similarity to the famous sourdough breads of northern California, which date from the days of the gold miners. *Naan* also bears a distinct similarity to the leavened breads of Syria and other countries of the Middle East. In fact there is a definite possibility that it may have come up to Afghanistan and then into India with the traders and conquerors.

I have had *naan* made with either white or brown flour and I really prefer the latter, which is closer to the Indian *atta* flour, used for *chapattis*. Try to get *atta* from an Indian or Asian grocery but if you cannot, then I suggest a mixture of flours. You can use yoghurt to achieve the characteristic sour effect.

Quantity: 6 breads

6 oz/1½ cups white flour
6 oz/1½ cups wholewheat flour
1 teaspoon salt
½ teaspoon baking powder
1 teaspoon sugar
4 fl oz warm milk
½ oz fresh yeast
4 oz plain yoghurt

extra plain all-purpose flour for working the bread
2 tablespoons melted *ghee* (clarified butter) (optional)
1 tablespoon poppy seeds (optional)

1 Sift the flours, salt and baking powder into a large bowl.

2 Dissolve the sugar into the warm milk; then stir in the yeast until it has dissolved also. Let the mixture sit for 5 minutes, or until the yeast begins to work a little; then stir in the yoghurt. Mix the liquid mixture thoroughly into the flours to form a smooth, soft dough. Transfer to a floured board.

3 With floured hands, knead the dough for about 8–10 minutes until it is the consistency of normal bread dough. Replace it in the bowl, cover and leave it to rise for up to 4 hours, or until the dough has doubled in bulk.

4 Preheat your oven to 500°F (250°C, Gas Mark 9) and place 2 baking trays inside.

5 Punch the dough down again and divide it into 6 balls. Shape each into a flat oval by slapping it from hand to hand until the ball lengthens and flattens. The shapes should be between ¼ and ½ inch thick.

6 Place 3 breads on each tray and bake in the oven for approximately 6–8 minutes, or until they are pale brown and a little crisp on the outside.

7 The breads may be served at this stage, or you may like to heat the grill, brush the top surface of each bread with *ghee* and sprinkle poppy seeds on top. Lightly brown the surfaces.

Notes: I have always preferred *naan* served hot but if you are going on a picnic this won't be possible. Cold *naan* wrapped around barbecued chicken or lamb and eaten in the open is delicious.

If you like, you can take a small lump of the uncooked dough and leave it in a warm place overnight, then experiment with using it as a starter for the next batch. The longer the starter is left, the more sour the ensuing bread. I think I would still use a little additional leavening, but leave out the yoghurt and make up the total amount of fluid with cold water.

Aloo parathas

•

These potato-filled breads are sinfully delicious. I adored them as a child and love them still. Funny, I can't eat the same large quantities of them as I used to!

Quantity: 16 small filled breads

6 oz/1½ cups white flour
6 oz/1½ cups wholewheat flour
½ teaspoon salt
5 tablespoons *ghee* (clarified butter)
1 small onion, peeled and finely chopped
½ teaspoon cumin seeds
1 clove of garlic, smashed, peeled and finely chopped

½-inch piece of fresh ginger root, peeled and finely chopped
¼ teaspoon turmeric
2 green chillies, finely chopped
2 medium potatoes, boiled, peeled and roughly mashed
1 tablespoon finely chopped coriander leaves
½ teaspoon salt

1   Sift the flours and salt into a mixing bowl and add 2 tablespoons of the *ghee*. Rub the fat into the flour then gradually pour in just over 5 fl oz of warm water, kneading and gathering up the dough until it holds into a compact ball.

2   Knead and fold the dough repeatedly for 7 to 8 minutes, until it feels soft and velvety and becomes elastic. Gather it into a ball again, replace it in the bowl and cover with a damp cloth. Let it rest in a warm place for 30 minutes while you make the filling.

3   Heat 1 tablespoon of ghee in a large pan and fry the onion and cumin seeds for 2 minutes. Add the garlic and ginger and continue to fry for another 2 minutes, stirring occasionally.

4   Add all the remaining ingredients and stir well until they are warmed through and thoroughly mixed. Take the pan off the fire and set it aside until the mixture has cooled.

5   Bring the dough back to the working surface and divide it into 16 equal portions. Flour your hands and, taking up 1 portion, form it into a ball and

then gently pat it into a thick circle. Use your thumb to make a depression in the middle and put 1 teaspoon of the filling into this hollow. Carefully coax and draw the edges of the dough up and over the filling and pinch them together at the top to seal. Turn the filled ball over on to the board, filled side down. Roll it out gently into a disc, about $3\frac{1}{2}$ inches in diameter. Repeat with the remaining portions of dough.

6   Melt the remaining *ghee* in a small saucepan and set it at one side of the stove. Place another pan on the stove and brush it with melted *ghee*. Fry the *parathas*, 1 or 2 at a time, until they are speckled brown on the bottom. Brush the top surfaces with melted *ghee* and turn them over. Fry the other sides for 2 minutes, pressing down with a spatula until they puff up a little. Repeat until all the *parathas* are fried. Serve hot or cold.

Notes: Peas can be added to the filling, or even a little leftover ground meat. Other vegetables, such as cooked cauliflower, broccoli or chopped beans, are nice additions.

Shami kebabs

•

In the earlier years of his career in the Royal Engineers, my father's work led him to tour and inspect some of the more distant areas of the north-west of what was then India. He was actively engaged in works projects, such as building bridges and roads, and the siting of these took him to many places: Gilgit and Chitral, Swat and Buner, Waziristan, Baluchistan, Quetta – he visited them all. Accompanied by the faithful Umar Khan, he rode horses, jolted along in all kinds of primitive transportation and often walked over most of the mountainous, rocky, barren and desolate lands of the Frontier. In later years he used to smile ruefully and say that it cost him a fortune in shoe leather.

By that time my father had passed the necessary interpretership exam in Pushtu, the language common to most of the area, so he was able to converse with whomever he met. And there was always a polyglot and picturesque assortment of people moving along the narrow tracks and mountain passes. Sometimes it was a party of Kohistanis, in moccasins and Gilgit caps, sometimes a lone old man, bearded and riding a donkey, or a fierce Afghani, with gun belt and firearms. Occasionally there would be a wedding party on its way to the next village, with banners and drummers and nautch-girls, singing and dancing. There were other objects of interest beside the remote paths. My father occasionally stumbled upon ancient

artefacts which had lain unnoticed since the time of Iskander and even earlier. One such find was the stone head of a lion from Gandhara. It was probably the carved finial of a banner, staff or tent pole. It still sits in pride of place in my mother's drawing room; its ageless and classic beauty is a testament to the great civilizations that have swept over the mountains of the north-west.

Among the most picturesque and memorable characters whom my father met was the Wali of Swat. The Swat Valley is about 130 miles long and is some eighty-four miles north of Nowshera, or north and west of Peshawar, over the high Malakand Pass. Called Udyana (garden) by the Buddhists some 2,000 years ago, the valley is very beautiful. Today, the Pakistanis call it their Switzerland, for it is surrounded by snowcapped mountains, their lower slopes covered with firs and deodar forests. The whole valley is strewn with ancient Buddhist ruins – a vast Buddha carved out of a rock face and remains of tumbled-down stupas. The capital, Saidu Sharif, is built near the site of an earlier civilization, probably dating back to the fifth century BC. The Swat Valley was conquered by Alexander, and was subsequently ruled by Indo-Greek kings, Indo-Scythians and then Kushans. But of all these rulers, probably none was so dedicated to his people nor so innovative as the Wali. My father met him in 1938, when the fierce old man was over sixty. He remembers him as tall, white-bearded and ruddy-cheeked, very upright and dignified. Although he was the blood grandson of the great Akhund of Swat, he had come to power after fifty years of internecine feuds and rivalries within the family; quarrels which had laid open a once-beautiful land to neglect and ruin. The Wali built and garrisoned eighty-five forts in the valleys of Swat and Buner. He laid telephone lines throughout the country, set up electricity in Saidu Sharif and built a hospital and a school. He also built a network of roads and this is where my father came into the picture. The British "gifted" the Wali with a road from Swat to Buner and my father built it. He got to know the Wali well and became on very friendly terms with his son, the Wali-i-Ahud (or heir-apparent). The son was educated at Islamia College and was a very English gentleman. He had designed and built the guest house at Saidu Sharif, an elegant building with all modern innovations, and his own home was as splendid as that of any of the Raj. In 1938 my mother and father stayed with him for a weekend, and dined at the palace with the old Wali. They both returned for the formal dedication and opening of the road.

What has all this to do with kebabs? Little, save that the Wali was a Muslim and ate as a Muslim. The following recipe for kebabs would be very familiar to Muslims from Baghdad to Kabul, and Peshawar to Saidu Sharif. They were probably prepared in exactly the same way for the Wali and my parents as our *khansamer* prepared them for picnics, for they are excellent finger food.

Serves 4–6

1 lb ground lamb
4 tablespoons pine nuts
1 small onion, peeled and
    finely chopped
1 teaspoon salt
¼ teaspoon freshly ground
    black pepper
1 teaspoon aromatic spice
    mix (see *Notes* below)
2 tablespoons finely
    chopped parsley

2 heaped tablespoons
    gram or chick-pea flour
    (*besan*)
4 fl oz vegetable oil for
    frying
2 large tomatoes, sliced
1 red onion, peeled and cut
    into rings
1 head of lettuce, separated
    into leaves
10–15 mint leaves,
    shredded

1   Place the lamb in a food processor or through a mincer and process or grind it to a fine paste. Place the meat in a bowl.

2   Add the remaining ingredients, down to and including the parsley, and blend and knead thoroughly until everything becomes a homogeneous mass. Chill for a few minutes.

3   Dusting your hands with flour, roll and form the mixture into small, fat sausages. Dredge them with the flour.

4   Heat the oil in a wok or deep pan to 325°F (170°C) and fry the sausages, 2 or 3 at a time, until they are crisp and brown on the outside. Drain them well on paper towels.

5   Serve the kebabs accompanied by the tomato slices and onion rings, mixed together, sprinkled with mint leaves and served on a bed of lettuce leaves.

Notes: The aromatic spice mix listed is similar to the *garam masala* mix but with a slight difference. Make it up in the quantities given below and store in a sealed glass jar in a dark cupboard. Use it to spice minced and ground meat mixtures.

Aromatic Spice Mix
    2 tablespoons ground allspice
    1 tablespoon ground cinnamon
    2 teaspoons ground nutmeg
    2 teaspoons ground cloves
    1 teaspoon ground ginger

Sakesar, a little hill station

It was the summer of 1925 and both the "Whitburn Sisters," my mother and her elder sister, Berenice, were up in Sakesar, in the Salt Range, for the hot weather. It was their first summer in India after finishing their seven years of schooling in England. In fact, Berenice was officially "out" but my mother was not. Nevertheless, my grandparents had decided that my mother should travel back to India with her sister. Consequently, at just sixteen, she was at rather a loose end that summer, with her activities somewhat curtailed because of her tender age. They both vividly remember Sakesar in 1925.

First, let me paint you a picture of the little summer settlement. It was not glamorous, unlike the large and famous hill stations of Simla, Darjeeling or Murree. The Salt Range hills stretch north-eastward above the vast Sind Desert, with the small town of Kushab to the south, Sargodha south and slightly east of that, and Rawalpindi quite a long way beyond the end of the range to the north. Sakesar lay at the Kushab end of the range at an altitude of between 4,500 to 5,000 feet, just high enough to get some respite from the heat. There was vegetation and trees but by no stretch of the imagination could you say it was thickly wooded. Its main advantage was that it was accessible to three administrative districts of the British: Mianwali, Attock and Sargodha, and the officials, such as the police, the deputy commissioner and other civil servants, including my grandfather, had their summer bungalows there. There were small villages scattered over the hills and the villagers trapped rainfall in ponds for irrigation. The ponds attracted wildfowl, so there was some shooting. Other than that, you rode, walked, or visited people who were up there from other districts.

The little hill station did not change much through the years. Lady Wilson described it in 1889 in *Letters from India*:

Blessings on the man who dreamt of Sakesar and made it an English home. I am delighted with our new quarters. You can't imagine the kind of material pleasure one has in material things that simply look English. The roof of this house enchants me, merely because it slants instead of being flat: the ceilings, because they are much lower than those at Shahpur and are plastered, so that the beams are concealed. The woodwork is actually varnished: the bow windows are really windows, not doors: the fireplaces are all in the right place; and now that our books, pictures, piano and general household goods have arrived, we are as cosy as cosy could be, and feel as if we had been established for centuries, instead of five weeks...

Our hill-top is sparsely covered with olives and wild figs, acacias and a few stunted fir trees, and has a narrow footpath running round it, giving us a two-mile walk in the evening, with tennis on the one little public tennis-court as an alternative form of exercise.

Dotted along the northern side of the hill are four bungalows, one called the Bannu Bungalow, another the Deputy Commissioner's, a third the Mission Bungalow, and the last the Policeman's. Add to these a little house by itself on a downward slope, in which an old gentleman lives with his Indian wife and children; a row which houses the Indian subordinate officials, with an Indian shop supplying their needs, and a temple, where an old Fakir spends his life meditating beside a small spring, and you can picture the extent and contents of our little hill station.

In 1925, it was little changed. My mother speaks:

You made your own amusement. There was a tennis court, but otherwise you rode your small pony or walked. It was very primitive. Our bungalow was separate from the others and looked over the Mianwali district and you could see for miles and miles. Father came up later to join us with two more men, and they went off grouse shooting up on the hillside. Toddles [family nickname for her elder sister], who was learning to be a good shot and who was old enough, went with them.

My aunt remembered:

Before the roads were built, the luggage went up on camels. You took the train to the last station on the line, then spent the night in the railway station rest house. At dawn the next morning, you would get up and ride fifteen miles along an arid track through hills covered with scrub.

My grandfather eventually built a road up to Sakesar, and my grandmother laid the foundation stone (*photo opposite*). But the big event in Sakesar, the one which the sisters remembered vividly, was the night of the panther.

My family was at dinner and a bearer came rushing up to my grandfather, saying "*Sahib*, they've seen a panther!" Of course, this caused great excitement. My grandfather immediately organized a shoot, gathering together a few of the young men who were up there, together with the *shikaris*, or gun carriers. The latter were good shots as well, and would scout out the game. They all went off down the hill towards the village with lanterns to catch the panther. Meanwhile, the rest of the family went to bed. My grandmother was inside the bungalow with her youngest daughter, Diana. My mother had taken her bed out on to the veranda – a common practice when nights were hot. But her elder sister had decided to get even more breeze and had pulled her bed out into the compound, just below the veranda, and was sleeping with her bull mastiff tied to the leg of her bed.

She was awakened by the call of a hyena, and she simultaneously felt her bed shaking. Then she realized that her dog was shaking with fear. She looked around and in a small, nearby copse of pines, she saw two gleaming yellow lights. At first she could not make out what they were; then she realized they were the eyes of the panther. He was about thirty feet away. He was after her dog, and he was hungry. She sat up in bed and shouted with fright.

At that moment, the shooting party was coming back up the hill, empty-handed, and heard the commotion. The *chowkidar*, or night watchman, was screaming "Panther, panther!" But the great beast did not move. He wanted the dog. My grandfather was actually ill-equipped to shoot big game, for all he had was his shotgun, suitable for birds, and four bullets. However, he raised his gun, aimed right between the eyes of the big cat, and fired. At the same time, the servants all came running out with lanterns, the beast moved, and the shot missed. The panther fled.

Some days later, the beast was killed. But my aunt never pulled her bed out into the compound at Sakesar again.

Raised game pie

•

The birds that were shot at Sakesar generally ended up in the pot, our family's, or at someone else's table. So, talking about small game (hopefully, not a panther), here is a pie recipe which utilizes game and at the same time is excellent provender for picnics.

Serves 6

veal knuckle or pork
    bones
1 large onion, peeled and
    quartered
6 peppercorns
1 large bay leaf
2 leaves of sage, torn
$\frac{1}{2}$ teaspoon salt
1 lb meat from partridge or
    pheasant
$\frac{1}{2}$ teaspoon freshly grated
    nutmeg
$\frac{1}{2}$ teaspoon ground white
    pepper
$\frac{1}{2}$ teaspoon ground cloves

$\frac{1}{3}$ teaspoon dried basil
$\frac{1}{3}$ teaspoon dried marjoram
$\frac{1}{3}$ teaspoon dried thyme
2 bay leaves, finely
    crumbled
$\frac{1}{4}$ lb calf's liver
8 oz sliced bacon
2 tablespoons finely
    chopped parsley
$\frac{1}{4}$ lb ham
1 lb/$3\frac{1}{2}$ cups flour
4 oz unsalted butter
1 teaspoon salt
1 egg, beaten

1   Place the bones, onion quarters, peppercorns, bay, sage and salt in a large saucepan and cover with 1 quart of cold water. Bring to a boil, skim the surface; then reduce the heat and let it boil gently for 2 hours, until the stock is reduced to just under one half. Cool, skim off the fat and strain the liquid. (It should jell as it cools.)

2   While the stock is boiling, dice the meat from the game birds and toss it in a basin, together with all the spices and herbs listed. Set it aside.

3   Mince the liver and *half* the bacon. (You may use a food processor.) Add the parsley and mix together vigorously until the forcemeat is well blended. Set it aside.

4   Cut the ham into julienne strips and set it aside.

5   Sift the flour into a mixing bowl and rub in the butter with your

fingertips until the mixture resembles fine breadcrumbs. Sprinkle the salt over the surface and lightly mix it in. Make a well in the middle and gradually pour in 6 fl oz of warm water, stirring until the dough adheres together. Place the dough on a board and knead it to a stiff paste. Let it stand for 10 minutes.

6   Roll out the pastry to $\frac{1}{2}$-inch thick. Take a cake tin with fairly high, straight sides and place it before you, right side up. Flour the inside of the tin. Reserve $\frac{1}{3}$ of the pastry for the lid and decoration. From the remainder, cut a circle to fit snugly into the bottom of the tin, and a long strip to line the sides. Pinch and press them together where they join at the base.

7   Line the bottom of the pastry form with *half* the bacon reserved in Step 3. Now place *half* the forcemeat from Step 3 in an even layer over the bacon. Over that, press in *half* of the seasoned cubes of game from Step 2. Top the game with *half* of the julienne strips of ham. Put in a layer of the remaining forcemeat, followed by the remainder of the game and then the last of the ham. Arrange the rest of the bacon over the top.

8   Roll out a circle of pastry just larger than the tin for a lid. Brush the edges of the pie with water and press the lid firmly on to the pastry sides, crimping the edges together decoratively to seal them. Cut pastry leaves from the scraps and attach them in a circle in the middle of the top with a little beaten egg. Cut a small hole in the middle. Fashion a pastry rose and place it over the hole but do not stick it down. Brush the top of the pie with beaten egg. Heat the oven to 375°F (190°C, Gas Mark 5) and bake the pie for 20 minutes. Reduce the heat to 350°F (180°C, Gas Mark 4), cover the pie lightly with a piece of foil to prevent it browning further, and bake for another hour and 40 minutes.

9   Remove the pie from the oven, reheat the jellied stock and pour it carefully through the hole in the top. Replace the rose. Let the pie sit in a cool place for 2 hours, then carefully take it from the tin. It may be chilled before you take it on your picnic.

Notes: Other game birds may be used, or you may substitute turkey and/or chicken meat in the filling.

Nargisi kofta

•

It is still a matter of debate as to whether the British took this recipe home and, gradually, it became the sausage-meat-wrapped eggs known as Scotch eggs, or vice versa. I suspect that India laid first claim to this dish because it is a direct descendant of the meat ball and meat patty, both of which have been prepared and eaten in the Middle East and India for many centuries. These *koftas* are eaten in India on feast days and holidays, either dry or in a rich, spiced gravy. The name, incidentally, comes from the word for the narcissus flower, *narga*, because, when the ball is cut in half, the pattern of yellow, white and brown is said to resemble the flower.

Serves 8–10

2 lb ground lamb
1 tablespoon *ghee* (clarified butter)
1 medium onion, peeled and finely chopped
1 clove of garlic, smashed, peeled and finely chopped
2 tablespoons of finely chopped coriander leaves
2 oz/$\frac{1}{3}$ cup *gram* or chick-pea flour (*besan*)
1 teaspoon salt

1 teaspoon *garam masala* (sweet spice mix, p. 293)
$\frac{1}{2}$ teaspoon ground cumin
$\frac{1}{2}$ teaspoon paprika
2 teaspoons ground coriander seeds
$\frac{1}{2}$ teaspoon freshly ground black pepper
10 hard-boiled eggs
2 eggs, beaten
vegetable oil for deep-frying

1   Place the lamb in a food processor or mincer and process or mince into a smooth paste. Place it in a mixing bowl.
2   Heat the *ghee* in a pan over medium heat and sauté the onion and garlic until they are soft. Empty them into the processor, together with all the spices, herbs and flour, and process until smooth. Add to the lamb and mix and knead the mixture into a stiff, smooth paste.
3   Divide the *kofta* mixture into 10 equal pieces. Shape each into a patty, about 4 inches in diameter. Dip a hard-boiled egg into the beaten egg and

centre it on a patty. Gently coax and shape the meat mixture around it, carefully pressing the meat around the egg and making sure there are no seams or irregularities. Roll the meat into a smooth sphere. Continue until all the eggs are covered.

4   Heat the oil in a wok or deep-fryer to 350°F (180°C). Dip each *kofta* in the remainder of the beaten egg then deep-fry to a rich, dark brown. Drain on paper towels and leave to cool.

Notes: The *koftas* can be accompanied by a dipping sauce made from mango chutney, or a fresh Indian coriander chutney. Recipe follows.

Coriander chutney

•

Quantity: 10 oz

4 oz coriander leaves and stems	2 small green chillies
1-inch piece of fresh ginger root, peeled and finely chopped	3 tablespoons tamarind liquid
	$\frac{1}{2}$ teaspoon salt
	1 teaspoon brown sugar

Place all the ingredients in a blender or processor and blend or process to a smooth purée, stopping the machine and poking the mixture down with a spatula if the blades do not immediately engage the ingredients.

Notes: You may vary this chutney by substituting an equal quantity of mint leaves for the coriander, and adding half a cooking apple which you have peeled, cored and diced just before processing.

Tamarind is available in various forms from Asian foodstores.

Spiced beef

•

This beef does take a time in its preparation but, if you plan ahead, the long marination can be accomplished with no trouble.

Serves 8

4 lb brisket of beef (chuck may also be used)

4 oz/½ heaped cup dark brown sugar

For the marinade

2 teaspoons juniper berries (optional)

2 teaspoons whole allspice

2 teaspoons black peppercorns

2 tablespoons coarse salt

1 pint white vinegar

2 small onions, peeled and sliced

1 bay leaf

1 3-inch stick of cinnamon

6 whole cloves

1   Wash the brisket well and pat it dry. Press the brown sugar firmly on to the brisket on all sides. Place it in a casserole and cover it. Refrigerate for 2 days.

2   Crush the juniper, allspice, peppercorns and salt together. On the third day, press ⅕ of the mixture into the meat. Repeat on each of the ensuing 4 days, covering it and returning it each time to the refrigerator.

3   On the eighth day, preheat the oven to 275°F (140°C, Gas Mark 1). Wash the brisket under cold running water and clean the casserole. Replace the meat inside and add the remaining ingredients. Cover tightly and bake in the middle of the oven for up to 3 hours.

4   Cool the meat and wrap it in foil. Refrigerate overnight with a heavy weight on top.

Notes: If you like to cook a shorter version of this recipe, omit the brown sugar coating and the daily spice rub. Merely marinate the beef in the vinegar and vegetables and spices at the bottom of the list of ingredients and then bake the next day. The beef will not have such a rich taste but it will still be exceedingly good.

Sardine curry puffs

•

Quite a way removed from the fish pasties which the Cornish branch of our family ate in Truro (their home town), but, nevertheless, delicious and good picnic fare. They were also very convenient for the *khansamer* to make because we always had sardines in the store cupboard.

Serves 6–8

1 bay leaf
2 whole cloves
¼ teaspoon cardamom seeds
1 tablespoon ground coriander
2 teaspoons ground cumin
1 teaspoon ground turmeric
4 small red or green chillies, finely chopped
2 cloves of garlic, smashed, peeled and finely chopped

2 tablespoons vinegar
3 tablespoons vegetable oil
1 small onion, peeled and finely chopped
12 sardines, drained from their oil
the juice of 1 lemon
1 teaspoon salt
1 lb puff pastry
2 eggs, beaten

1   Place the bay leaf and cloves in a heavy pan and dry-roast them over medium heat until the bay leaf browns and the spices become aromatic. Grind in a spice grinder, together with the cardamom pods.

2   Empty the powder from above into a blender, together with the coriander, cumin, turmeric, chillies and garlic, and add the vinegar. Blend everything into a paste.

3   Heat the vegetable oil in a saucepan over medium-low heat and fry the onion until it is soft. Scrape in the spice paste from the blender and fry for at least 3 minutes, stirring constantly.

4   Add 6 fl oz of boiling water and cook and stir the curry sauce for 10 minutes, until it is reduced and fairly thick. Now add the sardines carefully and stir once, gently, to ensure they are mixed in with the sauce. Sprinkle with the lemon juice and the salt and remove the pan from the heat. Stir once again and let the fish cool and marinate in the sauce.

5   Roll out the puff pastry to ⅛ inch and cut it into 5-inch rounds. Place a

large piece of sardine and a little sauce in each, brush the edges with beaten egg and then fold the pastry over and crimp the edges to seal.

6   Preheat the oven to 375°F (190°C, Gas Mark 5). Complete all the puffs, then glaze the tops with the remainder of the beaten egg. Bake in the oven for 25 minutes, or until the pastry is risen and lightly browned. (If you find them browning too quickly, place a sheet of foil lightly on top.) Serve the puffs hot or cold.

Aloo chops

•

Standard family fare for picnics, my mother remembers these with nostalgia. *Aloo* chops were also a common and unassuming supper dish, since they were a good way of using up leftover meat.

Serves 4

¾ lb cold meat (beef or lamb)

1 medium onion, peeled and finely chopped

½ teaspoon salt

¼ teaspoon freshly ground black pepper

1 or 2 small green chillies, finely chopped

½ teaspoon ground cumin

¼ teaspoon ground turmeric

the juice of half a lemon

6 medium potatoes, cooked, peeled and mashed

a little flour

1 egg, beaten

4 tablespoons breadcrumbs

oil or *ghee* (clarified butter) for frying

1   Mince the cold meat finely and combine it in a bowl with the onion, salt, pepper, chillies, cumin and turmeric. Sprinkle with the lemon juice.

2   Divide the mashed potato into 8 equal portions. Pat 1 portion into a round patty in your hands and place about 2 teaspoons of the filling in the middle. Top with another patty of mashed potato and pinch the edges together to enclose the filling completely. Repeat with the rest of the filling and potato until you have made 4 "chops."

3 Sprinkle the chops with a little flour and brush them on both sides with beaten egg. Press them gently into the breadcrumbs until they are coated.
4 Heat the oil and fry them on both sides until the surfaces are brown and crisp. Serve them hot for a supper dish or cold for picnics.

Notes: You may also add chopped herbs, such as fresh coriander leaves or parsley, to the filling.

Stewed brandied apricots

•

We ate fresh apricots all over the Punjab and the Frontier, as they were grown in many of the highland regions, including Hunza and Swat, and in certain areas of the Punjab itself. They were wonderfully sweet and juicy, and when we could not get them fresh we would buy the whole, dried apricots and stew them gently until they were tender for desserts, such as fruit fools and ice-creams. This dish of spiced, dried apricots was commonly eaten in Kashmir. It can be prepared and taken in an insulated jug for a picnic dessert.

Serves 6

½ lb dried apricots
2 tablespoons sugar
1 oz/⅛ cup blanched,
    slivered almonds
2-inch stick of cinnamon

2 cloves
pinch of cardamom seeds
a little apricot brandy
    (optional)

1   Soak the apricots in 12 fl oz of water for at least 6 hours or overnight, until they have softened. Put them on to boil with all the remaining ingredients, except the brandy. After they have come to a boil, lower the heat to a simmer and cook until the apricots are soft and plump and until the liquid has decreased by half and become syrupy. Remove the spices.
2   Remove the pan from the fire and let it cool a little; then add a little apricot brandy and stir. Transfer to a bowl and chill in the refrigerator.

Notes: I like to serve these with a little yoghurt into which some heavy cream has been blended. A pinch of grated nutmeg over the top is a nice addition.

Nimboo pani

•

The name of this drink can refer both to lemonade or limeade, depending on where you are in India and which fruit you prefer. My personal preference is for limes, but both are very refreshing. This was the staple drink when the *memsahibs* played tennis, gardened too hard, walked too far, or on any other occasion where one worked up a thirst.

Quantity: 12 glasses

6 fresh limes
4 or more tablespoons
    sugar

¼ teaspoon salt
12 ice cubes

1   Roll the limes on a cutting board using hard pressure with the palm of your hand. This loosens the flesh and makes the juice more readily available.

Halve the limes and squeeze the juice through a strainer, into a jug. Reserve the squeezed lime rinds, placing them in another jug, and cover them with the sugar.

2   Pour 1 pint of boiling water over the lime rinds and let them steep for 15 minutes. (This infusion draws the aromatic oil from the skins. Do not let them steep longer or the beverage will become bitter.)

3   Add the salt to this infusion and stir to dissolve it. Strain the warm liquid into the jug containing the lime juice. Add the ice cubes and refrigerate. When serving, fill each glass with about 4 additional ice cubes and pour in the limeade.

Notes: As mentioned above, this can also be made with lemons. The Indians drink it without sugar and increase the salt a little. In the hot Indian summer it is drunk to prevent heat stroke.

5

MEALS ON THE MOVE

•

Dak bungalows, camps and trains

These *dak* bungalows were dotted along the Grand Trunk Road the whole way from Calcutta to the Upper Provinces, at a distance of ten miles apart, and were kept up at the expense of Government for the convenience of European travellers. All you paid for this great convenience was one *rupee* for a term of twenty-four hours or half that sum for three hours. Your food was extra, according to what you ordered. There was not much choice. A *moorgee* (fowl), or "sudden death" as they were called, was cooked either as a curry, grilled or roasted. This with rice kedgeree, *dall*, boiled eggs or an omelette, constituted a *dak* bungalow menu.

An Englishwoman in India: The memoirs of Harriet Tytler, 1828–58

At the *dak* bungalows, our meals consisted invariably of chicken. When you arrived, you'd see your dinner scooting around the compound, then you'd hear it being caught, because there would be tremendous screeches. Finally, it was presented to you for dinner. You'd have roast chicken and custard pudding, nothing else. Then you'd have eggs and bacon for breakfast.

My mother, talking about the Punjab, 1928

One cannot say exactly that the *dak* bungalow was an institution beloved of the British in India. It was mostly regarded as a necessary evil to be endured while one moved around. But somehow it began to be regarded

---

1. The Khyber Pass, 1937; 2. The Deputy Commissioner (my uncle) on inspection tour; 3. The two sisters and friends ready to tour; 4. Johnny Johnston and "Aggie" Agelasto (Ralli Brothers Ltd) outside Lahore station, 1928; 5. My grandfather and the baggage camels outside a *dak* bungalow; 6. Solitary camp while on tour; 7. Victoria Terminus, Bombay; 8. Doing Puja to Ganesh, Bangalore. After prayers the offerings of food and drink are consumed; 9. The Chinbatti Loop; 10. Threshing rice, Mysore.

with a perverse affection, something on the lines of, "Do you remember when?", and its hardships retailed with pride. Since a large percentage of the British Raj were perpetually on tour for at least several months of each year, there was very little choice in accommodation; either one camped or one stayed at the *dak* bungalows.

Their name arose from the Hindi for the mail or post, *dak*, and the mail runners, or *dak-wallahs*, who ran in stages with rest-stops in between (approximately ten miles at a whack) and blazed the trail which eventually became dotted with these undistinguished landmarks.

Some of the better ones offered pretty fair accommodation, and the meals could approach mediocrity, but, good or bad, as Kipling rhymed, "Heaven-born, there's only fowl." If you wanted any variation, then after your day's work was done, you had better go out into the *mofussil* and shoot something for the pot.

My mother talked about going on tour with my grandfather up in the Salt Range when she was about seventeen:

After Kushab, there was a little place called Naushera – it sounded the same as the city, but was spelled differently – on the way to Sodi, and we spent one night there. It was just a rest house, no garden and very dusty. This *dak* bungalow was rather like a fort. You went through an archway into an open square and there were the verandas. In the middle was a sandy space. There were a few flowers trying to survive and maybe a tree – yes, it was a *kikka*, a thorn tree. And there were *charpoys* to sleep on, plaited fibres on a wood frame. (We also slept on *charpoys* when we went to the villages, but instead of fibre those were laced with flat webbing.) We sat on them and the local people brought us sweetened tea and hard-boiled eggs, which they insisted on peeling for us, and they'd be covered in black finger marks but we'd have to eat them. Then they'd bring us fruit, such as oranges, bananas and pomegranates.

It was not because the cooks did not care that the food was sometimes monotonous; the best of them certainly tried to please. It was just that chicken was the most available source of meat when one was "up-country," so the menu reflected it. In addition, many of these cooks had slightly strange ideas about "the *sahib*" and the food he ate. They regarded most of the British eating customs as odd at best and, in a lot of instances, as totally barbaric and unfathomable.

Camping was a far cry from a small tent, pitched in an English meadow, and a sleeping bag. The servants, whether they were one or fifty, took care of the needs of the Raj, down to the last detail. In the case of more elaborate arrangements, the servants would pack up the camp and travel ahead to set up at the next site. When the *sahibs* finished their work and entered the camp, everything would be set up exactly as it had been at the last stopping place, even down to the open book which the *sahib* had been reading – at the same angle on the table and open to the same page. Similar care was applied to the food. Contact would have been made with the nearest villagers or, if there were none, the larder would have been inventoried and a full meal planned and cooked. *And* one always bathed and changed for dinner. This continuity helped to alleviate the hardships and stress of a long tour and to provide at least a modicum of civilization.

The railways of India were and still are the veins of the country. The sheer size of the statistics is impressive in itself. According to one of the latest sets of figures, there are some 37,700 miles of track connecting 7,000 stations, and the trains carry approximately 10 *million* passengers daily. For almost the last hundred years of the British Raj in India, a train journey was bound to be a part of the life experience of the servants of the Crown. Every town in which the British lived had its railway department and generations of *sahibs* worked in "the railways." By 1910 there were more than 32,000 miles of track and the first electrification took place in 1925, although the old steam engine remained the romantic symbol of Indian railways. (To this day there are still some 7,000 great, sooty steam locomotives chugging and thundering across the hills and plains of the sub-continent.)

Of course, the style of transportation by train mirrored the class of society to which one belonged. From first class to third class was not just from private compartment to slatted wooden bench, but from top to bottom of Indian society. And, naturally, the Raj moved around in style, some more than others. In 1909 Lady Wilson (*Letters from India*) wrote:

After endless experiments and many fruitless quests, I have come to the conclusion that the only place on earth in which peace and rest can really be found is in an India railway carriage, reserved for any couple taught by the tread-mill of hard work to appreciate silent isolation. To start one evening and know that there in solitary confinement you will be at least for twenty-four hours, where no posts, no callers, no duties can disturb you: to sleepily remember that in the next carriage you have three silent, deft attendants, who will pack, unpack, waken, feed you, undertake in short each manual duty that should be yours in sterner circumstances; what more could even the tiredest bit of tired humanity in this twentieth century desire?

What a world away from the good-natured companionship and press of bodies which was an integral part of the Indians' train experience:

Travelling in a train you might suddenly discover that a man in the compartment hailed from the same village or town. There would be an immediate shout of, "*Lao, tusan te sade vatni hoay, sade apne ghar de, sade bhara, wah, wah!*" "Take it, you are our countryman, from our home, our brother, well, well!" A feeling of warmth welled up, especially if you were a long way from home. Everyone in the compartment felicitated you on this coincidence. In a strange part of the Punjab you both regarded yourselves as exiles, and commented on the air, water, milk, vegetables, dialect and everything else as being not quite what you were used to. You were abroad and such differences were to be expected, but it was good to have someone from your home. The locals would accept it all in good part, and remark that it was but natural that things away from home are never the same.

Prakash Tandon, *Punjabi Century 1857–1947*

Those were the attitudes dictated by class, and the physical trappings of the journey mirrored them accurately. Here are two different pictures of train travel, painted by Mark Channing in 1936, from his book, *India Mosaic*. First, the *sahib*:

... I had an entire first-class carriage to myself (a compartment three times the size of those we have in England, its two seats running longitudinally), with two overhead electric fans, a fragrant but dusty thermantidote, a tiled bathroom, slat sunblinds, glass windows tinted against the glare, and gauze shutters to keep out mosquitoes at night. Into this small palace on wheels, with much grunting, were thrust the bedding roll, the ice-box, the gun cases, the fishing rods, the two suitcases, the cartridge magazine, the helmet case, and the *tiffin* basket. As if by magic, they slithered into invisibility under the two seats, leapt on to the roomy racks, or vanished behind the bathroom door.

The majority of the travellers:

The third-class passengers were packed like the proverbial sardines. Cloth bundles of all shapes and sizes were stowed under their legs and bulged from the narrow racks above their heads, the overflow being piled in their laps. Their courtesy to each other was marvellous. A laden voyager would insist, for several minutes, that another equally laden passenger should precede him into one of the windowed sardine tins; every one apologized, either by word or gesture, even for falling over an obstructing platform-squatter. Whenever a fresh wedge of humanity was driven into the crowded complement of a third-class carriage by a muscular Anglo-Indian inspector, the apparently impossible was accomplished; room was made for the newcomer. The wedge, during its transit, never ceased to appeal to the others to realize his utter helplessness, a courteousness that elicited a babel of sympathetic assents, advice, and vigorous and helpful tuggings.

And what of the meals *en route*? For some of these train journeys lasted for many days. My mother describes the typical arrangement for the first-class passengers:

We'd stop at a station and the bearer would bring along *chota hazri*, a tray with buttered toast and tea. Then, in the middle of the day you'd stop at a station right out in the country; just a long platform and no sign of civilization. And there would be no sound, except for the hissing of steam and the occasional slamming of doors. Then a man would come along and say, "Lunch, lunch!" and you'd de-train and walk along the platform to the dining car where you'd get in and sit down and you would be served lunch. You'd probably have a soup, an entrée, a roast, and pudding, which was usually a baked or caramel custard. You had to sit there until the train stopped at another station where you'd get off and go back to your own compartment. We used to buy fruit at the stations, but of course we would have "*pinki-pani*," or permanganate of potash, to wash it in. When you stopped at a large station you would hear cries of "*Hindu pani*!" or "*Muslim pani*!" – which was drinking water specially for Hindus or Muslims – and "*Char! Gurram, gurram char*!" "Tea! Hot, hot tea!" The vendors walked down the platform with baskets on their heads and, on top of those, other flat baskets filled with sweets, fruit and all kinds of things. The station master would blow his whistle and you'd lean out of the window and buy as many things as you could, then the train gathered speed and off you'd go again. Then I always remember the lovely rhythm of the train it was eight-gauge – and at night it would lull you to sleep. Of course, you had to make sure all the windows were shut or you'd wake up the next morning as black as soot.

Whether it was by horse, car, carriage or train, the Raj moved around indefatigably, and rested their heads at night in dusty, echoing *dak* bunga-lows, flapping canvas tents or rocking railway compartments. And they ate, with hearty appetites, from china or beaten tin, everything from local food to tough roasted chickens and watery baked custards. In this chapter you will find an assortment of the dishes, but they have been re-created under easier circumstances and will, hopefully, reflect a higher standard of culinary skill than that endured by the Raj "on the road."

Ros-tos onion chicken

•

This recipe is a pure and unabashed hybrid; a creature born partly of tradition, partly of imagination and partly of inspiration. It takes the Indian love of marinades, spices and onions and uses them in a new way. It is also what the cook in a *dak* bungalow might do if he were faced with having to present a chicken in a slightly different way from his normal repertoire, but if he were still limited to a few simple ingredients.

Serves 4

4 large onions, peeled and finely chopped
3 tablespoons dark brown sugar
$\frac{1}{2}$ teaspoon salt
a pinch of ground cinnamon
a pinch of ground ginger
a pinch of ground cloves
$\frac{1}{4}$ teaspoon freshly ground black pepper
$\frac{1}{4}$ teaspoon cayenne
4 whole, boned chicken breasts, skinned and pounded flat
$1\frac{1}{2}$ tablespoons *ghee* (clarified butter), melted

1   Preheat a large, iron pan over high heat and then dry-fry the onions until they are a dark brown, almost black. Stir them constantly to prevent them from burning. They should be dry and crisp when you are finished. If they are not, dry them out by microwaving them on high for a minute at a time, or dry them in a low oven for 1–2 hours. When the onions are completely dry, place them, a little at a time, in a spice grinder and grind them to a powder.

2   Put the brown sugar and 1 tablespoon of water in a small saucepan and melt the sugar. Stir until it becomes a thin syrup.

3   In a bowl, combine the onion powder, syrup, salt and all the spices. Add a few drops of water until the mixture becomes a spreadable paste.

4   Pat the chicken breasts dry, then spread them with the paste on both sides. Let them marinate for 30 minutes.

5   Pour just enough melted *ghee* in a frying pan to coat the bottom thinly and place it over moderate heat. Sauté the breasts, smooth-side down, pressing them gently with a spatula until the cooked surface forms a rich

brown glaze (about 3 minutes). Now pour in a little more *ghee* and, turning them over, repeat for about 2 minutes on the reverse sides. Transfer to a serving dish.

Notes: You may add a little crushed garlic to the marinade if you like it. I suggest you serve the chicken with a few lightly and plainly cooked vegetables as a foil.

Dak bungalow murghi roast

•

While the last chicken dish could easily have been prepared in the kitchen of a speeding dining car, the cook's area at camp, or the back kitchen of a *dak* bungalow, this recipe, and the one following, would be standard *dak-*bungalow fare. But the difference, I hope, is that these versions should be far more appetizing than their originals. Of course, we are also using tender, plump chickens, instead of tough old compound warriors, who exercised their sinews in stark terror while they were being chased around the dusty yard by the cook wielding a knife.

Serves 4

1 whole 3½-lb chicken, cleaned (do not remove the skin)
½ teaspoon salt
the juice of 1 lemon
2-inch piece of fresh ginger root, peeled and chopped
2 cloves of garlic, smashed, peeled and chopped
2 green chillies, seeded and chopped
½ teaspoon turmeric
2 tablespoons yoghurt
½ teaspoon *garam masala* (sweet spice mix, p. 293)
3 tablespoons *ghee* (clarified butter)

1   Prick the chicken all over then rub the salt and lemon juice well into the skin. Set it in a bowl and let it marinate for an hour.
2   Place the ginger, garlic, chillies, turmeric, yoghurt and *garam masala* in a food processor and process to a purée.

3   Pour this purée into a plastic bag and place the chicken in the bag as well. Fasten the bag securely and shake it until the chicken is well covered with the marinade. Refrigerate it for 4–5 hours, or even overnight.

4   Preheat the oven to 375°F (190°C, Gas Mark 5).

5   Using either a wok or a saucepan large enough to take a whole chicken, melt the *ghee* over high heat. Drain the chicken from its marinade, reserving any left over, and brown the bird on all sides in the wok. Use a pair of wooden spoons or tongs to turn it. Do not pierce it with a fork. Now place the chicken in a baking pan and pour the *ghee* remaining in the wok over it. Let it bake in the oven for 30 minutes, loosely covered with a piece of foil. Half-way through the baking time, spoon any remaining marinade over the chicken, and then baste it with the juices and *ghee* in the bottom of the pan. Serve hot or cold.

Notes: If you serve the chicken hot, you may like to accompany it with roast potatoes and baked tomatoes, stuffed with peas. If you serve it cold, accompany it with a fresh salad of crisp greens and sliced tomatoes.

Baked rose custard

•

Here is an updated version of the old, familiar dessert. While the standard version is the dish which every cook in every *dak* bungalow could produce at command, with a little change it becomes a delicately perfumed surprise.

Serves 5

1 pint milk
4 tablespoons sugar
a pinch of salt
3 whole, beaten eggs, plus
  2 beaten yolks

½ teaspoon rose-water
1 tablespoon flaked
  almonds
a few rose petals

1   Preheat the oven to 300°F (150°C, Gas Mark 2).
2   Blend the milk, sugar and salt together.
3   Beat in the eggs and egg yolks.
4   Add the rose-water and mix well.

5   Pour into an oven-proof dish and bake for 1 hour.
6   Remove from the oven and sprinkle the top with the almonds.
Decorate with a few rose petals.

Notes: This custard may be served hot or cold.

Camp soup

•

While I often picture the travelling deputy commissioner for the district, or the chief engineer, or the commissioner for the railways relaxing at camp over a *chota peg* or, more likely if the day's work had been arduous, a *burra peg*, it is remiss of me not to remember the Indian Army at camp, especially since I am a soldier's daughter. The arduous campaigns on the North-west Frontier and their attendant discomforts were endured and even enjoyed by those in whose blood ran the traditions of the British Army. And it

seems that a large percentage of them wrote about it. Mostly, the books are about battles, campaigns, bravery, heroism and death. Occasionally one comes across descriptions that capture the imagination and fire the spirit. But, sometimes, there are those accounts of almost mundane things which capture the essence of time and place. This small excerpt from Mark Channing's book, *India Mosaic*, is one such description:

It is good to get into camp and see my transport delivering each regiment's baggage in its particular section of the camp as neatly as bottles of morning milk. From a hundred different points comes a sound that, once heard, is never forgotten – the *clink-clink* of iron picketing pegs being driven into the ground. The sun is setting stormily, and the smoke from the camp fires is Cambridge blue against black and purple. A golden haze of dust hangs over everything. The Transport is blamed for that, of course; and we *do* kick up a dust when we move; but there is digging going on – the clicking of picks and the chugging of spades. The camp is being encircled by trenches. The men whose turn it is to hold them are not envied. No one who has little sleep and a life-and-death responsibility can be envied. We Supply and Transport people can – *if* we can and *if* we will – sleep through a night attack on the camp. But we neither can nor want to.

After I have watched the mules being groomed, and inspected their backs, I stroll over to where a Highland regiment is bedding-down in the dust. It is good to hear their broad Scots accents; one feels curiously safe near them. I mess with the regimental officers, and I hear the day's news while we drink, very contentedly, dust-and-mutton-bone soup and split ration biscuits. Two British officers were killed this afternoon and I knew them both . . .

That account was written in 1938. This recipe is about fifty years older. I have omitted the dust!

Serves 6

2 tablespoons *ghee* (clarified butter)	1 teaspoon sugar
5 medium onions, peeled and thinly sliced	½ teaspoon freshly ground black pepper
2–3 lb meaty lamb bones	1 teaspoon salt
5 oz/⅔ cup *dhal* (lentils)	½ teaspoon dried mint (fresh, if available)

1 Melt the *ghee* in a stock pot over medium heat and fry the onions, stirring occasionally, until they are light brown. Add the bones, brown them on all sides and then pour in 1 quart of water. Bring to a boil.

2 When the water is boiling, add the lentils and cover the pan. Reduce the heat and let the soup simmer for 30 minutes, or until the lentils are soft and disintegrating. Add the sugar, pepper and salt and the powdered mint. Let it come to a boil once more, remove the bones and discard them and pour the soup into a tureen.

Notes: As you can see, while this soup has a good taste, it *is*, genuinely, the product of a sparse larder while in the field. I would suggest the addition of 2 peeled carrots and some stalk celery at the time the bones are added.

Baigan masala

•

The aubergine or eggplant is a wonderful vegetable for stuffing. In India, I ate many versions, so many that I think the cook would forget what he did the last time and just concoct a new filling for each occasion. Sometimes they were presented in traditional English fashion, stuffed with mince and breadcrumbs, but I far preferred them when he had used a gamut of Indian spices. Incidentally, we knew aubergines as brinjals, which was what the Anglo-Indians called them. It took a while after I returned to England before I understood what an aubergine was.

Serves 6

6 aubergines/eggplants
about 5 inches long
2 tablespoons *ghee*
(clarified butter)
1 small onion, peeled and
finely chopped
2 teaspoons ground
coriander
1 teaspoon ground
turmeric

$\frac{1}{2}$ teaspoon ground cumin
$\frac{1}{2}$-inch piece of fresh ginger
root, peeled and finely
chopped
$\frac{1}{4}$ teaspoon cayenne
$\frac{1}{2}$ teaspoon salt
2 tablespoons chopped
coriander leaves

1   Parboil the aubergines/eggplants for approximately 5 minutes. Let them cool a little, cut them in two lengthwise and scoop out the flesh. Reserve the skins.

2   In a pan, heat *half* the *ghee* over medium heat and fry the onions for 3 minutes. Add the coriander, turmeric, cumin, ginger, cayenne and salt and stir and fry for another 2 minutes.

3   Add the flesh from the vegetables and the chopped coriander leaves. Heat it and mix it thoroughly. Remove the filling from the heat.

4   Fill the skins and tie the lids on with thread.

5   Heat the remaining *ghee* in a saucepan over moderate heat and fry the aubergines/eggplants on all sides until they are slightly browned. Cover the saucepan, reduce the heat to low and cook them for 6–10 minutes. Untie them and serve them as a side dish.

Chick pea and smoked fish salad in tomato cups

•

... We are in the big mango-grove at Ratmugri Bagh. Our campbeds are set in the centre of a clearing; tired beaters are being paid for their day's work; tired horses are being rubbed down and fed; tired sportsmen are having their boots pulled off by yawning servants. At a clothless table in the centre of the beds, the Honorary Secretary of the Tent Club and the Honorary Surgeon are playing a game of piquet, with bottles of beer at their elbow, and cheroots, to keep away the midges.

Francis Yeats Brown, *Lancer at Large*

A fading sepia snapshot of the sporting life of the British Raj. Picture it inserted in photo corners on the black page of an embossed album. The title is written in copperplate hand in white ink, "Bareilly, 1910." Underneath would probably be the subtitle, "Unwinding at camp after a long day's pigsticking."

If you could step into the photograph and move around, without disturbing the tableau at the table, the smell of charcoal might lead you to another clearing lurking discreetly behind some mango trees. The *masalchi* is clattering the dishes slightly as he dries them with a *jarren* (cloth), and stacks them on top of a box. The cook is relaxing, cross-legged on the ground, near to the little stove, whose embers are now almost extinguished since dinner is over. The cook is content. He thinks the *sahibs* seem to have enjoyed the dinner. He gave them a cold entrée, almost a salad, and they ate it all. Then they had a roast. He mentally reviews his larder. Two more days in camp. He'll have to send his nephew – that lazy boy – into the village tomorrow to purchase some more vegetables. He heaves a sigh, then his face relaxes into a small smile. Allah be praised! There are no *memsahibs* along for the sport this time. He has to try twice as hard to please them, and then some are never satisfied. He lights his hookah, takes a deep puff and then looks up calmly at the stars.

Taking literary liberties with time and place, and culinary liberties with the menu, here is an adaptation of the entrée that might have been served.

Serves 6

6 large tomatoes
1 14-oz tin chick peas, drained

1 5–6-oz tin smoked kippers, drained of oil and chopped

½ cup chopped parsley

3 spring onions/scallions,
finely chopped

1 small clove of garlic,
smashed, peeled and
finely chopped

½ teaspoon paprika

¼ teaspoon dried oregano

½ teaspoon salt

6 lettuce leaves

1 Hollow out the tomatoes, chopping the flesh of 2 and placing it in a bowl. (Reserve the central flesh of the others for soup.) Turn the tomato shells upside-down to drain.

2 Add all the remaining ingredients, except the lettuce leaves, to the bowl and mix well. Spoon the mixture into the tomato cups and chill. Serve each on a lettuce leaf.

Notes: This salad may be made with sliced raw mushrooms instead of the fish. It may then be dressed with a little oil and lemon juice.

Keema mutter in pittas

•

The old saying in India went that all Royal Engineers were either mad, married or Methodist. Well, my father was not Methodist, and I did not detect any signs of the first except for his abiding passion for trains and an enormous collection of railway magazines. But this was a gentle obsession which he shared with so many "sappers." My father's degree of the railway madness was far less than that of some, who devoted whole rooms in their houses to model railway layouts, or who permanently commandeered the family dining table for oo gauge rails and chugging little engines. Perhaps, even as a girl, I inherited a little of his fondness for trains, and in my memory of the iron monsters of India the coaches always seemed to be clean and the engines magnificent. I know there were, and are, many sections of the system where the accommodations were less than perfect and the service less than grand, but the affection remains. Paul Theroux describes two such trains in *The Imperial Way*, his book on rail travel in India, but, nevertheless, his affection and gentle obsession shines through:

Just before Wazirabad at dawn there was a knock on the door of my compartment.

"You wanting breakfast?"

I could have been wrong of course, but it seemed to be the same brisk man who had asked the question ten years ago: it was the same bad eye, the same dirty turban, the same lined face. And the breakfast was the same – eggs, tea, bread on heavy stained crockery.

In one respect, the Kamrup Express was unusual: it had a dining car. For hours after we left, relays of men – only men – sat squashing rice and dal in their fists and flinging it into their mouths. Meanwhile, the kitchen staff boiled cauldrons of lentils and crouched between the cars peeling potatoes.

It had begun to rain. The kitchen fires were stoked again. The men were still eating, and lines of more men waited throughout the train to take their turn at the tables. In spite of the rain, it was very hot, and the fans in the dining car whirred and scraped. The rain was loud; so were the fans, so were the eaters. It was all motion and noise, and at midnight they were still at it.

Under these circumstances, the more fastidious passenger might have been inclined to purchase a snack from the vendors at a station. One such snack could have been this one, except that I have brought a traditional recipe into a more up-to-date milieu.

Serves 4

2 tablespoons vegetable oil

1-inch piece of fresh ginger root, peeled and finely chopped

4 cloves of garlic, smashed, peeled and finely chopped

1 large onion, peeled and finely chopped

a pinch of ground cardamom pods

3 whole cloves

$\frac{1}{4}$ teaspoon ground cinnamon

1 lb ground lamb or beef

$\frac{1}{2}$ teaspoon ground turmeric

$\frac{1}{2}$ teaspoon salt

$\frac{1}{4}$ teaspoon cayenne

4 oz/1 cup peas (fresh or frozen)

1 tablespoon chopped coriander leaves

2 wholewheat pitta breads

4 lettuce leaves, shredded

1 Heat the vegetable oil in a large pan. Add the ginger, garlic and onion and sauté until the onion is light brown. Add the ground cardamom pods, cloves and ground cinnamon, stir and cook for another 2 minutes.

2 Now add the meat, turmeric, salt and cayenne. Fry and stir for another 5 minutes. Stir in the peas, fry until they are just cooked and then stir in the chopped coriander. Put the pan aside.

3 Cut the breads in half. Take a smaller, heavy pan or a griddle and heat it. Press the breads lightly on the heated surface until they are just speckled with brown.

4 To assemble the breads: stuff the bottom of each pocket with lettuce and then fill them with the *keema* mixture.

Notes: Instead of lettuce, you may like to stuff the breads with a layer of onion slices – soak them in iced water to remove their pungency – and chopped fresh tomatoes, before filling them with the *keema*. These stuffed pockets would also be suitable for picnics.

First-class chicken fricassée

•

While chicken fricassée has been known to grace the tables of the Indian dining cars as an entrée, this version is upscale; perhaps what the cooks would have liked to produce if they had had the time, energy and money. For us, it is easy, and we do not have to crouch between the railway carriages to peel the onions either.

Serves 4–6

3 lb chicken pieces	4 cooked artichoke hearts,
3 tablespoons *ghee*	quartered
(clarified butter)	1 bay leaf
$\frac{3}{4}$ lb little onions, blanched	$\frac{1}{2}$ teaspoon chopped fresh
and peeled	tarragon leaves
$\frac{3}{4}$ lb fresh button	the juice of 1 lemon
mushrooms, halved	2 tablespoons chopped
4 fl oz white wine	parsley
4 fl oz chicken stock from	$\frac{1}{2}$ teaspoon salt
the chicken above	$\frac{1}{4}$ teaspoon ground white
6 fl oz cream	pepper

1 Place water in a steamer or steaming arrangement and bring to a boil. Put in the chicken pieces and steam them for 30 minutes. Cool and remove the meat from the bones, in as large pieces as you can effect. Measure out the stock.

2 Melt the *ghee* in a large pan over moderate heat and put in the onions. Brown them for 10 minutes, shaking the pan frequently. Drain them over the pan and set them aside.

3 Add the mushrooms to the pan and sauté them for 6 minutes. Use a slotted spoon to drain them and then set them aside.

4 Pour the white wine into the pan and scrape any browned fragments from the bottom. Bring to a boil. Now pour in the measured chicken stock from Step 1 and cook for 5 minutes, or until the liquid is reduced to about 3 tablespoons.

5 Pour in the cream and add the chicken pieces, artichoke hearts, onions, mushrooms, bay leaf and tarragon. Reduce the heat to low and simmer for

20 minutes. Stir in the lemon juice and parsley and season with the salt and pepper. Transfer to a warmed serving dish.

Notes: Serve the fricassée with plain rice. You could also make this dish with the white meat from a turkey.

Railway lamb curry

•

Whatever else was on the menu of the dining car, there was always curry, generally lamb or chicken. In fact, "lamb" was a misnomer, for it was mutton more often than not. But it was cooked well and was very tasty. In the original recipe the meat was boiled to tenderize it before being incorporated. But with the lamb we have available, there is no need for this step.

Serves 4–6

the bones from a shoulder
    of lamb
2-inch piece of fresh
    ginger root
½ teaspoon of salt
6 small red chillies, seeded
    and chopped
7 cloves of garlic,
    smashed, peeled and
    chopped
1 teaspoon cumin seeds
2 tablespoons coriander
    seeds
½ teaspoon ground
    turmeric

3 tablespoons *ghee*
    (clarified butter)
1 large onion, peeled and
    finely chopped
6 curry leaves (*curry pak*)
1 lb boned shoulder of
    lamb, trimmed of fat
    and cut into 1-inch
    cubes
2 large potatoes, peeled
    and cut into 1-inch cubes
6 fl oz coconut milk
4 tablespoons tamarind
    liquid
1 teaspoon salt

1 Make a concentrated stock from the lamb bones, *half* the ginger and the salt. (Use enough water to cover the bones and then let the bones simmer until the stock is reduced to about 8 fl oz. Strain it and reserve.)

2 While the stock is boiling, place the remaining ginger, the chillies and

garlic in a processor or mortar and process or pound to a paste. Grind or pound the cumin and coriander seeds to a powder and add them to the paste, together with the turmeric. Add a teaspoon of water to mix the paste thoroughly.

3   Melt the *ghee* in a large saucepan over medium heat and fry the onion and curry leaves, stirring constantly, until the onion is soft. Add the spice paste from the last Step and stir and fry it for 3 minutes. Then pour in the stock from Step 1. Bring to the boil and then add the meat, potatoes and the coconut milk. Reduce the heat and let the curry simmer, uncovered, for at least 30 minutes, or until the lamb and potatoes are tender. The gravy should have reduced and thickened also by this time. Add the tamarind water and season with the salt. Serve with plain rice and, perhaps, a *dhal* to accompany it.

Notes: This curry will taste even better if it is made the day before and reheated. A note here on the vagaries of coconut milk. When coconut milk is introduced into a meat dish, it will separate unless the pan is left uncovered and the heat is turned low. The separation only detracts from the appearance and not the flavour. If it does occur, you can stir in a little thick coconut milk at the end of the cooking to add a creamy texture to the gravy again.

Tamarind is available in various forms from Asian foodstores, as are curry leaves.

Bhuna chicken

•

In 1943 we undertook a marathon train journey down the entire length of India. The "we" consisted of my mother, my English nanny, two brindle Great Danes, one liver-roan cocker spaniel, one Muslim bearer, twenty-seven pieces of assorted luggage and one small girl. And the reason for this trek was that we were leaving the Punjab and joining my father, who had come back to India from Burma and was taking up a staff job in Southern Command, in Bangalore.

India, during that period, was undergoing one of the spasmodic upheavals that eventually led to the departure of the Raj. In this instance, a tribe called the Gonds were in a state of insurrection and were systematically derailing trains in the central part of India. So, to the accompaniment of dire warnings from our well-meaning friends, we boarded the first of many trains that were going to take us from Rawalpindi, in the north, along some 2,300 miles of track to Mysore State in the south, our destination.

I remember our departure as being quite chaotic. My mother, suitably clad for the trip in a dark blouse and pair of slacks, had Jeannie and Silver, the Great Danes, on leashes, as well as Kim, the spaniel. The bearer was shouting commands at several porters who were sweating and straining to get all our luggage crammed in the coach. My nanny was fussing over the nursery equipment, which meant those things considered necessary for the welfare of a rather small girl, and the friends were all talking at once and placing garlands around our necks, and the servants we were leaving behind were moaning and salaaming and crying. I thought it was all great fun and high adventure.

Amazingly enough, we settled down fairly quickly to the routine of the journey. It was to take five days and nights, and some sort of order began to prevail in the compartment, in spite of our having to edge around stacks of tin trunks and boxes to go to the bathroom. The *bhistra-bund* bundles, or bedding rolls, were laid open and the bunks made up each night. When the train stopped at a station, my mother put the dogs on their leashes and walked them up to the far end of the platform for exercise. This promenade, of course, was considered an astonishing sight to the other people, both on the train and the platform, and quite often she was followed by a large and staring crowd, upon which our bearer would keep a close watch.

Our meals were generally taken in the dining car, although sometimes they were delivered to the compartment. I thought it delightful to sit by the window of the dining car and watch the flat, endless plains rush by, their monotony broken sometimes by a small, earth-walled village, or a lone tree, standing sentinel over the fields. I could see a distant plough, pulled by a brace of oxen, wearily and slowly scratching its line in the dusty earth. It reminded me of the little, gaily painted, carved models that you could buy in the bazaar, or even on the platforms of the stations. At night the

great, dark bowl of the Indian sky arched over the earth, pierced by millions of stars, and we seemed to be the only thing awake and moving through the dark. Sometimes in the middle of the night I would wake feeling the cessation of motion as the hissing monster stood quietly by some deserted station. A jackal would howl in the distance, starting up a chorus of barking from the dogs of a village. Then the train would start once more, picking up motion with a squeak of wheels, and tug us southward again, and I would sleep, lulled by the "biddle de dah" of the rails. And then came the trouble.

I woke one morning, disoriented. There was shouting and slamming of doors. People were hurrying by the window and I could hear exclamations and cries. My mother stuck her head out of the window and called her bearer. "*Yay tho kiah hai?*" she asked. "What's going on?" "*Khudaah! Memsahib!*" His voice was horrified. He told her. The Gonds had derailed the train before ours; a third-class train, carrying pigs, kerosene and luckless passengers. He told us that workmen were labouring as hard as they could to clear the wreckage off the line and mend it so we could go through. We stayed, motionless, as the day grew hotter and hotter. Then, finally, they pronounced the line mended and we began to inch along. "Don't look!" said my nanny. But to a child, the order is tantamount to a command to do the opposite. I wished I hadn't, for, to this day, it is engraved on my memory. The engine and first three coaches lay in a heap of twisted metal and splintered wood, wedged between the hillside and the track. The rear coaches were far below down the *cud*-side (mountain-side). Tins of spilt kerosene, piles of pigs' carcasses, and other things we shall not mention, lay scattered everywhere. For the next hundred miles or so, I was convinced it would happen to us too, and the motion of the train became a dreaded rhythm, pulling us towards some unnameable horror. But it abated. We kept going and we arrived, long after, in a steamy-hot city called Bangalore, perfumed by hundreds of flowering trees, to be greeted by one very relieved head of the family.

It is anticlimactic to follow such a story with a recipe, but that journey gradually became overlaid with many others, including the wonderful, toy-like Blue Mountain Express, which chugs up into the Nilgiris, past billows of spreading trees, lush vegetation and wild arum lillies. The appetite, sharpened by the clean, bracing air of the hills, would demand something very satisfying, something like this dry chicken curry.

Serves 6

4 cloves of garlic,
smashed, peeled and
chopped

1 large onion, peeled and
finely chopped

1 bunch of coriander
leaves, washed and
finely chopped

1-inch piece of fresh
ginger root, peeled and
finely chopped

1 teaspoon ground
turmeric

1 teaspoon salt

2 teaspoons *garam masala*
(sweet spice mix,
p. 293)

1 teaspoon cayenne

2 tablespoons *ghee*
(clarified butter)

3 large tomatoes, peeled
and chopped

2 tablespoons plain
yoghurt

3 lb chicken pieces,
skinned

1 tablespoon dried
(desiccated)
unsweetened coconut

the juice of 1 lemon

1   In a food processor, blend the garlic, onion, coriander leaves and ginger to a purée. Add the turmeric, salt, *garam masala* and cayenne, turning the blades briefly to mix them in well.

2   In a large saucepan, melt the *ghee* over moderate heat and fry the paste from the processor, stirring continually and scraping the bottom of the pan, for 3–4 minutes or until the aroma mellows and the paste is cooked. Add the tomatoes and yoghurt and stir well.

3   Put in the chicken pieces and, stirring to coat them, fry for 5 minutes. Reduce the heat to low, cover the pan and simmer until the chicken is tender (20–30 minutes).

4   Uncover the chicken and increase the heat as necessary to evaporate any remaining liquid. Add the coconut and lemon juice and cook, stirring, for 2 more minutes, before transferring the curry to a serving bowl.

Notes: For ease of eating, you may cut the chicken pieces through the bone into smaller pieces before cooking. A heavy cleaver is the best utensil to use, but a very large kitchen knife will do.

Sweets and snacks from the station vendors

Lord, what a noise there was! All over the platform were squatting groups of Indians, chattering at the top of their thin metallic voices. Laden third-class passengers, making for the train, fell over them. But it did not matter; everybody was sympathetic with everybody else. There were recumbent sleeping Indians too, swathed corpse-wise in white sheets, who had come to take a train that would start . . . in twelve hours' time? Well, whenever it might be. It, too, did not matter. In India time is not money; it is *maya*, illusion. The piercing cries of the vendors of "*Cha-garm-dudh*" ("Hot tea and milk"), "*Mithai*" ("Sweetmeats"), "*Mewra, baray achchay mewra*" ("Fruit, very good fruit!"), and half a dozen others, rose and fell pleasantly upon my not too attentive ears.

Mark Channing, *India Mosaic*

Was it really as hectic as I remember? Yes, it was. A constantly shifting kaleidoscope, a ceaseless swarm of motion, like an anthill disturbed by a well-placed kick, and a cacophony of noise that only a symphony orchestra tuning up together with a brass band and a jazz ensemble could provide. Wait! Add to that three simultaneous announcements from loudspeakers and the anticipatory crowd sound at the beginning of a football Cup Final. Don't forget the olfactory assault; the mingled smells of curries, fried *puris* and *samosas*, rose perfume from the *gulab-jamuns*, sandalwood and incense, marigolds from the tinsel-and-gold farewell garlands, and jasmine, jasmine everywhere.

Here are some of the utterly delicious sweetmeat delicacies available. A few are rare, regional snacks, like the *peras*, which my mother remembers as a child and which she still looks for, without success, in any Asian shop she encounters. Others are the rich and mouth-watering traditional sweetmeats from all over India.

Khoya, granulated khoya and rabadi

One really cannot think of making Indian sweets without knowing something about these milk products. Basically, they are made by reducing (evaporating or condensing) milk by slow cooking and stirring. It is a long, tedious process and while there are Indian cooks who insist that there are no short cuts or substitutes, there are others who do suggest them and, probably, others who use substitutes although they wouldn't shout it from their kitchen doors. Let us take a look at them, one at a time.

Rabadi

•

I have taken this product first, because it is actually an intermediate stage in the making of *khoya*. *Rabadi* is milk which has been reduced to the consistency of a thick, fluid cream; milk which has been reduced to a third of its volume. Let us assume you have started with 2 quarts of whole milk. Place it in a large, heavy, non-stick saucepan over medium heat. Stir it constantly and bring to a boil. This will take about 15 to 20 minutes. Now lower the heat and simmer the milk, stirring often, for about 50 minutes or so. The milk will thicken and reduce by a third. It will resemble tinned evaporated milk, with a warm, milky, caramel-type smell. Let it cool in the refrigerator. In this form, it can be used as the base for several Indian sweets. The short cut to *rabadi* is tinned evaporated milk, sometimes combined with a little sweetened condensed milk if the sweetened form is needed.

Khoya and granulated khoya

•

Khoya is milk which has been cooked down to a solid. The loss of volume is, of course, very large. The same 2 quarts of whole milk will produce 8 oz of *khoya*. So your end product will be an eighth of the original. After you have reached the *rabadi* stage, you merely continue cooking and reducing the milk over low heat, stirring constantly to prevent it sticking or burning. This should take between 15 and 20 additional minutes. As the milk reduces right down, it will sizzle with the last drops of moisture. Continue to stir until the sizzling stops. When it is at the stage of completion, the milk will be in a slightly sticky lump, with the consistency of soft pastry. Cool it and refrigerate. After refrigeration, it will lose its stickiness and have the consistency of fudge. In this form, it is used to make a whole variety of sweetmeats. Granulated *khoya* is also called *danedar*. It is made in the same way, except that when the milk first comes to the boil, tartaric acid (about $\frac{1}{8}$ teaspoon to 1 pint of milk) or lemon juice (the juice of 1 lemon per pint of milk) is stirred in and the milk then separates into curds. The reduction process then continues in exactly the same way. Indian sweet-makers insist that the granulated *khoya* is used to make *barfi*, the deliciously creamy Indian toffee. Again, at a pinch, some cooks substitute powdered milk, stirred into a little whole milk, for the traditional *khoya*. If this is done, the proportion should be 6 tablespoons of powdered milk to $1\frac{1}{2}$ tablespoons of liquid milk. The mixture is then cooked and stirred over low heat until it reaches the consistency of real *khoya*. (I have tried this and experimented using evaporated milk together with powdered milk. I found this combination to be closer to genuine *khoya* than any other short cut.) Incidentally, powdered milk is sometimes used instead of *khoya* to make *gulab-jamuns*.

Chenna and paneer

•

These two curd products are also ingredients in Indian sweetmeats. *Chenna* is actually soft curd cheese. *Paneer* is *chenna* which has been drained longer and then compacted by being pressed under a heavy weight.

To make both of these products, you may either use home-made yoghurt, called *dhai*, or, if you wish for a quicker method, you may merely separate the milk into curds and whey with lemon juice or tartaric acid. In either case, you should bring the desired volume of fresh milk up to just under boiling point, then let it cool to lukewarm. If making yoghurt, you may add up to 3 tablespoons of home-made or commercial yoghurt to 1 quart of milk, stir, cover the bowl with a towel, insulating it well, and then put it in a warm place for 5 hours or overnight. If you are using lemon juice or tartaric acid, you may add it before the milk has cooled. Let the pan sit off the heat for 15 minutes and then process the curds. Either form should be placed in a muslin bag and allowed to drip overnight. The resultant *chenna*, or soft curd cheese, is placed on a board and kneaded until it is soft and creamy.

If you wish to make *paneer*, the *chenna* should be hung until every trace of excess moisture is gone. The hard curds can then be shaped into a flat cake and put on a plate. Cover this with another plate upon which you have placed a weight, such as an iron. (A warning: do not get too enthusiastic and think you can do the job more efficiently by doubling the weight; you will merely split the cheese.) The hard curd cheese is solid enough to be fried, or simmered in liquids.

Peras

•

These are creamy, slightly sticky sweets, with a consistency of soft fudge. They are rich and sinfully delicious.

Quantity: 10 *peras*

1½ pints whole milk	1 teaspoon ground
1 teaspoon *ghee* (clarified butter)	cardamom pods
4 oz/½ heaped cup sugar	20 hulled pistachio nuts, chopped

1   Make *khoya* (see p. 171) by reducing the milk to a solid mass. There should be approximately 4 oz of *khoya*. Let it cool and refrigerate briefly.

2   Melt the *ghee* in a saucepan over very low heat. Take the lump of *khoya* and crumble it over the saucepan. Stir the milk solids and butter together over the low heat for 5 minutes.

3   Now add the sugar and mix it in well. Remove the pan from the heat and use a wooden spoon to beat the mixture until it is smooth and pliable. Let it cool until it can be handled.

4   Divide the mixture into 10 equal pieces. Take 1 portion in your hands and form a flat, round biscuit shape. Place it on an oiled or non-stick surface. Continue until you have made all the *peras*.

5   Sprinkle the top surfaces with the ground cardamom, patting down lightly. Now press a little of the chopped pistachio nuts into each. Let the *peras* dry out slightly in the air. They can then be wrapped in wax paper and stored in an airtight tin.

Notes: You may like to substitute freshly grated nutmeg for the cardamom. Chopped almonds make a nice alternative to the pistachios.

Luddoos

•

There are several varieties of these semi-hard balls with a fudge-like consistency. They are made from either lentils or semolina; sometimes a mixture of both. Traditionally, luddoos are part of the food offerings to the elephant-headed god, Ganesh, during his festival in the late summer. The most delicious ones come from around the Bombay area. These particular *luddoos* are made with semolina and have a slightly chewy, fudge texture.

Quantity: 18 balls

6 tablespoons *ghee*
  (clarified butter)
6 oz/1 heaped cup super-
  fine semolina
6 oz/scant 1 cup fine
  brown sugar
3 tablespoons powdered
  whole milk

$2\frac{1}{2}$ fl oz whole milk
pinch of saffron (powder
  or threads)
1–2 tablespoons slivered
  almonds
1 teaspoon ground
  cardamom

1   Melt the *ghee* in a heavy, non-stick saucepan over low heat and add the semolina. Stir for 10–15 minutes, or until the semolina begins to toast slightly and gives off a sweet, nutty smell. Now add the brown sugar and stir for 2 more minutes.

2   Add the remaining ingredients and stir well. Continue to cook, stirring continually, until the mixture draws away from the bottom and sides of the pan into a solid mass and becomes a little shiny from the butter oil. Remove the saucepan from the heat and let it rest until the mixture is cool to the touch.

3   Pinch off pieces and roll them into balls of just over 1 inch in diameter. Place on a shallow dish to harden.

Notes: You may add 2 tablespoons of sultanas to the pan with the nuts.

Jellabies

•

These are saucer-sized coils of crisply fried batter filled with rose-flavoured syrup. The secret lies in getting the *jellabies* to absorb the syrup without losing their crispness, and this is why they must be served when they are freshly made. This has given rise to the traditional Indian phrase of all-inclusive contempt for an inept housewife: "She runs the kind of house where you expect to be served stale *jellabies*!"

Serves 8

1 lb, 2 oz/3¾ cups flour
5 tablespoons rice flour
¼ teaspoon baking powder
¼ teaspoon saffron strands, soaked in 1 tablespoon hot milk
¼ teaspoon dry yeast
vegetable oil for deep-frying

2 lb/4 cups sugar
⅛ teaspoon cream of tartar
1½ teaspoons yellow food colouring
7 drops of red food colouring
1 teaspoon rose-water
a large pinch of crushed cardamom pods

1   Combine the flours, baking powder, saffron liquid, 1 pint of lukewarm water and the yeast in a bowl and beat until you have a smooth batter, the consistency of thick cream. Let it stand in a warm place, uncovered, for 12 hours.

2   Pour the oil into a wok and heat it to 350°F (180°C).

3   Combine the sugar, 1½ pints water and the cream of tartar in a saucepan and stir over moderate heat until the sugar has dissolved. Bring it to a boil and boil briskly for 5 minutes or until the syrup reaches 220°F (105°C). Remove it from the heat, stir in the colouring, rose-water and crushed cardamom pods. Set it near the stove.

4   Fill a pastry bag or funnel with batter and pour batter in a steady stream and in a circular motion over the oil in the wok, making spirals or figures of eight. Do not make more than 4 coils at one time. Keep your finger near to the tip of the funnel so that you can stop the flow immediately when you have enough batter.

5   Fry the coils, turning them once, until they are crisp and golden. Lift them out of the wok with tongs or a slotted spoon, then drop them immediately in the syrup and leave them for 1 minute. (The hot fried batter will absorb the syrup without losing its crispness.)

6   Lift the coils, draining them over the syrup, and place them on a shallow dish to cool. Try to accomplish both the frying and syrup-dipping processes as quickly as possible, before the syrup begins to cool and thicken. You may delay this by placing the pan of syrup inside a larger pan filled with hot water.

7   When all the *jellabies* are completed, transfer them to a clean dish and serve.

Mango lassi

•

Lassi is the thirst-quenching Indian drink made from yoghurt. The Indians drink it diluted with water, shaken with cracked ice and a little salt. A pinch of spice might be added: sometimes cumin, or it might have a touch of rose-water and sandalwood. Variations include fruit juices mixed with the yoghurt and, since I always loved mangoes, I was very fond of this *lassi*. It really approximates to a kind of Indian milk shake.

Serves 4

8 oz plain yoghurt
1 pint milk
chopped flesh of 3
   mangoes
¼ teaspoon roasted and
   ground cumin seeds

2 teaspoons sugar
cracked ice
a few drops of *kewra*
   (screw-pine, pandanus)
   extract (optional)

1   Depending on the volume of your blender, you may need to make this in 2 batches. First, place the yoghurt and milk in the blender container and blend until bubbles appear.

2   Add the rest of the ingredients and blend on high until the drink is smooth and frothy. Pour into glasses.

Notes: Another variation of this *lassi* may be made using the yoghurt but substituting orange juice for the milk and adding slices of fresh peaches instead of the mango. Delicious!

6

THE RAJ AT TEA-TIME

•

Teas and garden parties

... and we all sat and had tea together in my Mother's sitting-room. Our old *khansamah*, Kajoo by name, brought in the tea and cakes, and I remembered him perfectly from the days of my childhood, and also the old Abdar.

Emily, Lady Clive Bayley (1848), *The Golden Calm*, ed. M. M. Kaye

It is a cottage with a verandah, built on a steep slope and buried deep in shrubbery and trees. Within all is plain, but exquisitely neat. A wood fire is burning gaily and the kindly tea-tray is at hand. It is five o'clock. Clean servants move silently about with hot water, cake, etc ...

Aberigh-Mackay, on the "grass widow" in Simla, 1884, quoted in Pat Barr and Ray Desmond's *Simla, A Hill Station in British India*

The late-afternoon sun paints broad bars across the pillars of the veranda and stripes the rush mats on the cement floor. It glints on the silver tea-pot and hot-water jug on the lace-covered tea trolley. From the garden comes the scent of newly watered grass and the heady perfume of carnations. The flame-coloured cannas stand to attention like soldiers in the silver rain of the watering-can as the *mali* moves slowly and patiently along the rows, his bare feet squelching in the grass.

---

1. Afternoon tea for British troops on leave, Delhi, 1944; 2. Tea pickers, Silent Valley Estate, Munnar, Kerala; 3. Prize giving, 1906; 4. Garden party in the grounds of the Palace of the Maharaja, Kapurthala; 5. My aunt Berenice and her fiancé Mark, later Sir Alexander MacFarquhar; 6. Tea at the club; 7. Wartime wedding in Murree, 1940.

Sandwiches have been arranged in precise, geometric stacks on the doily-covered plates by the bearer. The cakes and scones are elevated in tiers on the silver cake stand. Little blue-glass beads edge the net cap over the milk jug and tinkle gently as my mother removes it to pour a measured amount into the cups. A few feet away, the dogs lie obediently but attentive; their eyes following the movements of our hands.

Although the places and houses varied, that picture was essentially the one which lingers throughout my childhood in India. In Murree, in the hills, it was followed by the big "tropical" radio being turned on for the news. That was all-important because the gathering clouds of war increasingly affected our lives and eventually led to my father's prolonged absence during the Burma Campaign. Later, in 1944, the family teas continued, but this time in our flat in the West End Hotel in Bangalore. But the Great Danes still lay obediently on the Afghani rug near the balcony – one wave of their tails would have sent the tea things flying – and tea was still a time of relaxation and domestic calm before the quickening pace of the evening.

Tea arrived in England in the seventeenth century, at first through foreign traders and then through the East India Company in 1664. By the next century there were several types of both black and green teas such as Imperial, Bohea, Pekoe, Souchon, Twankay and Gunpowder. It was still a very expensive beverage, costing between £1 and 3 guineas a pound. The East India Company followed its successful importation with little china tea sets, but the cups were after the Chinese pattern and had no handles. Thomas Twining opened the first tea shop in London in 1717 and, shortly thereafter, tea gardens opened; the most famous being the gardens at Vauxhall. By the middle of the eighteenth century, a little milk was being added to the tea and bread and butter was making an appearance as an accompaniment.

As the dinner hour slid later and later during the eighteenth century, from around two or three o'clock to six or seven in the evening, so the drinking of tea, padded out with light refreshments, helped to bridge the gap between meals in the afternoon.

While the habit of drinking tea was becoming firmly entrenched into the British way of life, the saga of the

plant in India was just beginning. Tea was found growing wild in Assam in 1820. Twenty-one years later, an enterprising doctor in the Indian Medical Service, named Campbell, brought tea from China and planted it near Darjeeling. The plants grew and thrived. By 1866 there were some 10,000 acres of tea growing in the area alone, and the British were in a wild fever to plant it all over India and see if the bush would grow. From Assam to Cochin, plantations were started. Naturally, in some regions it thrived, but in others, get-rich-quick schemes withered and died along with the plants. By 1888 tea grown in India had finally won the lead over tea exported from China and the total crop was worth some £4 million a year. The lead was never lost.

As a meal, tea served more than the mere social habit of meeting and gossiping. It began to fulfil a uniquely useful function of providing an occasion wherein people could be entertained informally without the rigid class strictures that invaded luncheons and dinners. There was no "order of precedence" to teas, except in the context of garden parties, which I talk of a little more later. Lady Wilson, in *Letters from India*, found tea a useful opportunity to entertain some regimental football teams in Simla for a tournament:

One day it occurred to us that it would be a great pleasure to us, and also a pleasant change for the soldiers, if one or two of the Scotch teams came upon different afternoons to have tea with us. We consulted some of the officers, who happened to be old friends of our own, and they welcomed the suggestion.

So behold us seated round two tables in the dining-room last Tuesday, Jim presiding at one, and I at the other, with half-a-dozen ladies, born, by good fortune, on the right side of the Border, to add by their presence to "the gaiety of nations," and "the gallant Gordons" in their element, very discursive, very punctilious, delightfully homely and frankly enjoying themselves.

There was also the formal side to the tea-time occasion – that English institution, the garden party. In India, they were generally held to mark an occasion such as the King's birthday. In the cities they would be given at Government House. In the smaller towns, the affairs would be hosted by the commissioner or, if it was a large military cantonment, by the commanding general. My mother remembers:

They were just like going to a garden party at Buckingham Palace. You all dressed up in your best frocks, with hats and gloves and uniform or morning dress for the men. There was a military band playing light music, like Gilbert and Sullivan. The governor and his lady would circulate among the guests, and there would be big tents, or *shamianas*, set up on the lawns or among the trees, with refreshments and tea. The top Indian officials would be invited and the Muslim and Hindu women would be in gorgeous *salwar khameez* and *saris*. The colours were so brilliant, they looked like tropical birds.

Even so, she really didn't like going to them very much, but they were an obligatory part of the social structure and protocol was all-important. "I couldn't wait to get home and take my shoes off and have a drink!" she said.

Fortunately there were other teas for large gatherings that were far more fun for the participants, such as tennis teas, teas at the gymkhanas and tournaments, and teas at the fêtes given for charity. The last, of course, were numerous between 1914–18 and 1939–45, because the British in India were motivated by patriotism. It could also have been that a tiny piece of guilt had its place in the drive to do good works: there was a large contrast between the leisurely, servant-attended pace of life on the subcontinent and the hardships that the English were enduring at home.

Whatever the reasons, the British Raj loved and valued their teas and tea-time occasions. So did their Indian cooks, for it gave them the opportunity to show their skill with sugar confectionery. For Indian tea snacks were every bit as numerous as those of the British and, eventually, a strange give-and-take of recipes, a cross-pollination of pastries occurred. Some of each are here, together with the beloved tea-time classics of the Raj.

Bangalore club sandwiches

•

On special occasions, the cooks at the hotel in Bangalore would make wonderful club sandwiches. These slices of layered bread with their strata of different fillings were an intriguing combination of textures and tastes. The layers were not always the same either. They varied according to the inspiration of the cook on that particular day.

Quantity: 15–20 sliced sandwiches

1 day-old, unsliced, white loaf	1 bunch of watercress, washed and drained
butter	mayonnaise

3 hard-boiled eggs,
 shelled
mango chutney
2–3 oz cooked chicken,
 finely shredded
½ teaspoon curry powder
1 tablespoon yoghurt
1 heaped tablespoon
 cream cheese

1 large tomato, skinned,
 seeds and juice removed
2 sun-dried tomatoes,
 drained of oil and finely
 chopped
1 tablespoon chopped
 parsley
salt and pepper

1   Cut the crusts off the loaf and then slice it lengthwise into 5 slices, each ¼ inch thick. Butter them lightly.

2   Chop the watercress roughly and place it in a processor together with about a tablespoon of mayonnaise. Process to a rough spread. Transfer it to a bowl and set aside.

3   Chop the eggs finely and place them in a bowl. Take about a tablespoon of mango chutney and finely chop any whole pieces of mango. Mix it with the eggs. Set aside.

4   Place the shredded chicken in a bowl and add the curry powder and the yoghurt. Mix well. Mash the cream cheese and blend it into the chicken. Season with salt and pepper to taste.

5   Chop the tomato finely and place it in a bowl. Blend in the minced sun-dried tomatoes and the parsley. Season with salt and pepper to taste.

6   Spread each filling on a length of bread, making sure that the layer is even and covers the bread right to the edges. Reserve the fifth slice of bread for the top.

7   Assemble the sandwich by starting with the egg layer and placing it on a board, spread side up. Cover this with the watercress layer, placing it carefully on top. Follow with the chicken layer and, lastly, with the tomato layer. Invert the reserved piece of bread and place it on top.

8   Wrap the reassembled loaf carefully in foil and chill it in the refrigerator. When it is quite firm, unwrap it and slice it carefully.

Notes: This layer sandwich is even more attractive if you use a white loaf and a brown loaf. Make twice the amount of filling and assemble two loaves, alternating the slices between white and brown.

Carrot and raisin spirals

•

These sandwiches borrow their sweet filling from the ingredients of the traditional carrot *halva*. Besides appealing to children, they are also very nutritious.

Quantity: 60–70 sandwiches

1 large carrot, peeled and finely grated	5 oz cream cheese, mashed and beaten
2 tablespoons finely chopped raisins	a pinch of ground cardamom (optional)
$1\frac{1}{2}$ tablespoons clear honey	1 unsliced, wholewheat loaf

1   Mix together the carrot and raisins and stir in the honey and cream cheese. Add the cardamom and stir it well. Continue to stir until the mixture has a spreadable consistency.

2   Remove the crusts from the bread. Then cut slices lengthwise, about $\frac{1}{4}$–$\frac{1}{2}$ inch thick. Spread each slice with the carrot/raisin mixture, taking care that the entire surface of each slice is covered.

3   Roll up each slice tightly and evenly. Place all the rolls, seam side down, tightly together on a dish. Cover with plastic wrap and chill in the refrigerator.

4   Slice each roll crosswise into slices, $\frac{1}{2}$ inch thick, and arrange on plates. The slices may be covered and refrigerated until serving time.

Notes: For more texture, you may add finely crushed walnuts to the filling mixture. The crunch is rather nice.

Droppies

•

I know that the official title of these little pancakes is drop scones, and that in England, south of the border, they are known as Scotch pancakes but they were always called Droppies in our family and I can speak of them by no other name.

Serves 4

8 oz/1⅔ cups flour
⅛ teaspoon salt
1 teaspoon cream of tartar
1 teaspoon bicarbonate of
   soda

1 heaped tablespoon sugar
1 egg
5 fl oz milk
a little butter for greasing
   the pan

1   Preheat an iron griddle or pan.
2   Sift the flour, salt, cream of tartar and bicarbonate of soda together into a bowl and then stir in the sugar.
3   Beat the egg and milk together and then gradually add it to the dry ingredients, beating until you have a thick, bubbly batter.
4   Grease the griddle and drop a spoonful of batter on to the surface, enough to make a small pancake, about 3½ inches in diameter. When after a few seconds you see bubbles appearing on the surface, turn the pancake over and cook the other side. (It should be a light, even brown.)
5   Work on, cooking 3–4 pancakes at a time. Stack the completed pancakes in a warm oven, covered with a towel.
6   Serve them warm and freshly spread with butter and honey or jam.

Rawalpindi potato scones

•

These scones do not have to go near an oven, which is probably why our *khansamer* liked to make them; his kitchen was hot enough without the oven going. Because they don't contain baking powder or any raising agent, they are heavier than the usual scone, but, served hot with butter, quite delicious. I am reminded of this cosy scene described by Lady Wilson in Simla, in 1906:

We had such a cheery home-coming. The house had been dressed up to look its best, repainted and polished, with flowers everywhere, and our chairs drawn up by the drawing-room fireplace, the tea-table set, while Komal's best scones and his crispest toast were brought in by the smiling butler, before we had time to sit down.

Quantity: 8–9 scones

2 medium potatoes,
   cooked, mashed and
   kept warm
1 tablespoon butter

2 oz/½ cup flour
2 teaspoons *ghee* (clarified
   butter)

1   Work the butter into the mashed potato while the latter is still warm and then knead in as much flour as the potato will take to make a pliable dough.

2   On a floured board, roll out the dough to ½ inch in thickness and cut out rounds with a 3 inch cutter. Prick the rounds with a fork.

3   Grease a griddle or heavy iron pan with the *ghee* and heat it over a moderate fire. Cook the scones 4 at a time for about 3 minutes each side. Press them down lightly with a spatula. Keep the first batch warm as you make the remainder. Serve at once, buttered.

Notes: These are also good if a pinch each of dried sage, dried oregano, dried thyme and dried basil are mixed into the dough, together with a little freshly grated Parmesan cheese and some paprika.

Sev

•

I share with the rest of my family a passion for this snack. My aunt always bought great big bags of it and kept them in the house, to the detriment of our waistlines. I buy *sev* in Asian shops with the avowed intention of bringing it home to have with drinks. I come home after shopping, but instead of the *sev* I bring with me a big guilt complex because I have generally eaten it in little handfuls before I get it home. Which brings me to a wry conclusion. For many of us expatriates and remnants of the British Raj, one of the biggest legacies that India has left with us is a rapidly spreading area around our midriffs!

Quantity: enough for a polite group of 6 people, 1–2 greedy ones

12 oz/2 cups *gram* or
   chick-pea flour (**besan**)
½ teaspoon cayenne

1½ teaspoons salt
⅓ teaspoon ground
   turmeric

1 teaspoon of any of the following:	poppy seeds
parsley seeds	2 tablespoons melted *ghee* (clarified butter)
onion seeds	vegetable oil for deep frying
celery seeds	
cumin seeds	

1   Sift the flour, salt, turmeric and cayenne into a bowl and stir in whichever seeds you have chosen. Pour in the *ghee* and mix well. Add enough warm water (up to 3 fl oz) to form a stiff but pliable dough. Knead it for about 5 minutes.

2   Roll out the dough on a floured board to ¼ inch thick. Cut the dough into 6-inch strips and then cut each strip crosswise into very thin strips (about the width of linguini).

3   Heat the oil in a wok or deep-fryer to 370°F (190°C). Fry the *sev*, a handful at a time, until crisp and light brown. Drain on paper towels. When they are cool, store in an airtight tin.

Notes: You may leave out the cayenne and the seeds if you wish, and then you have the basic *sev*, but I think the spiced version is far more interesting.

Flagstaff House chocolate éclairs

•

Once upon a time in India, there were three children, and their names were Robert and Lucy and Edgar. (They had an elder sister, called Berenice, but she doesn't count because she was busy doing all the grown-up things that elder sisters do.) And they lived in a bungalow with a large garden at 7 EI Lines in Karachi. Now these children were very bad. They used to get up to all sorts of pranks and play up their poor old fat *ayah*.

The house they lived in had a very nice, English sort of street in front, but at the back, the dusty road led to the Indian bazaar. And Robert and Lucy and Edgar would escape from their *ayah* and jump on to the trams and ride down to the bazaar, where they would buy sticky Indian sweets for one *picer*, and their poor old *ayah* would be pulling her hair out and wailing because she didn't know how she could face the *burra memsahib* until the children came back. But they always did. Now these children built themselves a tree house in the front garden, and then they would climb up and hide from their *ayah* among the leafy branches. They found themselves a length of rope and they would lasso people who walked up the gravel drive below. (They learned how to use a lasso from the Tom Mix movies they saw at Saturday matinées at the bioscope in Karachi.) Then they would hold these people to ransom.

Now it was the year of 1917, and the Great War was still going on, and everybody was doing their bit for the war effort. The children's father was in charge of shipping things for the army in a place called Kemari, the port of Karachi. Their Aunt Effie, who lived with them, was working for the general as an aide. And she would get a lift home from the office in a big, grey, open tourer, called a Napier. One day the children were up in their tree house, hiding from their *ayah*, when they saw the big car coming down the drive with their aunt sitting in the back alongside a man in uniform. So the naughty children whirled that lasso, and down it came through the air, whistling and snaking, and lassoed the man in uniform. Well, you guessed it. It was the general, General Fowler. Their aunt was very angry, but they didn't care. They were going to hold him for ransom. Happily for Robert and Lucy and Edgar, the general was amused. He paid the ransom. He invited them to tea at Flagstaff House, and they went: just their aunt, the three children, and the poor fat, old *ayah*. And they had cakes with sticky icing, and buns, and all the things that boys and girls like, including chocolate éclairs. And Lucy really liked those. What little girl of seven wouldn't?

Well, Lucy grew up, as all little girls do, and even when she was grown up, she still loved chocolate éclairs. How do I know? Lucy, now called Lucette, is my mother.

Quantity: 12 éclairs

3½ oz/⅔ cup all-purpose
   flour
⅛ teaspoon salt
¼ lb unsalted butter
3 eggs, beaten
8 fl oz heavy cream

1 oz/⅓ cup
   icing/confectioners'
   sugar, sifted
4 drops of vanilla extract
4 oz dark chocolate

1   Preheat the oven to 400°F (200°C, Gas Mark 6). Have the eggs at room temperature.

2   Sift together the flour and salt. Pour 7 fl oz water into a saucepan and add half the butter in small pieces. Bring to a boil.

3   Immediately add all the flour at once and stir quickly with a wooden spoon. As the mixture becomes smooth, stir faster. When the paste becomes dry and leaves the side of the pan, remove the pan from the heat. Keep it off the heat for 2 minutes and then add the eggs, a little at a time, beating briskly between each addition. Continue to beat until the dough no longer looks slippery.

4   Place the dough in a large piping bag fitted with a tube or star nozzle, and pipe 4-inch lengths on to a greased baking sheet.

5   Bake the cases for 15 minutes. Reduce the heat to 350°F (180°C, Gas Mark 4) and bake them for 25-35 minutes longer, or until the cases are firm to the touch. Let them cool, then cut them horizontally with a sharp knife.

6 Meanwhile, whip together the cream and sugar and add the vanilla extract. The cream should be standing in sharp peaks.

7 Pipe the cream into the pastry cases, closing each one as it is filled. Place the chocolate, broken into pieces, in the top of a double boiler. When the chocolate is melted, stir in the remaining butter. Dip the tops of the éclairs in the chocolate and let them harden.

Notes: Variations include adding a spoon or two of hot, very strong coffee to the chocolate. While many people fill éclairs with *crème pâtisserie*, or even add chocolate to it, my mother still prefers real cream. However, a spoon of toasted, flaked almonds, stirred into the cream after whipping, is a nice addition.

Granny Whitburn's pound cake

•

Indispensable to the serious tea table, nothing really surpasses a good pound cake. Even when it is surrounded by all manner of cream confections and *pâtisserie*, it still appeals to the appetite. Perhaps it is because of a well-founded expectation that it will taste just as we remember it; that the texture will be just as firm as it should be, that the moisture will be exactly in the right proportion. There will be no unpleasant surprises. Too often, the eye is seduced and the appetite tempted by continental pastries and then the reality falls below the level of expectation. The cream is ersatz, the pastry soggy or the taste unpleasant. Thank the gods of the kitchen, a pound cake is a pound cake, as solid and dependable as the British Empire in its heyday. Here is my grandmother's version.

Quantity: 1 large pound cake, enough for 10 people

18 oz/3¾ cups combined all-purpose and cake flour	¼ lb unsalted butter
	8 oz cream cheese
3½ teaspoons baking powder	11 oz/1½ cups suga
	3 eggs, beaten
½ teaspoon salt	3½ fl oz milk
	1 teaspoon vanilla extract

1   Preheat the oven to 350°F (180°C, Gas Mark 4).

2   Sift the flour, baking powder and salt together into a bowl.

3   In another bowl, cream together the butter and cream cheese until they are well blended. Gradually beat in the sugar, until the mixture whitens and becomes fluffy. Beat in the eggs, a little at a time, completely blending in each addition before adding more.

4   Now add the sifted ingredients alternately with the milk, blending in each addition before adding another. Finally, stir in the vanilla.

5   Turn the cake batter into a greased and floured 10 × 4 inch deep baking ring/tube pan and bake it for 1 hour.

Notes: Some people add a few drops of rose-water or a tablespoon or so of brandy, together with the vanilla.

7

BUFFETS
AND
GRAND TAMASHAS

•

*Refreshments at the club, fêtes, fairs,
weddings and gymkhanas*

Their proposals are that the Cricket Club should include in their programme the games &c., proposed by the promoters of a *gymkhana* Club, so far as to not interfere with cricket, and should join in making a rink and lawn-tennis, and badminton courts, within the cricket-ground enclosure.

Pioneer Mail, 3 November 1877, from Yule and Burnell, *Hobson-Jobson*

By way of change there was football, cricket, clay-pigeon shooting and tent-pegging for the young men, tilting the ring for the young ladies who, Lady Dufferin remarked, loved to go "galloping about, lances in hand, their hats falling off, looking very energetic and very much amused". It was all good clean competitive fun – polo-matches and gymkhanas, horse- and dog-shows, postillion races, steeple- or paper-chases and rickshaw-races...

Pat Barr, Simla, 1888, *The Memsahibs*

---

1. Indian marriage ceremony, *c*.1920; 2. Guests of the Begum of Mandhote near Ferozepur. The Begum, mother, me, nanny, 1940; 3. Berenice and Alexander MacFarquhar's wedding, Sargodha, 1929; 4. My great uncle Edgar's house and guest house of 8,000 bottles, near Tikamgarh, 1937; 5. At the races; 6. Sargodha races; 7. St Fillan's Church, Sargodha; 8. Indian idler.

The club was a peculiarly Anglo-Indian institution. A lot of fun has been poked at club life in India, without those who indulged in this sort of sport realizing how vital a part of the life it was. Getting together for games and exercise and talk was really a very important part of our life. It was the social centre of the civil and military station.

Charles Allen, *Plain Tales from the Raj*, 1986

Sargodha, where my family lived for so many years, would really serve as a model for the typical smaller British civil station in India. It was a new town, part of the phenomenon of development in the Punjab. The land between the rivers had been covered by the new canal system, which brought water to the area and, in its wake, roads, communications and railways. Then the Land Settlement officers set about attracting Punjabis to this new land of opportunity. Wherever a few families settled together they made a village. Then the British government founded towns to act as focal points for the marketing of the ample agricultural produce the newly farmed lands were producing. Sargodha was one such town. It was not higgledy-piggledy like the old Indian towns and cities, but was built in a square, bounded by the new canal on one side, and the new railway line, which bisected the canal at a right angle, to form the second side. A belt of gardens and orchards formed a third side, while there was a wholesale produce market, next to the railway station, on the fourth. The actual town was divided into two, as were so many others; the city and the market on one side of the railway line, and the civil station on the other.

The civil station was built in a large rectangle along the railway lines. There were bungalows for the officials as well as some privately owned residences, and my aunt remembered there being about twenty-five British families there at that time, about 1926. The streets were tree-lined and wide and straight. As my grandfather was the district engineer, the family bungalow was large. It had seven rooms, with each member of the family having his own bedroom and dressing room. There were four bathrooms, furnished with tin tubs, wooden-grids, floor mats, and towel rails. In each was also a metal or enamel wash basin, a tin bathtub and water jugs and jars. In the corner was a wooden commode – familiarly termed "the thunder box," and enclosing an enamel toilet. The other rooms had *dhurries* (woven cotton rugs) and *numdahs* (embroidered, pressed-felt rugs) covering the floors, and old-fashioned *punkahs* (wooden frames covered with heavy material with a frill at the bottom) hung suspended from the ceilings. The bungalow had thick, plastered walls, whitewashed every year, and deep verandas, which made the rooms rather dark and gloomy. Behind the main house were the servants' quarters, the kitchen and the stables. In front there was a horseshoe-shaped drive around a sunken garden, which my aunt had planted with a profusion of roses. A menagerie of dogs, chickens, ducks and geese completed the household, in addition to the horses.

This was how the Whitburn family lived, and so did the majority of the families that formed the small, closed community of the civil station. Besides the engineers, there were the waterworks people, those with the police, the deputy commissioner, the assistant commissioners (always young, unmarried men, as were most of the assistants), one man in irrigation, and two people with the Imperial Bank of India. The community was a young one, with most people being in their early thirties, except for the deputy commissioner and my grandfather, who were then, respectively, in their middle and early forties. So everybody was willing to work hard and play hard and make their own fun, for the nearest city with amenities was Lahore, 107 miles away. The other close source of activity was the Remount Depot, about five miles from Sargodha, where horses were broken, trained and allotted to various regiments. My grandfather sent his two daughters there for riding lessons and, as there were never enough people to exercise the horses, the girls could ride any mount they liked, so they almost lived in riding britches.

The Sargodha Club was the focal point of social life. My grandfather was elected club secretary and he set about raising money energetically for all kinds of activities. The clubhouse was a large, low building of red brick with very deep verandas in front and on one side. The verandas were protected by cane *chicks* (blinds) lined with navy-blue canvas to keep out the glare. In the winter the *chicks* were let down and laced together like tents to provide sitting-out room for dances. For those occasions, *dhurries* were put on the floor, and the verandas decorated with vases of flowers. Little charcoal stoves were scattered around for warmth.

My mother remembers the club:

You walked into the deep, main hall. On the left side was the ladies' room, a drawing-room commonly known in most clubs as "the snake pit." It was full of wicker easy chairs with bright cotton cushions and had a large fireplace. On dance nights, its polished floor made it suitable for a ballroom. Off that room was a little library on the left. On the other side of the drawing-room was the ladies' cloakroom. The right-hand side of the club was "men only." There was a big billiard room which had a bar that was also strictly male. But off that was the bridge room, into which ladies were allowed.

The club grounds were large with rolling green lawns in the front. A pathway led through a magnificent hedge of yellow Marshall Neil roses to the tennis courts and a half-size court with a wall, against which my mother would play for hours. Tennis tournaments were held all through the winter and were fully subscribed because there were some very fine tennis players among the residents of Sargodha.

Besides dances, Sunday services were also held at the club and presided over by the deputy commissioner, for it was not until a few years later that my grandfather built the church, St Fillan's. When it was completed, the Protestant minister would visit once a month to hold a service, and my aunt played the small pedal organ for the hymns. After my aunt married, my mother took over that task. Coincidentally, the first wedding to be held in the newly built church was my aunt's in 1929. Then, although there were christenings and funerals in the intervening years, the next wedding at St Fillan's was my mother's, in 1933. The Roman Catholics in Sargodha were shepherded by a young Belgian Jesuit, Father Damien, who became a close friend of the family. He was multi-talented and something of a character, covering the large distances necessary for tending his flock on a motor bike. He also played the piano for the Saturday-night dances, ending punctiliously at the stroke of midnight. According to my aunt, he instructed our family in the making of an excellent raisin wine.

It seems that my grandfather mixed business with pleasure for, as district engineer, he built the Sargodha racecourse and, later, a golf course. The former was constructed on a rather arid and scrub-filled piece of land called Kirana, quite far from the station, with a few kikka trees near a large lump of rock termed "the hill." In the middle of the racecourse oval, he also laid out a greyhound-racing track. To his credit, he succeeded in the unusual feat of growing real grass in the paddock and laid out a garden. It was all really quite civilized.

With the racecourse, Sargodha's position as a racing and horse-breeding centre became established. Its British population was growing rapidly as more railways and roads were built and additional people were brought into the expanding administration. The Remount Depot was growing too, and horse-breeding was becoming very popular. This was due to the British government's Griffin Scheme, wherein horses or fillies could be leased from the *jemadars* and landowners and trained for racing, with the winnings split fifty-fifty between owner and trainer. So the Punjabis were encouraged to breed really fine horses. During the winters, there were now two races each month, as well as several gymkhanas and the Sargodha Horse-show.

My mother recounts the opening of the main track at the racecourse:

That winter, the Governor of the Punjab, Sir Malcom Hailey, and his wife came for the horse-show and opened the main course for the racing season. They stayed with the deputy commissioner, Archie McNab. It was quite an occasion. They drove down the racecourse in an open carriage with four horses, and all the ladies turned out for the opening in flowered chiffon dresses, hats and gloves, and the men in morning coats. Lady Hailey presented "The Hailey Cup" for the Sharpur Stakes – three-year-olds, the best country-bred of all the districts. Lady Hailey was a character; little, bird-like and cheerful – like a cockney actress – and she didn't give a hoot for anybody. She was rather fond of the bottle, too. Well, there was a gala celebration at the club after all this. Father was secretary of the club, and his word was law. The VIP party arrived and he duly met them and escorted them inside the hall. Lady Hailey wandered off into the bar, in spite of the aide-de-camp trying to restrain her. There she was, lifting a glass quite happily. Father went up to her as club secretary and said, "With due respect, Your Ladyship, this bar is for men only, and ladies trespassing have to pay a fine." With which, she looked across at her husband and said, "Malcom, pay him!" That was that. She stayed where she was and it became a big joke in Sargodha.

So, with horse-racing, horse-shows and gymkhanas, tennis matches, golf tournaments, dances and weddings, life in Sargodha was fun, gay and full of activity. As with so many other stations in India, the club became the hub and the venue for many of the parties held after such events. But unless the affair was very large or important, in which case catering would be handled by Nedous, Filettis or Larangs from Lahore, the regular refreshments were provided on a member-pitch-in basis, with the various cooks of the households showing off their skills. And these refreshments covered the range from petite bridge-tournament sandwiches to full-bodied buffets, together with the accompanying fruit cups and punches.

Some of these foods are in this chapter, together with recipes for a few of the excellent alcoholic libations, many of which have become hard to locate because of the long years intervening since those halcyon days.

Of horse-shows and gymkhanas

Practically every station of consequence put on a horse or cattle fair during the cold season. They were often held around the racecourse and were, in fact, a combination of fair, horse-show and races. These events were known as Weeks, although they lasted for as little as three and as much as ten days, and every city or station that could support such an event scheduled it carefully so it did not coincide with other similar *tamashas*.

The focus of attention was the horses and for many who attended, buying, selling, breeding, riding, training or just watching, it was a serious event. But for most it was a glorious holiday. The Punjabis turned up *en masse*. Crowds of men in their best clothes (those that had them) – baggy trousers topped by *kurtas* (long, loose shirts), and heads swathed in *puggarees* (turbans) – wandered past the enclosures where sheep and goats bleated and butted their heads against the barricades. Lowing cattle or squawking chickens added to the cacophony. Those who had no relatives to stay with, carried blankets or shawls over their shoulders, into which they would huddle or roll up like corpses when the chill of the night descended. They would sleep on *dhurries* in makeshift encampments, or squat round camp fires and smoke while they discussed the price of grain, the quality of the cattle, or the prospects of a big sale for their horse. In the dark, the myriad lights of their twinkling camp fires dotted the darkened plain like stationary fireflies.

The next day, there would be competitions and judging for the best in breed, with rosettes and prize money, and even exhibitions of fruit and vegetables. The farmers and the *malis*, or gardeners to the British, would enter these, proudly clutching their produce in baskets or bundles of cloth.

There were Punjabi women there too, but they were local. The men from the provinces did not bring their womenfolk with them. The females clustered round the stalls that displayed bright glass bangles and glittering beads. Other vendors sold local crafts; gaily painted wooden toys for children, cup-and-ball, crude ceremonial effigies of elephants on wheels or spinning tops. The food stalls were always well patronized, the *chapattis*, stuffed *parathas*, *samosas* and sweetmeats adding tantalizing smells which rose above the heads of the throng. In a more sedate fashion, other stalls displayed heaped piles of grains: raw lentils, rice, millet and wheat, or various kinds of cattle and livestock feed.

But the big excitement was reserved for the racing, dogs as well as horses, for not only were the Punjabis keen horsemen, but they also hunted rabbits with greyhounds.

For the British Raj, the Weeks were exciting too, but the emphasis was different. Few of them mingled with the crowds at the fair; they had their own entertainment during the period. Every resident of the area in which the event was being held had house guests from other districts. And there were non-stop entertainments: parties, balls, tennis matches, polo. Of course, the British were also keen participants in the horse-show. Those who owned and trained horses were very involved. Many took part in the competitive events such as jumping, dressage, and ladies' hacks. There were feats of horsemanship such as tent-pegging, at which the Indians were excellent also. Then there were two-horse carriage races – called "depot tongas" in Sargodha – and the four-in-hand races, the heavy artillery of the events. The latter were incredibly exciting, with the horses thundering down the course and the crowd roaring and everyone cheering their own teams.

The racing part of the Week would open with the greyhounds, followed by the gymkhana races. Then the main events would run – the trophy and cup races. During these, the jockeys were local lads and the crowd betting at the totalizer was heavy. The Punjabis loved to gamble and so did the British. Large wagers were made, side bets placed, and the result was either bottles of champagne all round or a painful visit to the manager of the bank after the festivities.

While the Indians ate from the food stalls, the Raj ate in *shamianas*, large decorated tents. There the catering would be done by one of the well-known hotels or restaurants – you always knew which one because the bearers would be dressed in the livery of the establishment. It was just like "back home." The luncheon tents had buffets of cold meats and more elaborate dishes, such as chicken in aspic, or grouse stuffed with pâté, and salads. The tea tents featured strawberries and cream. Membership for the Week included admission into the refreshment tents. But in the members' tents of the larger clubs, such as the Lahore Race Club, or the Delhi Club, it was strictly members and guests only. Then there were the bar tents where you paid for your drinks and celebrated the coup that your horse won – whether he was in fact yours, or merely the horse you had backed for that race.

Of course, then there was always music provided by regimental bands, which made the Raj feel very much a part of the abiding Empire and very patriotic. It was all magic and noise and excitement and breath-taking feats and sinew-stretching competition. It was, of course, THE WEEK!

Stuffed pomfret rolls in aspic

•

I have left the original fish in the name of the recipe, because the delicious pomfret was the fish most commonly used in India for this type of dish. I suggest that you substitute any fine white fish fillets.

Serves 8

8 fish fillets
6 oz small shrimps, shelled and finely chopped
2 green chillies, seeded (optional) and finely chopped
1 teaspoon grated lemon zest
$\frac{1}{4}$ teaspoon ground cumin
1 anchovy, mashed, or 1 teaspoon anchovy paste
2 tablespoons fresh white breadcrumbs
1 egg, beaten
8 large shrimps or prawns, shelled and cleaned
$2\frac{1}{2}$ tablespoons gelatine
$1\frac{1}{2}$ pint warm fish stock, strained through cheesecloth

1 tablespoon capers
3 tablespoons white wine
$\frac{1}{2}$ teaspoon salt
8 oz sour cream
1 teaspoon finely chopped parsley
1 teaspoon finely chopped tarragon
1 teaspoon finely chopped chives
1 bunch of watercress, washed and drained
$\frac{1}{2}$ cucumber, scratched along the skin with the tines of a fork, then thinly sliced
6 radishes, washed, then cut into roses

1   Heat some water in a steamer. Line the tray with wax paper, pierced in several places to admit the steam.
2   Trim the fish fillets and lay them on a board.
3   In a bowl, combine the small shrimps, chillies, grated lemon zest, cumin, anchovy, breadcrumbs and beaten egg. Spread the fillets thickly with the mixture, leaving a space for rolling at one end. Roll them up and fasten them with thread.

4   Place the fish rolls in the steamer and steam them for 15 minutes, adding the shellfish 5 minutes before the end. Remove, untie the rolls and let everything cool.

5   Meantime, chill a large mould in the refrigerator. Place the gelatine in a very large jug or lipped bowl and dissolve it in $\frac{1}{4}$ of the fish stock, stirring constantly. Add the remainder of the fish stock and stir in the capers, wine and salt.

6   Pour a little of the aspic into the mould and chill until it thickens. Arrange the fish rolls decoratively, alternating them with the large shrimp or prawns. Pour half of the remaining aspic around them and chill again until that thickens. Then, as a second layer, pour in the remainder of the aspic. Let the mould chill in the refrigerator until it is very firm.

7   While it is chilling, place the sour cream in a bowl and blend in the finely chopped herbs.

8   Turn the aspic mould out on to a large platter. Surround it with dollops of the sour cream and tuck watercress sprigs in between the mounds of cream. Garnish with slices of cucumber and place the radish roses round at intervals as highlights. Refrigerate it until you are ready to serve.

Notes: In hot weather, such as we had in India, you may add a little more gelatine for a firmer mould. A few freshly cooked green peas, scattered evenly in the thickening aspic would also be a nice touch. You could decorate the actual mould further by placing slices of hard-boiled egg at intervals in the second layer of aspic. A freshly made, thick mayonnaise may be substituted for the sour cream.

Shamiana chicken liver pâté

•

The light inside the *shamianas* was at once mellow and cool, as if one was inside an old parchment shade. The grass was soft under one's feet, like an old carpet, although after a hundred or so people had trooped in for refreshments, it became trampled and there was a smell of old hay, appropriate to the occasion. The bearers hurried to and fro, although there was not so much for them to do, since the food was buffet-style and one simply had to get it and sit at a table. None the less, there were fingers raised in an imperial summons for "more water" or "another fork" and the bearers rushed around and appeared very attentive, which was also a tribute to the caterer for whom they worked. Race cards were tucked into handbags which, in turn, were put down on the grass beside one's seat. Glasses of beer, punch or champagne were poured and fragments of conversation could be heard.

Serves 8

6 oz unsalted butter

1 lb chicken livers, washed and patted dry

1 medium onion, peeled and chopped

3 cloves of garlic, smashed, peeled and chopped

2 tablespoons fine white breadcrumbs

1 teaspoon salt

$\frac{1}{2}$ teaspoon freshly ground black pepper

$\frac{1}{4}$ teaspoon allspice

1 tablespoon Worcestershire sauce

3 hard-boiled eggs, 2 peeled and chopped, 1 sliced

1 tablespoon cognac

6 or 7 sprigs of parsley

8 slices buttered toast, crusts trimmed, halved diagonally

1   Melt the butter in a large pan over medium heat and fry the chicken livers until they are brown on the outside, but slightly pink on the inside. Turn them into a bowl, together with the butter.

2   Add the onion, garlic, breadcrumbs, salt, pepper, allspice, Worcestershire sauce, and the 2 chopped eggs. Mix it all well together and then pour in the cognac.

3   Place it, one half at a time, in a processor and process to a rough paste. Form it into a mound, or place it in a greased mould and chill until just before needed.

4   Turn out the pâté, decorate with the slices of hard-boiled egg and then garnish with the parsley. Surround it with the slices of buttered toast and serve.

Notes: If you wish, the remaining hard-boiled egg may be finely chopped and sprinkled on top.

Bloody Mary shellfish mould

•

This is dedicated to the memory of those stalwart "old *kohais*" who would rather drink their meal than eat it. Perhaps this might have lured them in from the bar tent to the buffet.

Serves 8

3 tablespoons gelatine
1 pint warm fish or
  chicken stock, strained
  through muslin
8 fl oz tomato juice, plus 2
  teaspoons tomato paste
2 tablespoons vodka
½ teaspoon celery salt
1 teaspoon Worcestershire
  sauce
5 drops of Tabasco
1 teaspoon of finely
  chopped fresh dill
the meat from 1 large
  cooked lobster, cut into
  chunks
10 cooked prawns/large
  shrimp, 6 of them
  shelled

4 tablespoons freshly
  made thick mayonnaise
the leaves of 1 head of
  lettuce
3 large avocados, seeded
  and the meat cut into
  cubes
3 tablespoons freshly
  squeezed lemon juice
6 tablespoons olive oil
1 teaspoon Dijon mustard
1 clove of garlic, smashed,
  peeled and finely
  chopped
¼ teaspoon salt
¼ teaspoon freshly ground
  black pepper
2 hard-boiled eggs,
  shelled and quartered
sprigs of parsley

1   Dissolve the gelatine in ¼ of the fish stock. Pour in the remainder of the stock and stir well. Add the tomato juice and tomato paste, vodka, celery salt, Worcestershire sauce, Tabasco and dill. Stir everything together well.
2   Chill a large ring mould, and pour ¼ of the tomato and stock mixture into it. Chill it until it begins to thicken. Arrange the chunks of lobster meat in the mould, alternating with the cooked, shelled prawns/shrimp, cut

in half, lengthwise. Pour just over half of the remaining stock and tomato mixture around the shellfish and set the mould back in the refrigerator to let the next layer thicken.

3 Stir the mayonnaise into the remaining tomato stock mixture and blend it in well. Remove the mould from the refrigerator and pour in the pale pink, creamy mixture. Put it back to chill completely.

4 Line a large platter with the lettuce leaves.

5 Place the avocado cubes in a bowl. Blend together the lemon juice, olive oil, mustard, garlic, salt and pepper into a dressing and pour it over the avocado. Mix it well.

6 Remove the mould from the refrigerator and turn it out carefully on to the lettuce-lined platter. Fill the middle with the dressed avocado and garnish with the quartered eggs and sprigs of parsley. Take the remaining unshelled prawns and drape them over the top of the mould at equal distances. Chill until you are ready to serve.

Notes: This is a very pretty two-tone mould. The vodka may be omitted by those who wish.

Cucumber stuffed with Roquefort and hazelnuts

•

These stuffed rounds of cucumber are both interesting and attractive. They are also very quick to make, and become a convenient side dish for a buffet table.

Quantity: 24 stuffed slices

1 cucumber (about 1 foot long), washed, ends trimmed, then cut in half, crosswise

$\frac{1}{4}$ lb Roquefort cheese

1 tablespoon cream

1 teaspoon lime juice

$\frac{1}{2}$ teaspoon ground white pepper

$\frac{1}{2}$ teaspoon caraway seeds

15 hazelnuts, peeled and finely chopped

12 hazelnuts, peeled and halved

1 Hollow out the seeds and about a $\frac{3}{4}$-inch diameter column from the middle of both halves of the cucumber. Pat them dry with paper towels and up-end them to drain.

2 Break the Roquefort into a food processor, add the cream and blend on high for a few seconds. Scrape down the sides of the bowl with a rubber spatula. Add the lime juice, pepper and caraway seeds and blend again for a few seconds. Scrape the sides again and add the *chopped* nuts. Blend a final time just long enough to distribute the nuts.

3 Stuff and fill the tube inside the cucumber halves with the mixture from the processor, using a table knife. Force and tamp the stuffing from both ends to eliminate air pockets.

4 Refrigerate the stuffed cucumber for at least 30 minutes.

5 Slice each half into $\frac{1}{2}$-inch-thick disks and garnish each disk with a halved hazelnut. Refrigerate until ready to serve.

Notes: The cucumber may be stuffed one day in advance, refrigerated, and sliced just before serving.

Roulade of duck

•

This recipe might, at first, seem a little ambitious, but it is quite easy; it only looks impressive. The chief trick is to remove most of the duck's skin intact, or in as large a piece as you can manage, because you will need it to be the wrapper for the roll. It takes patience and a very sharp, small-bladed knife so you can nick it carefully in the places that attach it to the carcass.

Serves 6–8

1 5-lb duck, plucked and dressed, together with its heart, liver and giblets
4 oz ham
2 hard-boiled eggs, peeled
6 pitted black or green olives
1 medium onion, peeled and finely chopped
¼ lb unsalted butter
1 tablespoon Worcestershire sauce
4 tablespoons tomato paste
4 tablespoons finely chopped coriander leaves
1 tablespoon olive oil
½ teaspoon salt
¼ teaspoon freshly ground black pepper
2 tablespoons grated orange zest
the yolk of 1 egg
2 tablespoons honey
watercress

1   Place plenty of water in a steamer, just below the level of the cooking surface, and slowly bring up to heat.

2   Remove the skin from the duck, trying to keep as much as you can in 1 big piece. Lay it on a board.

3   Remove the meat from the duck, keeping 6 or 7 slices on one side. Chop the remaining meat finely and then the ham, hard-boiled eggs and olives. A food processor can be used for this. Combine the ingredients in a bowl.

4   Add the onions and butter to the mixture in the bowl, and work it all well together.

5   Now add the Worcestershire sauce, tomato paste, coriander, olive oil, salt, pepper and grated orange zest and combine everything thoroughly.

6   Place the reserved slices of duck in a layer on the duck skin. Form the

mixture from the bowl into a sausage and place it on top of the slices. Roll up into a firm roll with the mixture on the inside, surrounded by the slices of duck and then by the skin as an outer wrapping. Use a poultry needle and thread to stitch up the roll, or wind it with thread so that it is firmly fastened. Wrap the roll in muslin or cheesecloth which you have first wrung out in a little oil so that it does not stick to the skin. Wax paper may be used instead.

7   Steam the roll for 45 minutes, adding more water if necessary.

8   Meanwhile heat the oven to 450°F (230°C, Gas Mark 8).

9   Carefully unwrap the cooked roll and paint it with the egg yolk mixed with the honey. Place it in the oven and bronze the outside skin, turning it from time to time. (Approximately 15 minutes.)

10   Let the roll cool, then unsnip any thread and remove. Serve the roll, sliced, on a bed of watercress.

Notes: You may like to garnish the roulade with slices of orange, in addition to the watercress.

Polo pilaff

•

At Shighur I first saw the game of the *Chaughan*, which was played the day after our arrival on the *Mydan* or plain laid out expressly for the purpose ... It is in fact hocky on horseback. The ball, which is larger than a cricket ball, is only a globe made of a kind of willow-wood, and is called in Tibeti, "*Pulu*" ... I can conceive that the *Chaughan* requires only to be seen to be played. It is the fit sport of an equestrian nation ... The game is played at almost every valley in Little Tibet and the adjoining countries ... Ladakh, Yessen, Chitral, &c.; and I should recommend it to be tried on the Hippodrome at Bayswater ...

G. Vigne, *Travels in Kashmir, Ladakh, &c*, 1838,
from Yule and Burnell, *Hobson-Jobson*

The horses wheel in the field; a sharp click as mallet hits ball, and clods of earth are flung upward from gouging hooves. Helmets shine white in the sun and the hard breathing of man and horse is audible. A tattoo of hoof beats, then the figures dwindle rapidly and are silhouetted against a china-blue sky. From the perimeter of the field comes a scattering of polite applause.

A headlong charge thunders down the rocky plain, squeezed between high mountains. There is a crash like that of opposing armies, and the landscape is filled with struggling horses and men, weaving and colliding. Sticks cross and break, blood flows from angry welts in the flesh of both riders and steeds alike. The mêlée of locked and frantic figures resembles a classic battle scene except that, somewhere, there is a ball.

Two thousand years separate the first scene from the second and yet the game is the same, polo. It is said to have started in Persia as a battle-training exercise for cavalry during the reign of Darius I – a free-for-all enacted by one hundred players a side! But it was much too much fun and excitement for mere commoners and the Persian royalty and nobility adopted it. Even queens and their entourages played. In those days it was called *chaugan*, after the Persian term for a stick or mallet. Then the Arabs adopted the game, and the Mohammedans who were Moguls introduced it to India in the thirteenth century. As the Mogul emperors died out, the game lapsed with them, except a very crude form played by the men of the mountains bordering the north. In Tibet the game finally took its name from the Tibetan for ball, *pulu*.

In the mid-nineteenth century, some British tea planters saw polo being played in Manipur, near Assam, and pronounced the game as fit for the Raj, and the first polo club was formed in Silchar in 1859. Almost simultaneously the British in Kashmir were also exposed to polo, and it was adopted and became an institution in the North-west Frontier Province and the Punjab. British cavalry units, namely the 10th Hussars, took up the game, but it was then still being played by eight men a side (a form which did not change until the early 1880s). Soon every maharaja worth his salt had a string or two of polo ponies, and the game had run the full cycle, back to royalty again.

In Sargodha there were a lot of horses to choose from and a lot of young men, so there would be polo three times a week at the Remount Depot. My mother used to play "stick and ball" by herself:

One day I was playing, riding off illusionary horses, when up came a young man, Cumford by name, and said, "Lucette, would you like to play a chukka with us?" I was absolutely delighted. It turned out they were one man short. I remember the team was called Sargodha Fillies, and that winter they went on to play very well in the polo matches held during the horse shows. The following year, they went on to win the Northern Punjab Tournament. Their *sowars* (rough-riders) trained their ponies, and they used to lend them to me once they knew I was interested in the game. It was the greatest fun.

So it was for the spectators, too. As a child, I loved to go out on to the field at half-time and help tread down the chunks of earth up-turfed after a hectic game. Part of the ambience was the tea or lunch served in the refreshment tent, where everybody excitedly discussed the prowess of experienced riders, the mistakes of the comparative novices, and the fortunes of their teams. This *pilaff*, regal enough to serve as fare for maharajas and the Raj alike, would be excellent for a polo buffet lunch.

Serves 8

4-inch piece of fresh ginger root, peeled and finely chopped

2 cloves of garlic, smashed, peeled and finely chopped

$\frac{1}{2}$ teaspoon salt

1 small onion, peeled and finely chopped

$\frac{1}{2}$ teaspoon powdered saffron

4 oz plain yoghurt

1 teaspoon aniseed

2 bay leaves, broken into pieces

the juice and grated zest of 1 lemon (keep separate)

the meat from 1 large lobster, cut into 1-inch chunks

1 dozen small oysters, shucked

2 tablespoons *ghee* (clarified butter)

4 oz/$1\frac{1}{3}$ cups slivered almonds

1 lb/$2\frac{1}{3}$ cups best-quality long-grain rice, washed well in cold water, drained and dried

8 whole cardamom pods, crushed

4 cloves

1-inch stick of cinnamon

1 teaspoon salt

2 tablespoons chopped parsley

1   Place *half* the ginger and the garlic, salt, onion, saffron and yoghurt in a food processor and process to a purée. Grind the aniseed and bay leaves to a powder and add it to the processor, together with the lemon juice, giving the blades a few more turns to mix them in.

2   Place the lobster meat and oysters in a bowl and add the purée from the processor. Mix well and then cover the bowl and let the seafood marinate for 2 hours in the refrigerator.

3   Melt the *ghee* over low heat in a large saucepan and fry the almonds until they are a golden brown. Drain them over the pan with a slotted spoon and set them aside. Increase the heat to moderate and, in the same *ghee*, fry the rice, together with the remainder of the ginger, adding the lemon zest, cardamoms, cloves and cinnamon, stirring until the rice becomes opaque. Now add water to a level of $1\frac{1}{4}$ inches above the surface of the rice. (This is just above the first joint of your index finger, if the tip is placed lightly on the surface of the rice.) Cover the pan and bring to a boil.

4   As soon as the water boils, uncover the pan and add the seafood and its marinade from Step 2, and the salt. Stir once, then cover the pan again and bring to the boil. Turn the heat very low and let the *pilaff* simmer for 20 minutes.

5   Uncover and stir in the fried almonds from Step 3, and the parsley. Cover the pan, turn off the heat and let the pan sit for 10 minutes.

6   Transfer the contents of the pan to a flat serving dish, picking out and discarding the cinnamon stick. Take care to place some of the lobster meat and oysters on the top of the rice.

Alabaster chicken

•

Indian weddings are the greatest show on earth for "people-watchers" and connoisseurs of good food, although nowadays they are not as extravagant as they were in the times of the Raj. Then, celebrations went on for days and the wealthier the Indian family, the more lavish the festivities and feasts. Less wealthy families would borrow money from the moneylenders at exorbitant rates to marry off their daughters, and spend the rest of their lives repaying the debt. It was a matter of pride, and the gossip of neighbours, that compelled them to put on a big show, way above their means.

And then there were all the dowry requirements: chests of *saris*, linens, bedding, pots and pans – busy arrangements, begun months beforehand, kept the women of the family twittering and accumulating treasure like nesting birds.

A wedding reception that I attended in the Punjab was given by a wealthy Muslim businessman. It commenced at twilight. *Shamianas*, enormous marquees with open sides and pitched roofs edged with scallops, were erected on rolling green lawns; torches or flambeaux flared from the borders of flowers and strings of lights festooned the trees. The arriving guests were given flowers – jasmine bracelets for the women and roses for the men's lapels. The brilliant silk *saris* of the Hindus, embroidered with gold and silver, and the swaying, ankle-length skirts and tight jackets of the Muslim women were set off by glittering jewels on wrists, fingers, necks, ears and even noses. The shifting hues were punctuated by the formal, black, high-necked jackets or gold brocade tunics of the Indian men and, here and there, one could see the full-dress "blues" of the British military or the white tropical dinner jackets of the civilians. The air was heavy with expensive perfumes, sandalwood, jasmine and attar of roses. The plaintive rippling melody of a sitar could be heard.

Uniformed bearers passed among the multitude with huge silver trays of hors-d'œuvres, accompanied by traditional fruit drinks for the devout and champagne for the British. At the feast itself, the guests sat on Persian rugs at low tables. Out of deference to the Raj, chairs and higher tables were placed for their convenience – an arrangement which always made one feel very conspicuous and isolated.

The food was abundant. All manner of kebabs over flaming charcoal, rich *kormas* and rice *pilaffs*, or *birianis* sprinkled with rose-water, were proffered by relays of servants. Pyramids of fruit and silvered sweetmeats ended the meal, with *paan* for the Indian guests, and bowls of scented water with which to rinse the hands. Of course, everyone was encouraged to eat far too much, and it would have been an insult to the hospitality of the host to have done otherwise.

In some areas of India, an all-white rice *pilaff* is served at wedding feasts, and I have re-created the dishes below to echo that tradition. The delicately spiced, creamy chicken is mounded on a snowy, fragrant rice, accented with pine nuts. Even if there is no wedding occasion, it would be perfect for a June evening. Serve it on a large, silver platter or an elegant, dark dish for contrast, and ring it with frosted green grapes and pink roses.

Serves 6

3 tablespoons *ghee*
(clarified butter)
1 large onion, peeled and
chopped
1-inch piece of fresh
ginger root, peeled and
chopped
4 cloves of garlic,
smashed, peeled and
chopped
3 lb skinned chicken
pieces, i.e. the legs
(drumstick) divided
from the thigh, the
wings left whole, and
the breast separated
down the middle then
halved again, crosswise

12 oz plain yoghurt
1 teaspoon ground white
cumin
1 teaspoon ground white
pepper
1 teaspoon salt
1 teaspoon ground
cardamom
8 fl oz double cream

1   In a large, heavy saucepan, heat the *ghee* over a medium-high setting and fry the onion, ginger and garlic (in that order), stirring, until the onion is just translucent and shiny.

2   Scrape the contents of the pan into the bowl of a food processor, fitted with a metal blade, and whirl at high speed until a coarse purée is formed. Transfer it back to the pan on heat.

3   Add the chicken pieces and all the remaining ingredients, except the cream, to the saucepan. Stir everything well to coat the chicken with the yoghurt and spices.

4   Cover the pan, reduce the heat to low and simmer until the chicken is tender but not falling off the bone (about 30 minutes).

5   Uncover the pan and stir in the cream. Increase the heat to medium and cook, stirring gently, for 5 more minutes.

Notes: Either serve the dish at once with your own accompaniments, or put the chicken on hold in a low oven while you prepare the following rice.

White pilaff with pine nuts

•

Serves 6

6 green or white
  cardamom pods
1 3-inch stick of cinnamon
8 whole cloves
2 bay leaves
5 tablespoons vegetable
  oil
2 large onions, peeled and
  finely chopped

23 oz/3 cups best-quality
  long-grain rice
  (preferably Basmati),
  washed well, then
  drained and dried
1 teaspoon salt
1 tablespoon sugar
1 tablespoon melted *ghee*
  (clarified butter)
3 oz/1 cup pine nuts

1   Fill a kettle or medium saucepan with water and place it over high heat for use in Step 5.

2   Place the cardamoms, cinnamon, cloves and bay leaves in a small square of cheesecloth or muslin and tie it into a little bag with string – much as you would make a *bouquet garni*. Set it aside for use in Step 6.

3   Place a large, heavy saucepan (with a tight-fitting lid) over medium-high heat and add the oil. When the oil is up to temperature, add the onions and fry, stirring constantly, until they are translucent and shiny, but have not turned golden.

4   Now add the rice and thoroughly stir it until every grain is coated. Pour in enough water to cover the surface of the rice by $1\frac{1}{4}$ inches.

5   Measure in the salt and add the bag of spices. Cover the pan and bring the rice mixture to a boil. Reduce the heat to low and let it simmer for 20 minutes, or until the rice is just cooked.

6   Remove the lid and discard the spice bag. Now add the sugar and *ghee*, blending them into the grains. Stir in the pine nuts and turn the *pilaff* on to a large serving platter. Serve at once.

Notes: If you postpone serving the rice for some time, you may keep it warm in a low oven, covered with a damp cloth.

Tipsy laird

•

Passed to my mother by a member of the MacDonald Clan, this Scottish recipe for trifle is just a little different from others. The difference is, of course, the noble liqueur, Drambuie. Let the trifle grace your buffet table with the other desserts and I promise it will disappear before most of the others.

Serves 8–10

12 oz (approximately) sponge fingers/ladyfingers, each split in half

16 oz good raspberry jam

2 small boxes of fresh raspberries, washed and drained

8 fl oz sweet sherry

8 tablespoons Drambuie

7 egg yolks, beaten

$2\frac{1}{2}$ oz/$\frac{1}{3}$ cup sugar

1 pint milk

1 tablespoon cornflour/cornstarch dissolved in 4 fl oz of the above milk

$\frac{1}{2}$ teaspoon vanilla extract

16 fl oz heavy cream

5 glacé cherries, halved

3 tablespoons blanched, slivered almonds

1 $\frac{1}{2}$-inch piece of angelica, sliced into diamonds

1   Spread all the fingers with a coating of raspberry jam. Line a 6-quart (approximate) glass bowl with them, standing up, jam-side inward. Sprinkle the raspberries over the sponge fingers. Combine the sherry and 4 tablespoons of the Drambuie and pour it over the sponge and fruit. Cover and chill while you make the custard.

2   Stir the egg yolks and sugar together in a small bowl. Scald the milk in the top of a double boiler and stir about 1 tablespoon of the hot milk into the yolk mixture. Pour the egg-yolk mixture into the upper saucepan with the milk and stir it constantly until it thickens to the consistency of heavy cream, but does not set (approximately 15 minutes), adding the cornflour mixture to hasten the thickening.

3   Remove the custard from the heat and place the pan in a large bowl filled with ice. Stir in the vanilla and let it cool and thicken for about 10 minutes, stirring from time to time to avoid a skin forming on top. Pour

the custard over the chilled cake and fruit mixture and cover the bowl, returning it to the refrigerator.

4   Refrigerate a whisk and mixing bowl. Beat or whisk the cream until it forms stiff peaks. Add the remaining 4 tablespoons of Drambuie and continue beating for several more seconds until it is blended in.

5   Spoon the cream over the custard. Smooth the edges and decorate with the cherries, almonds and angelica. Cover and refrigerate until you are ready to serve.

Notes: You may like to add a layer of peeled and sliced fresh peaches over the raspberries.

Byculla Club soufflé

•

It is quite unnecessary for us to say how a Soufflé should be made as it is the one dish that every Indian cook knows and in which he excels. If he should fail at any time and the Soufflé should be not properly risen it is probably not because of the preparation but because he has had his oven too hot. A hot Soufflé requires a slow oven. The basis of the Soufflé whether it be hot or cold can be left to the imagination as anything sweet will do. Blackcurrant jam, coffee or mango pulp are three suggestions which the average cook does not generally think of. Cold Soufflés should always have some sort of liqueur in them. Some people unfortunately seem to think that any cold Soufflé should be called Byculla Soufflé. This is quite incorrect as the secret of the preparation of that dish exists with the Byculla Club in Bombay and depends upon an extremely skilful blending of liqueurs.

Karachi, 1923, C. C. Lewis, *Culinary Notes for Sind*

Well, there you have it; a genuine reference and tribute to the original Byculla Club soufflé, whose fame has reached almost mythic proportions among the world's wanderers, and whose existence is now only a dim memory among most of the dwindling numbers of the British Raj. I do use the word "most," for I was determined that if I was going to write this book, then it must include the Byculla Club soufflé. Without it, there would be no book, for it embodies the epicurean standards of the Raj at their best.

I was lucky and my perseverance – or importuning – was rewarded. My mother's younger sister, Gery Scott, or Diana, as she is known to our family, had managed to acquire the original recipe and had hoarded it through the years. Perhaps rival claims to possession of the genuine article could start a heated correspondence in *The Times. This is the real thing* – I have eaten it and it is ambrosia. It justly lives up to its hallowed reputation.

The Byculla Club

Serves 8

6 large, fresh egg yolks
3 tablespoons sugar
1 tablespoon gelatine, softened in 3 tablespoons of cold water
16 fl oz double cream
2 tablespoons kümmel

2 tablespoons green chartreuse
2 tablespoons orange curaçao
2 tablespoons Benedictine
3 tablespoons crushed macaroons, or other sweet biscuits

1 Chill a whisk and a large mixing bowl.
2 Place the egg yolks in another bowl over hot water and beat them, gradually adding the sugar, for 10 minutes or until they are thick and light. Remove the bowl from the hot water and continue to beat for a further 2 minutes. Set aside.

3 Place the softened gelatine in a small bowl over a pan of hot water and stir until it is dissolved. Set it aside to cool and thicken slightly.

4 Pour the cream into the chilled bowl and whisk it until it becomes thicker but is still shiny.

5 Stir the liqueurs, in the above order, into the gelatine.

6 Fold the egg mixture and the gelatine/liqueur mixture into the cream and combine gently.

7 Spoon into your best crystal bowl and sprinkle the top with the biscuit crumbs. Refrigerate for at least 3 hours.

Notes: The Byculla Club soufflé may be presented in classic style, by choosing a soufflé dish and fastening a paper collar around the top. It may be also served in individual goblets.

The Raj imbibes

In a land where "sociability was gauged in very large measure by drinking habits" and where whisky came at less than three rupees a bottle, it was nevertheless a severe crime "to drink too much or to be seen to drink too much before your Indian servants."

Charles Allen, *Plain Tales from the Raj*

We never drank cocktails as known in these days, but we had a mixture of our own, called "pink peg" or "Khaitola cocktail," made up by a local chemist, which consisted of Justerini and Brooks's best brandy (may we be forgiven because of our youth!) lashed with a small quantity of chloroform and ether. To this terrific tipple we added soda and bitters. Its effect was like letting in the top gear of a racing car; but we never drank it until the sun was over the yard arm.

Francis Yeats-Brown, *Lancer at Large*

On 11 October 1877, for example, there were fourteen guests to *tiffin* and thirteen to dinner. They drank between them six bottles of champagne, eight of claret, two of sherry, two of German beer, two of whisky; their personal servants accounted for four more clarets, three beers, four pints of porter and six glasses of brandy.

Pat Barr and Ray Desmond, an account of Government House in Simla during the term of Lord Lytton as Viceroy of India, *Simla, A Hill Station in British India*

There is no doubt that the British Raj enjoyed drinking. Alcohol was employed as the oil to help the wheels of Anglo-Indian society revolve, and the active social life was a necessary counterbalance to hard work, often performed under difficult circumstances. But the code of a gentleman generally prevailed. The knife-edge distinction between drinking and being drunk was maintained by the upper classes, albeit precariously. It is a distinction difficult enough under any circumstance, but even more so in a climate where the body needed copious amounts of fluid to offset the tropical heat.

There were, of course, exceptions who were unable to preserve the balance. India had more than its share of characters and eccentrics among the "old *kohais*" and quite a few of them carried a high enough level of alcohol in their constitutions to cause any mosquito to turn into an instant

sake-soaked *kamikaze* pilot. They swore it was "to prevent malaria," or "to squelch the damn fever I picked up in Madras in '96," but their servants knew better, although out of loyalty they would never speak to anyone about their *sahib*'s peccadilloes.

As C. C. Lewis remarked, good wine was not part of the libations available in India, since it did not survive the long voyage on unrefrigerated ships, nor the sharp changes in climate. Beer and spirits had to substitute and much ingenuity was employed in devising interesting and palatable ways to disguise the inferior wines that did make the journey, or to use the available spirits and liqueurs. Indeed, our drink "punch" derives from the

Hindustani word "*panch*," meaning five, or five ingredients in the traditional drink. In the seventeenth century, these consisted of: arrak, sugar, lime juice, spices and water.

In the eighteenth century, tea was substituted for the spices, possibly owing to efforts on the part of the East India Company to promote their export before a wider audience. By two centuries later, punch had become the name for any drink made of rum, whisky, brandy, wine or other liquor, in combination with water, fruit juice and sugar – served from a large bowl into cups or glasses, either very hot or well iced.

Champagne cups and fruit cups were very popular for club buffets on such occasions as gymkhanas, tennis tournaments and dances. But for everyday drinking, whisky and water or soda, in large glasses and well diluted, was the normal tipple of choice; but not until 6 o'clock or sundown. After a full day's work, followed by a long ride or several chukkas of polo, or a hard, competitive tennis match, there was nothing nicer than to relax in creaking rattan or wicker chairs on the veranda of the club, watching a *mali* watering the lawn, enjoying the first cooling breezes of the evening, while gossiping about the day's doings in the station or cantonment with a *burra* or *chota peg* (large or small measure) at one's elbow and a satisfying sense that all was well in the world of the Raj.

At weekends the unspoken proscription against drinking during the day was relaxed. The hour or two before Sunday *tiffin* was the time for several pristine gimlets or pink gins but, again, the rules applied. The drinks were as straightforward and honest as the people who drank them. Cocktails were not very popular, except at times when one "lived it up" in the larger hotels: times such as being on leave in the hill stations; during the Weeks (see p. 197) in places like Delhi, Calcutta or Bombay; or as part of the round of celebrations for those who were leaving India. In the 1920s and 1930s, when cocktails became the rage of the smart international set, then they did catch on in India, but not to the same extent as in Europe or America.

The libations that follow are the memorable inventions of bartenders of the more renowned hotels in India, of the major clubs in the areas where the Raj congregated, or of the regiments and, in some cases, of individuals whose inspirations added a little sparkle to life in India.

In some of the recipes that come next, there are a few inflexible rules to take note of:

1   Use fresh fruit.

2   If carbonated beverages are to be used, add them at the very last minute so the sparkle is not lost.

3   Chill all the ingredients before placing in the bowl.
4   Use only a large block of ice. Small ice dilutes and weakens the beverage too quickly, particularly in hot weather.

A classic gimlet

•

1 jigger dry gin
½ teaspoon lime cordial

½ teaspoon sugar syrup
   (optional)
a slice of fresh lime

Take a big, wide-mouthed champagne glass and put in the gin, followed by the lime cordial, then stir in the sugar syrup, if you need to use it. Fill up with chilled plain water, add an ice cube and a thin slice of big, green lime.

Notes: The sugar syrup should correct any lack of sweetness in the particular lime cordial you use. Some people omit the water and merely fill up the glass with ice cubes. To my mind, the drink then only becomes perfect about half-way through, when the ice cubes have melted sufficiently.

Pink gin, according to the "Expert"

•

Take a thin, stemmed cocktail glass and shake in 4 or 5 dashes of Angostura bitters. Tip the glass to a drunken angle and twirl it between thumb and fingers. Whatever Angostura sticks to the glass through capillary action is precisely the right amount, although many "old *kohais*" prefer a heavier measure in order to stimulate their heat-faded appetites. Pour off the superfluous bitters and fill the glass with dry gin. That's all.

Notes: I personally prefer to twist the thinnest curl of lemon peel on top, for its aromatics, but this is not a classical approach.

Sargodha Club tennis cup

•

For the purist, the chief difference between a cup and a punch is that the former is mixed with soda water or another sparkling beverage. Punch is generally diluted with water. The exception to this is champagne punch, for obvious reasons.

8 fl oz sugar syrup	8 fl oz sherry
1 pint freshly squeezed lemon juice	3 bottles of dry white wine
8 fl oz brandy	1 cucumber, peeled and thinly sliced
8 fl oz strong Indian tea	1 quart soda water

1   In a large bowl, mix together the sugar syrup, lemon juice, brandy, tea, sherry and wine. Add the cucumber and let it stand for 30 minutes.
2   Remove the cucumber and discard. Carefully place a large block of ice into the bowl and pour in the soda water.

Notes: Reserve the cup for *after* the tennis match, not during it, because the sight of an otherwise good player trying to hit two balls simultaneously is enough to make a grown man cry.

Karachi Club champagne cup

•

½ small cucumber, cut into slices	1 orange, sliced
4 tablespoons orange curaçao	1 lime, sliced
12 fl oz sherry	2 bottles of champagne
12 fl oz cognac	20 fl oz soda water
4 fl oz noyau	20 fl oz carbonated lemonade
4 tablespoons sugar syrup (optional)	

1   Place the cucumber in the bottom of a punch bowl and add the curaçao, sherry, cognac, noyau and sugar syrup. Let the mixture steep for 30 minutes, then remove the cucumber.
2   Place a block of ice in the bowl and add the orange and lime slices. Pour the champagne, soda water and carbonated lemonade over the ice.

Note from the sahib: For those who have not come across it before, noyau is a colourless or pale pink liqueur, tasting of almonds.

Lahore claret cup

•

half a large pineapple,
   peeled and cut into
   wedges, lengthwise
half a cucumber, peeled
   and sliced
3 oz/1 cup
   icing/confectioners'
   sugar
the juice of 1 large lime

$\frac{1}{2}$ teaspoon freshly grated
   nutmeg
10 fl oz sherry
5 fl oz maraschino
2 bottles of claret
   (Bordeaux)
1 quart carbonated
   lemonade

1   Place the pineapple and cucumber in the bowl and cover with the sugar. Add the lime juice and let the fruit marinate for 30 minutes to 1 hour.
2   Grate the nutmeg over the top and then add the sherry, maraschino and claret. Place a block of ice in the bowl and pour in the carbonated lemonade.

Notes: Some hosts like to add a couple of ounces of orange curaçao for an added fillip.

Bengal Lancer's punch

•

Quite a special punch. Reserved for such celebratory occasions as when the regiment won the polo tournaments.

4 fl oz freshly squeezed
orange juice
4 fl oz freshly squeezed
lime juice
4 fl oz freshly squeezed
pineapple juice
2 oz/¾ cup
icing/confectioners'
sugar

6 fl oz Barbados rum
6 fl oz cointreau
2 bottles of claret
(Bordeaux)
1 bottle of champagne
20 fl oz soda water

1   Place the juices in a bowl and stir in the sugar.
2   Add the rum, cointreau and claret.
3   Place a block of ice in the bowl and pour in the champagne and soda
water.

Notes: A friend of ours in the 10th Hussars used to make a very similar
punch. I don't really know who first laid claim to it, but I would rather
stay out of the way and let them battle it out on the polo field.

Oddennino's own hot punch

•

8 fl oz blended whisky
2 tablespoons brandy
1 tablespoon gin
½ tablespoon orange
curaçao

1 teaspoon kümmel
the juice of 12 lemons
3 oz/1 cup
icing/confectioners'
sugar

Place all the ingredients, in the listed order, with 12 fl oz boiling water, in
a heated bowl or large jug. Stir and serve.

Notes: A most deceptive drink. Innocuous to the taste, it is dangerous in
the long stretch. Reserve for a cold winter's day when you don't have to
drive anywhere.

Gulmarg Golf Club mulled wine

•

Another hot drink, this one would definitely warm up those avid golfers who insisted on playing right at the end of the season when it became really cold.

2 limes, quartered	6 whole allspice
½ a firm banana, cut in half	2 bottles of burgundy
2 3-inch sticks of cinnamon	8 fl oz dark Jamaican rum
12 whole cloves	4 oz/½ cup packed brown sugar
4 whole cardamom pods, crushed	8 fl oz soda water
	curls of lemon peel

1   Tie the fruit and spices into a bag of cheesecloth or muslin and place it in a saucepan. Add the burgundy and heat it until the steam rises.
2   Discard the bag of spices and add the rum and brown sugar. Stir until the sugar is dissolved.
3   Add the soda water and serve, foaming, with a curl of lemon peel on top of each cup.

Notes: Do not let the wine boil or you will lose the alcoholic content and turn the drink bitter.

His Highness's champagne burra peg

•

When I was very young, two years old to be precise, we went to Bhopal to see my grandfather's younger brother, Edgar, who was a civil engineer and also somewhat of an eccentric. One does not normally remember much of life at two, but the circumstances were so bizarre, they stuck in my memory. Uncle Edgar had constructed himself a small house and a guest house, way out in the middle of nowhere, at Tikhamgarh, many miles north of the city of Bhopal. The main house was rounded at one end and the walls were thick, the thickness of a bottle. And that is what he had done, built himself two bottle houses, the walls being constructed of bottles, layered in cement. He announced that there were eight thousand bottles in the construction of both houses and that he had a hand in drinking the contents of all the bottles himself. We sat there, and the adults talked over drinks until it grew dark. And outside I heard the roar of a prowling panther. It was an evening I never forgot.

Uncle Edgar had befriended many maharajas. This classic champagne cocktail was, he assured us, always the first choice of one of them.

3 fl oz good, well-chilled cognac	Angostura bitters
1 lump of sugar	dry champagne
	curls of lime peel

1   For each person, take a very large goblet, 14–16 fl oz in capacity. Pour in the measured amount of cognac and, dousing a cube of sugar with Angostura, place it in the glass.
2   Fill the glass with champagne and top with a twist of lime peel.

Notes: Edgar preferred 4 fl oz of cognac to a glass. I have heard these champagne cocktails referred to as "French seventy-fives" in some other circles, but I prefer Edgar's term of reference.

The Royal Bombay Yacht Club East India cocktail

•

Once the epitome of elegance and the height of society for the Raj, the Royal Bombay Yacht Club stood as a Victorian monument to the permanence of the Empire. The Residential Chambers were particularly ugly, or beautiful, whichever way you looked at them. Five storeys of solid masonry, with arched windows, turrets and mock-Tudor gables, it housed the Servants to the Queen. When the "servants" were not about their business in the port city, they could be seen lounging comfortably in deep chairs, quaffing cocktails such as the following.

1½ jiggers cognac	1 teaspoon orange curaçao
1 teaspoon pineapple syrup	2 dashes of Angostura bitters
⅔ teaspoon maraschino	twist of lime peel

Put the ingredients in a cocktail shaker, fill with fine ice and shake well. Strain into a cocktail glass and garnish with a twist of lime peel.

Notes: Some people use orange bitters instead of Angostura.

Athol brose

•

In 1927 the then head of the Imperial Bank in Sargodha, a man called Hutcheson, known to everyone as "Hutch," decided to give a Christmas party at the Bank house. He and my aunt got together and determined that it would be a totally different party from the usual affairs, something which everyone would remember. It was to be a pyjama party. So all the females ordered silk and satin lounging pyjamas, made by the *durzis*, and duly arrived. My mother remembers:

Instead of going in the front door, we were ushered up to the roof. (Outside stairs led up to the usual flat roof, on which people would sleep during the hot weather.) On the other side of the roof were more stairs which had been turned into a slide. You got on a mat and slid down, and, at the bottom, was a bearer standing there with a tray of "custard drinks." I thought it was the greatest fun and kept on climbing up to the roof and sliding down. Of course, every time I did, I was handed another custard. I could not understand, after a while, why I was feeling so dizzy. In those days, I did not drink alcohol, and the delicious "custard" that I was downing with gusto, was Athol brose!

The party was cleverly planned. In the main room were big tar barrels, filled with bran. The twenty or thirty guests fished deep down in them and pulled out packages. When opened, they either yielded a trinket, or toy, or something to eat. Unfortunately, many of the guests thought that these were all the refreshments there were, and they went back to the barrels again and again. But there was a sumptuous buffet laid on in the dining room. Music was provided by a band, and everyone danced. Hutch's party set a standard not topped by many others in Sargodha.

1 lb oatmeal	6 pints double cream
2 lb good Scottish honey	3 bottles (75 ounces) Scotch whisky

1   Crush the oatmeal and soak it in a deep pan of cold water for 24 hours.
2   Strain the liquid and combine it with the honey and cream.
3   Stir in the Scotch whisky and then refrigerate until chilled.

A strange but sad coda: on Easter Sunday, in 1930, my mother was staying with her then married sister, in Ferozepore. She woke feeling very depressed for no apparent reason, and at breakfast she did not want to eat. She could not shake off the feeling. In the middle of the meal, there was a long-distance call for her from Peshawar (to where Hutch had been transferred). A voice informed her that Mr Hutcheson and Mr Dinsmore had been shot and killed on the Khyber. Dinsmore had come out from the head office in England and he and Hutch had taken a Bank car and had gone up the Khyber – as many people did. They had reached Landi Kotal, where there is a fort. Directly below the fort there is a headland from which you can see far into Afghanistan. Hutch and Dinsmore were standing at this viewpoint, looking out, when their own guard, who had accompanied them, shot them both in the back. The sentry on duty at the fort promptly shot the man. There was no explanation except that it was said that he had gone mad. My mother and the family lost a close friend ... but that was the way it was on the Frontier.

Prairie oyster

•

My father was a firm believer in the efficacy of prairie oysters as a "morning-after" remedy for whatever ailed you. He tried hard to convince my mother to follow his suggestion but, since the mere idea of a raw egg would send her back to bed, he had to swallow them by himself. He mixed them or rather poured them into a shot glass and downed them while my mother shuddered. I thought it all rather funny, but then, I didn't drink!

1 egg yolk, unbroken	1 teaspoon Worcestershire
a good pinch of salt	sauce
1 teaspoon lemon juice	2 drops of Tabasco

Place the ingredients, in order, in a shot glass. Close your eyes, make a face and swallow it in one gulp.

Notes: Probably better to take 2 tablespoons of oil the night before in preparation for the evening's entertainment. Failing that, I can recommend 2 more hours in bed as a remedy. If you *have* to swallow a prairie oyster, this works as well as any. Some people add vinegar and tomato sauce as well, but, to my taste, that's a bit much.

"NEARLY THERE"

8

CHILDREN'S FARE: FESTIVALS AND EXTRAVAGANZAS

•

Christmas celebrations, birthday parties, etc.

The women attendants are called *ayahs*; they wear white saris, gold bangles and nose rings. One carries a pale-faced little child in long petticoats and over the infant's head a native man holds a parasol; then comes a small carriage drawn by a man, and in it sits another child. The processional ends with a pony on which is a little boy. He is held on by an attendant while another leads the animal; both the young charioteer and the rider are protected from the sun by other servants carrying parasols, and thus they all creep on for an hour every evening at the same funereal pace.

Pat Barr, *The Memsahibs*

Of course I recollect nothing of my life till I was a little over two years old, when my father and mother decided to send my eldest sister and two eldest brothers home to England, not only for their education, but more principally on account of the climate being so trying to English children, for in those days we had no Himalayas to go to. My mother was twenty-six years in India, and I might almost say had never heard of the Hills, not that they did not exist, but simply we had

---

1. Fancy dress party in Murree, 1940. Probably the last year I could dress in that costume; 2. One recruit to the British Raj. Myself and Nanny onboard the *Viceroy of India*, 1936; 3. The centre of Murree and the post office; 4. Sheila Hutchinson and myself, next-door neighbours and best friends, Bexley Hotel, Murree, 1939; 5. Nannies and their charges. April Marsden's birthday, Murree, 1940; 6. "Marmaduke", Nowshera, 1937; 7. Alex Hugh transported, Gulmarg, 1937; 8. Christmas Day, Nowshera, 1938; 9. A juvenile dancing class in the Shalimar gardens, Lahore.

no sanatoriums so far back as the early days of my parents' sojourn in India. Nowadays everybody goes to the Hills, as we call these gigantic mountains. Consequently, children can be kept in India in as perfect health as in the Mother Country, by a summer's visit to any of the Hill stations.

Harriet Tytler, *An Englishwoman in India*, ed. Anthony Sattin

As a third-generation member of the British Raj, there were no major adjustments to my childhood in India. My mother, born in Calcutta and raised in Karachi, spoke Hindustani fluently and regarded life in India as naturally as if she were in her own country, which in a sense she was. She did not want me spoilt and indulged by *ayahs*, so she engaged an English nanny at the time that I was born, in England, and that admirable woman, as upright and strict as Mary Poppins, with a loving heart beneath a prickly, starchy exterior, shaped my early life in the exotic surroundings I regarded as "home."

Nanny ruled the nursery world, and I was encapsulated and protected by that discipline. Although I was too young to remember, there was a period during my first two years when Nanny went home to England and I had a temporary *ayah*, but I suspect the thought gave my nanny no peace. Didn't *ayahs* slip opium into babies' bottles to make them sleep? So she soon returned to India and to her "charge," the term she used for her beloved children.

In our bungalows in Nowshera, Peshawar and Rawalpindi, her domain usually consisted of the day nursery, the night nursery and her bedroom and bathroom. She sailed serenely through the ups and downs of daily life in India. The servants gave her no problems; Nanny had that air of authority which caused even senior army officers to tiptoe around her. I have a clear memory of the starched crackle of her white apron as she tucked me in the cocoon of my mosquito net every night, with military precision.

Whenever we moved to a new station, on her first day off she would visit the post office and the cemetery. Then she was both oriented and comforted. The English names on the gravestones assured her of a degree of continuity and permanence in a strange place.

My childhood routine was probably that of most children in India. *Chota hazri*, tea, toast and a glass of milk, was brought in by Farid Khan, the nursery bearer – the tea and toast for Nanny, the milk for me. Then breakfast, after which she taught me the essentials of reading, writing and arithmetic. (When I was seven, she announced to my mother that I should go to school because she had taught me all she knew. "She's gone right through Arthur Mee's *Children's Encyclopedia*!") After lessons, there would be the morning ride.

When I was young, lunch was eaten in the nursery – just Nanny and me. But when I grew older, and when my father was away in Burma, I sometimes joined my mother for the meal. After lunch, there was a nap, considered obligatory for children in India. Even if one was too old to sleep, one was obliged to lie still. This was followed by the afternoon outing. In Rawalpindi we often went to the club, which had a large playground for children, and all the nannies gossiped together and knitted or embroidered while they kept a watchful eye on their "charges."

My hair was always worn short (for the hot climate), and cut by my mother ("Keep still or I'll cut your ear off!"), and Nanny always parted it on one side and tied a large hank of it with a bright ribbon bow, chosen to match whichever freshly ironed dress I wore. On one afternoon walk, when I was two or three, I remember we went to a park where we encountered a British soldier with a small monkey on his shoulder. Of course, I was fascinated, and Nanny and the soldier were chatting away when the animal suddenly reached down and yanked at the bright hair ribbon. He got it, with all the hair bound up in it as well. Nanny was mortified, but I had a bald patch for quite a while.

Tea was the time I enjoyed the most. I joined my parents for the meal, and we sat on the broad veranda with the lace-covered tea trolley, looking out over the sweep of garden; tall shade trees, freshly mown lawns and the carnations or chrysanthemums in pots, lining the driveway. After tea, my father and I would exercise the dogs by chasing them over the grass until we were out of breath; then we repaired to the drawing room, where my parents had *chota pegs*, and we listened to the six o'clock news on our large tropical-band radio. My parents then went to bathe and change into evening dress for a dinner party or other adult function, or there would be brother officers and their wives in for drinks. I disliked that, for I was always brought in from the nursery and paraded for the guests and I had to kiss all the "uncles and aunts" good-night.

The daily pace changed when we moved up to "the hills" for the summer. When I was very young, we went to Kashmir and stayed in Srinagar or Gulmarg. A pram was out of the question on the hilly terrain and I was transported in a *dooley* – a large, woven wicker litter suspended on two poles. There was also a large woven basket, carried on the back of a patient and uncomplaining porter, in which the baby faced backwards while being carried up the steep hills.

Between 1939 and 1942 we went to Murree every year and stayed at the Bexley Hotel. It was not a large building but a collection of small private bungalows, scattered up and down a steep hillside, around a central building which contained the dining room and lounge. We always stayed in the same bungalow; a three-bedroomed cottage, with a drawing room, small veranda and lattice-fenced garden that bordered on the steep hillside. It was here that Jeannie, one of our brindle Great Danes, had seventeen puppies on the day that war broke out, and all the prospective buyers for the puppies dropped out because of the prevailing uncertainty. It was here, too, that we acquired Humpy Doo, a strident green parrot, and Clarabella, a turkey originally purchased to be fattened up for Christmas, but who became a household pet.

I loved shopping trips into Murree, when we would sit on the balcony of Nedou's and eat ice-cream. The houses and shops were all perched precariously on the hillsides, the middle of the town being the only fairly even ground. It encompassed the post office and the stone church, where I went every week for Sunday school and collected Bible stamps which I carefully stuck in a book that was my attendance record as well. This was also cigarette-card collecting time – one series was the Coronation of King George VI – and I couldn't wait for the circular "tropical tins of fifties"

(Du Maurier for my mother and Craven A for my nanny) to add to my album.

The Bexley Hotel also catered for all the birthday parties, and their cook made the most incredible edifices of hard-sugar piping, which rose like fragile cages or fairy palaces above the birthday cakes. There were always birthday parties and fancy-dress parties, and the *durzis* from the bazaar were kept busy stitching costumes for the children.

On my sixth birthday – which falls in the summer, when we were always up in "the hills" – my mother decided to make some of the sweets which were wrapped in crêpe-paper for the guests to take home after the party. She decided to make peppermint creams – an ambitious project since we had no access to a kitchen, she had no cookbook, and, in those days, did not cook much either. She bought quantities of sugar and peppermint extract in the bazaar. We formed it into a sticky kind of paste which, she announced with conviction, we would just roll out and stamp into sweets. But with what? We had nothing. Inspiration struck me. I would get the little tin lid to my child's teapot set. It worked. Each peppermint cream had a funny little hump in the middle where the tin was cut and raised to form a knob, but nobody noticed. Later, at the close of the party, when the children started looking around to see where their expected gifts might be, my father suggested he should play the piano before everyone left. This was greeted with much enthusiasm, as he was an excellent pianist. He stood at the piano and raised both hands, looking at the assembled children and commanding their attention. He brought his hands crashing down dramatically into the opening chord ... and nothing happened. There was a curious muted twang and a rustle. The nannies and *ayahs* giggled. With great solemnity he said, "Perhaps there's a mouse in the piano!" Shrieks from the children and the more timid edged towards the door. Then he lifted the lid of the upright piano and exclaimed with exaggerated surprise, "My word! Look at this!" Everybody

crowded around, and there, stuffed against the strings, were bags and bags of bright crêpe-paper, bulging with sweets (and the home-made peppermint creams).

Every Christmas there would be the garrison Christmas party for all the children. They were invariably enormous affairs, with anywhere from 100 to 500 guests, English and Indian, and they were always held in the open air. They were really more like fairs than ordinary parties, for the organizers and the garrison engineers went to extreme lengths to provide everything a child could desire. There were conjurors and magicians, puppet shows and food stalls, balloons and ice-cream and sometimes even elephants and camels to ride.

One year the engineers constructed a model railway and parents and children alike chugged along the rails, like Gullivers in Lilliput. There was always a military band, and that *rum-ti-tum* made you feel excited and patriotic the moment you heard it. But the high point of the party was always the arrival of Father Christmas. Sometimes he rode in on a camel, sometimes grandly on an elephant and, on one more ignominious wartime occasion, in a jeep. Many of the Indian children didn't know who he was but the English kids would rush up and surround him, dragging their nannies and *ayahs* behind them. I remember one time the red-clad figure with the white woolly beard called out, "Ho! Ho! Ho!" in a stentorian bass voice (I think he may have been the regimental sergeant-major) and a little Indian boy beside me burst into tears. He thought the figure was a demon.

But the war was looming larger in our lives, although I was not directly aware of it. I remember my father leaving, and my mother being at once sad and brave, and we left the north and travelled down India by train to Bangalore. Mother took permanent accommodations in the West End Hotel for herself, Nanny and me, and became a very junior staff officer in Southern Command. We made new friends, and exercised the Great Danes and the spaniel on the racecourse near the hotel. There were brave military displays of soldiers and guns and army vehicles, and I was allowed to climb inside and inspect one of the tanks. There were anti-British riots too, but I didn't know, for the adults would talk in hushed tones and stop when I entered the room. There were war cartoons and big black headlines in the newspapers, and teas for wounded soldiers and, big excitement, American soldiers were billeted at the hotel. I made friends with my first three Americans, tall, strange-spoken gods called Ted, Butch and Hank, and learned to play the recently installed fruit-machine in the hotel lobby. My new friends gave me bubble gum but I didn't know you weren't supposed to swallow it. In a friendly way, I shared some with the two Great Danes, and couldn't really understand why my mother was upset.

Of such bright and funny and sad things is the childhood kaleidoscope made. The world for children in India was a wonderful place and one I shall never forget. By the food we ate I can remember so many events, and the following small set of recipes brings it all back vividly to me.

Pish-pash

•

My mother remembers this dish from her childhood in Calcutta and Karachi. She, in turn, gave instructions to the *khansamer* to make it for me as a child. I still make it on occasions when someone is not feeling too well, since it is very digestible, but, at the same time, delicious.

Serves 4

1½ lb lamb (best neck, ribs or loin)
1 bay leaf
1 large onion, peeled and chopped
½ lb/1 heaped cup short-grain rice, well washed

1 teaspoon salt
3 whole cloves
3 whole peppercorns
1 3-inch stick of cinnamon

1   Cut the meat into chops and trim it of fat and fell. Put the meat into a large saucepan and set it to boil with enough cold water to cover the meat. Put in the bay leaf and onion and cover the pan. Reduce the heat to simmer and cook it for 15 minutes.

2   Uncover the pan and add the rice, salt and spices. Cover the pan again and bring it to a boil; then reduce it to simmer until the rice is soft and almost to the point of disintegrating. The rice should be soft and digestible and of a slightly sloppy consistency. If it is still a little dry and not quite soft, add a little hot water and let it cook longer.

3   Uncover, remove the bay leaf and spices. Turn it into a bowl and serve.

Chicken hot-pot

•

As the pathetic little gravestones with their heart-rending inscriptions testify, the graveyards adjacent to the English churches in India are full of the children of the Raj. The chances of any baby born in India achieving a full life-span were very slim, and especially the children of the British before the discovery of antibiotics. There was hardly a family, during the last century, that had not lost one child to some tropical fever, or to snake or scorpion bite. During my first year of life, I contracted dysentery but, although I was a small, rather skinny baby, I survived. My cousin, almost the same age, did not. My childhood was punctuated by visits to the doctor at regular intervals, during which I was punctured with a series of inoculations and vaccinations against everything you could think of. It seemed that I was always in the state of having one arm, reddened and swollen, in a sling. Of course, I disliked it intensely, and suffer a degree of needle-phobia to this day. But I was lucky that my span of life in India coincided with the use of immunization.

Some sort of legacy of childhood illness was manifested in an early inability to eat fried foods (which I adored), or anything too highly spiced. Curries were considered bad for me, although *dhal* was allowed. However, I remember mainly the hot-pots which the various cooks were instructed to produce for lunch or dinner. In true Indian style, they were to make sure that no germs penetrated the wholesome dishes, and the lids over these stews were tightly sealed with dough. They arrived at the table in that fashion, with my nanny breaking the seal and inspecting the contents in the manner of a royal taster. Only when she had pronounced the dish satisfactory, was I allowed to eat.

This is a close cousin to one of those hot-pots. We have no need of a pastry seal as it bakes in a lidded casserole.

Serves 4

2 tablespoons/1 oz
unsalted butter
2 lb chicken pieces,
skinned

1 teaspoon salt
½ teaspoon freshly ground
black pepper
1 teaspoon sugar

$\frac{1}{4}$ teaspoon thyme

2 tablespoons finely
   chopped parsley

2 large onions, peeled and
   cut into rings

$\frac{1}{4}$ lb fresh mushrooms,
   sliced

2 lb potatoes, peeled and
   thickly sliced

15 fl oz home-made
   chicken stock

5 fl oz cream

1   Preheat the oven to 350°F (180°C, Gas Mark 4).

2   Melt the butter over medium-low heat in a large pan and sauté the chicken pieces, turning them until they are golden. Lay them in the bottom of a deep, lidded casserole.

3   Mix the salt, pepper, sugar, thyme and parsley together in a small bowl; then sprinkle a quarter of the mixture over the chicken.

4   Layer *half* the onions, mushrooms and potatoes, in that order, over the chicken, sprinkling a little of the herb seasoning over each layer. Repeat the layering with the remainder.

5   Pour the chicken stock and cream, mixed together, over the ingredients and close the casserole. Bake the casserole for $1\frac{3}{4}$ hours, removing the lid for the final 15 minutes and turning the oven up to 400°F (200°C, Gas Mark 6), to brown the potatoes.

Notes: In true style, the casserole would be cooked, closed, for the entire time, but I prefer the dish with a browned topping.

Dhal and rice with poached eggs

•

My earliest memories of eating this dish are as a child in Rawalpindi. But I also associate it with an unusual trip we made up to Murree in the winter. I think we had gone to visit my mother's elder brother and his three children. Prior to that time, I had always thought of the hill station as a summer place. I had also never seen snow, and now it lay about three feet thick on the ground, pristine white and pure. I thought it was incredible and magic and I was dumbfounded because there was no frame of reference for this strange stuff in my short life. Our two Great Danes were also astonished by it and the expression on their faces when they took their first, tentative steps out of the car were comical beyond belief. I remember we then went back to my cousins' house and had *dhal* and rice and eggs for lunch.

Serves 4

3 tablespoons *ghee* (clarified butter)

3 medium onions, peeled, 1 onion sliced, the others chopped

½ lb/1 heaped cup lentils, any variety

½ teaspoon ground turmeric

1 teaspoon salt

½ teaspoon cayenne

½ lb/1 cup long-grain rice, washed and drained

3 tomatoes, blanched, skins removed, chopped

4 eggs

1   Heat 1 tablespoon of *ghee* in a pan over medium heat and fry the *sliced* onion, stirring, until it is crisp and brown. Drain it on paper towels and reserve.

2   Place the lentils, turmeric, salt and cayenne into a saucepan, add 1 quart of boiling water and cook, uncovered, until the lentils are tender.

3   Place the rice in another saucepan and add sufficient cold water to cover the rice by 1½ inches. Cover, bring to a boil and then reduce the heat to medium. Cook for 20 minutes, or until the grains have absorbed all the water and are dry and fluffy. Depending on your timing, the rice may then be placed in a shallow dish in a low oven until you are ready to assemble the meal.

4   While the lentils and rice are cooking, heat the remainder of the *ghee* in a pan and add the *chopped* onions and the tomatoes. Fry them, stirring, until the onions are brown. Add them to the lentils and cook the dish uncovered, stirring, for 5 more minutes. Leave it on low heat while you prepare the eggs. (The lentils should be thick but soupy.)

5   Poach the eggs, drain them and keep them warm.

6   To assemble: Place a helping of rice on each plate, and top it with a ladle of lentils in the middle. Make a slight depression in the central part of the lentils and slide a poached egg on to each plate. Sprinkle the rice surround with the fried onions from Step 1 and serve.

Notes: This makes a dish ideal for lunch or supper. It is digestible and very nutritious. In India, it is eaten by both the poor and the wealthy.

Spiced mince with croutons and mashed potatoes

•

Sometimes one turns to the simple fare of childhood as food for reassurance in the complexities of adult life. Thus do we reward ourselves when work has been particularly trying, when family traumas wash up against our door, or merely when we feel a little under the weather. Over the years, I have tinkered with this classic, particularly in the spicing of the meat. Each time, it turns out a little differently as a small inspiration strikes me and I reach for a different accent in the seasoning. I am particularly keen on this version.

Serves 4

2 potatoes, peeled and cubed

4 slices of bacon

2 tablespoons vegetable oil (optional)

2 slices of white bread, trimmed of crusts, each slice cut diagonally into four

1 tablespoon *ghee* (clarified butter)

1 large onion, peeled and finely chopped

1½ lb lean ground beef

½ teaspoon salt

¼ teaspoon freshly ground black pepper

a pinch of ground cinnamon (about ⅛ teaspoon)

a pinch of cayenne

1 teaspoon Worcestershire sauce

¼ teaspoon ground coriander

1 large tomato, blanched, skinned and finely chopped

1 tablespoon finely chopped parsley

1 tablespoon/½ oz butter

2 tablespoons cream

salt and pepper to taste

1 tablespoon very finely chopped onion

1   Put the potatoes on to boil.

2   Fry the bacon until well done. Drain over the pan, reserving the fat. Crumble the bacon and set aside.

3   Fry the triangles of bread in the reserved fat, adding the oil if necessary. Remove the bread when it is golden brown. Drain on paper towels and keep warm in a low oven.

4   In the same pan add the *ghee* and, when it is up to heat, fry the onion until it is translucent and lightly browned. Add the meat and stir and fry for 2 minutes. Now add all the seasonings up to and including the coriander, and stir and fry for 2 more minutes.

5   Add the tomato and parsley and continue to cook the meat until the tomato has disintegrated. (At this point add 1–2 tablespoons of water, if you prefer your meat to have a little gravy.) Add the parsley and stir and cook for 1 more minute. Turn off the heat under the pan.

6   Drain the potatoes and mash them, adding the butter, cream and salt and pepper to your taste. When they are thoroughly creamed and fluffy, stir in the onion.

7   Warm up the meat briefly, then spoon it into the middle of a flat serving dish. Surround it with the mashed potato in a ring. Take the fried bread triangles from the oven and stick the points at regular intervals into the outer edge of the potato ring. Serve at once.

Notes: Our *khansamer* always served it with green peas, but crisp green beans or broccoli, spiked with almonds, would be just as nice.

Peshawari pasande

•

This is a wonderful dish from the North-west Frontier Province and, perhaps because it was not a curry, I remember having it on an occasion when we were out. We may have been visiting Indian friends but I am not sure. I do not recall it as fiery, and if it was I would not have been allowed to eat it. The amount of chillies, however, may be varied.

Serves 6

1 boned, 3-lb leg of lamb, trimmed of fat and skin

20 oz yoghurt

1 teaspoon ground ginger

2 cloves of garlic, smashed, peeled and finely chopped

1 teaspoon salt

3 tablespoons *ghee* (clarified butter)

3 large onions, peeled and sliced

1 tablespoon ground coriander

1–3 small red chillies, finely chopped

$\frac{1}{2}$ teaspoon ground
   turmeric

2 tablespoons ground
   poppy seeds

5 tablespoons ground
   almonds

$\frac{1}{4}$ teaspoon powdered
   saffron

1 teaspoon ground
   cinnamon

$\frac{1}{4}$ teaspoon ground cloves

$\frac{1}{4}$ teaspoon freshly ground
   black pepper

$\frac{1}{4}$ teaspoon ground
   cardamom

2 hard-boiled eggs, peeled
   and sliced

1   Slice the lamb thinly and then beat the slices until they are even thinner, with a mallet or heavy rolling pin.

2   Mix *half* the yoghurt, all the ginger and garlic and *half* the salt together in a large bowl. Place the lamb in the marinade and mix well. Let it marinate for 1 hour.

3   Meanwhile, heat the *ghee* and fry the onions over a medium setting until they are completely brown and crisp. Drain them over the pan and blot them dry with paper towels. (If you like, you may complete their crisping in a slow oven or microwave.) When the onions are dry and crisp, let them cool and then grind them to a powder.

4   Empty the remaining *ghee* from the fried onions into a large saucepan over medium heat. Place the lamb and its marinade in the pan together with the coriander, chillies and turmeric. Adjust the quantity of chillies from 2–8, according to your taste and tolerance. Fry everything, then place the lid on the saucepan and reduce the heat to a simmer. Simmer for 30 minutes, or until the meat is tender and the gravy has evaporated.

5   Now add the onion powder from Step 3, the remainder of the yoghurt and salt and the ground poppy seeds, almonds and saffron. Cook uncovered, over medium-low heat, stirring from time to time, until the gravy is thick.

6   Mix the remaining 4 ground spices together and sprinkle them over the top. Turn the *pasande* into a serving dish and garnish with the slices of egg.

Notes: In true northern style, this dish is accompanied by *chapattis* or *parathas* – unleavened bread, not rice.

Poppadams

•

Poppadams, or *pappads* as they are also termed, are the flat, round, crisp wafers that often accompany curries and which are broken up and sprinkled on top of the food for textural contrast. They have a seductive taste, which, combined with their crunchiness, quickly makes them a popular Indian item. Poppadams are usually made commercially and they are available from most Asian foodstores in packets of twelve, spiced with cracked peppercorns, or plain. Bought dried, they must be fried briefly over a hot flame, whereupon they puff up and become brittle and light.

Because of their commercial availability, Indians do not generally make them at home so, correspondingly, it is very difficult to find a recipe for them. This dismayed me, for I have loved poppadams since my childhood in India and I have often lived in places where Indian ingredients are not available. After much searching and questioning over a number of years, this recipe eventually came to light. It is from southern India.

Please bear in mind that poppadams are a store-cupboard item and should be kept in airtight tins until needed. You will want to prepare them when you have plenty of time, not just before you intend to cook an Indian meal.

Quantity: 20–30 poppadams, depending on size

2 tablespoons bicarbonate of soda/baking soda
2 tablespoons salt
2 lb/7 cups *arhad dhal* flour (see p. 115)

1 tablespoon cracked, coarsely crushed black peppercorns
1 teaspoon dried red chillies, seeded and finely chopped
2 fl oz vegetable oil

1   Heat 1 quart of cold water until it is hot to the touch. Stir in the bicarbonate of soda/baking soda and the salt until they are dissolved. Remove from the heat, let the solution cool and then strain it through a cloth.

2   Measure out and reserve about 2 oz/½ cup of *arhad* flour. Place the remainder in a basin and mix in the spices. Add enough cooled water to form a stiff dough. Knead it for 2 minutes, place a cloth over the basin and set it aside to rest overnight.

3   The next day, knead the dough for 10 minutes or until it is very smooth and elastic. Divide it into balls the size of a small lime.

4   Dip each ball into the vegetable oil. Sprinkle some of the reserved flour on a pastry-making surface and roll out each ball into an extremely thin, round wafer, about 5–6 inches in diameter.

5   When all the wafers are rolled out, they may either be dried in the sun for a few days (assuming you are in the middle of a spell of hot, dry weather), or placed in the oven, with just the pilot light (if it is a gas oven). If your oven is electric, then you may be able to dry them by setting it to its lowest position. (A fruit-and-vegetable drier also works well.) The wafers should be *completely dry* before they are stored.

6   To prepare them for the meal, either deep-fry them until they puff up and become light and crisp, or fry them on an almost dry griddle, pressing them down with the spatula to help them puff up. They may also be toasted with tongs over an open flame, but only if you are in complete command of the situation!

Notes: Poppadams are extremely brittle and fragile after they have been dried, so handle them carefully or all your efforts will be wasted.

Khansamer's lemon pudding

•

This is so simple and so delicious.

Serves 4–6

4 oz unsalted butter	the juice of 3 lemons and
6 oz/$\frac{3}{4}$ cup sugar	the grated peel of 1
6 eggs, separated	4 tablespoons freshly
	grated breadcrumbs

1   Preheat the oven to 350°F (180°C, Gas Mark 4).

2   Cream the butter and sugar together until the mixture is white and fluffy. Work in the egg yolks, 2 at a time. Gradually add the lemon juice, lemon peel and breadcrumbs.

3   Butter a baking dish, pour the mixture in and bake for about 20 minutes,

until the top is lightly browned. Serve at once, while the pudding is still puffy.

Notes: As an alternative, try the same formula with the equivalent amount of juice and peel from tangerines. It is very refreshing.

Kulfi malai

•

I always knew when we were going to have ice-cream because my mother would send the bearer down to the ice supplier, and he would ride back in a *tonga* with a large block of ice, wrapped in gunny sacking, beside him on the seat. The next thing I heard was a series of thumps from the back regions behind the house, as the ice was cracked into small pieces. Indian ice-cream, or *kulfi*, is quite unlike our soft, whipped ice-cream. It is intensely rich and frozen hard into blocks. A spoon, dug with pressure into it, will yield a firm, cold mouthful which melts deliciously on the tongue. Because *kulfi* contains no gelling agents, it does not hold its shape when it begins to melt, so it must be eaten quickly after it is served.

One day, when I was about four, Farid, our bearer, called me from the door to the nursery. I followed him. It was a treat arranged by my mother. There, on the floor of the dining room, was the ice-cream-making apparatus. If you picture even a hand-cranked freezer you would be wrong. We made it in the primitive but effective way that Indians did. There was a galvanized tin tub which was filled with ice, salt and saltpetre. Inside this was a bucket into which were jammed the long metal cones containing the ice-cream mixture. Farid unscrewed the lid of one and showed it to me. I was breathless with anticipation. He started to rock and turn the bucket in the ice. Of course, I begged to help him (which is what my mother had intended) and rocked and turned it to the best of my ability. But my short arms soon grew tired and my short attention span did not hold. Farid teased me, saying that if I did not churn it there would be no ice-cream. But I had faith in him. I wandered out into the garden and forgot about it, but only until Nanny called me to come inside and wash before lunch. Then *kulfi* was right in the forefront of my mind and, soon, in my mouth. Scrumptious!

Serves 4

2½ pints whole milk

8 fl oz thick cream, or an equal quantity of clotted cream (*malai*)

3–4 tablespoons honey (depending on your taste for sweetness)

1 teaspoon ground pods from green cardamoms

2 tablespoons ground almonds

¼ teaspoon *kewra* (pandanus) extract, or 1 tablespoon of rose-water

1 tablespoon blanched, slivered almonds

1 tablespoon hulled, chopped pistachios

1 Place 3 to 4 (unsectioned) ice-trays (depending on capacity) in the freezer.

2 Pour the milk into a saucepan and heat until it boils. Reduce the heat to low and let it simmer until it is reduced by half and is creamy. (You have just made *rabadi*, see p. 171.) Remove it from the heat and stir in the cream and honey. Replace it on the low heat and stir for another 5 minutes.

3 The mixture should now be the consistency of custard. Turn off the heat and stir in the cardamom and ground almonds, blending to ensure there are no lumps. Add the *kewra* extract (or rose-water) and nuts.

4 Let the mixture cool until it is barely warm and then pour it into the ice-trays. Freeze until there are ice crystals forming around the sides of the trays. Remove them from the freezer and stir, scraping the sides into the middle to break up the crystals. Return the trays to the freezer and freeze them until the ice-cream is hard.

5 Turn out the blocks. Quickly cut them into large cubes with a sharp knife. Pile the cubes into ice-cream glasses or dishes and serve immediately.

Notes: *Malai* is actually the Indian version of clotted cream and is paste-like in texture. If you are using it instead of thick cream, you will have to blend it in completely until smooth. If you are in a hurry, you may use an equivalent quantity (to the fresh milk after reduction) of evaporated milk, but the taste and texture is slightly different. You may vary the *kulfi* by using almond extract instead of the *kewra* or rose-water, and by leaving out the pistachios but doubling the slivered almonds. You may also make banana or mango *kulfi* by either adding 2 bananas, thoroughly mashed, just before freezing (omit nuts and extracts), or by adding ½ cup of sieved mango pulp (again omit the nuts and other extracts).

My grandmother's sponge cake

•

Christmas in India was always fun. If you were up in the North-west Frontier provinces or in the Punjab, then the weather was seasonally cold and frosty. Of course, if you had stayed up in the hills, there was deep snow. I remember one Christmas party my parents gave for me in Rawalpindi, for which my father had borrowed a film projector. This was a great treat, for children seldom went to the cinema. One of the black-and-white films was of diving beauties – of course they all wore very modest, one-piece swim suits and bathing caps. I think it must have been out of a sense of mischief that my father put it on backwards; all the children erupted in peals of laughter to see a little fountain of water, out of which popped a girl who zoomed up and backwards on to a diving board. The children were rolling all over the floor with mirth by the time my father rewound the reel.

My mother remembers her own Christmases as a young woman:

Father got a Christmas tree from somewhere for that year. The servants entered into the spirit of it all for they loved festivals and went to endless lengths decorating and helping. They were just like children. There was always the custom of "dollies" at Christmas. They were trays of food and other goodies which were presented by the Indians. It was their custom to take gifts to their employers on their and our holidays. The rule of the government was that only fruit and sweetmeats could be accepted. Anything larger might be construed as a bribe. Father and mother would sit on the veranda, side by side, in two basket chairs which looked like thrones, and trays of sticky sweets would be presented, and they touched them symbolically in acceptance. Then they were taken away and divided up among the household servants. And that was called "getting a dolly." If there were many, which there often were, since father was a contractor, then he would take them around to the local hospitals.

Many years later, on the Frontier, one of my father's contractors got in touch with his bearer because he wanted to give him a very special Christmas gift. On Christmas morning my father was on the veranda when this large tray of fruit was presented. For some reason, perhaps instinct, my father did not merely touch it, but lifted a piece of fruit from the middle. There was a glint of silver. He pulled at it and there, in solid silver, was a life-size replica of my mother's evening sandals. My father was extremely angry with his bearer but he did not show his anger in front of the contractor. He merely said, with a smile and a slow shake of the head, "Take them away." They were removed. Later that evening, when my mother was changing for the Christmas night celebration, she saw the solid silver sandals had magically reappeared in her cupboard. She called the bearer and patiently explained why she could not keep them and told him to return them to the contractor. Later she remarked to my father that she didn't know why on earth he had chosen to copy her evening sandals, because she could hardly wear solid silver shoes. My father laughed and called her Cinderella for a few days.

My grandmother and the cook always put out extra effort over Christmas. In fact, our *khansamer* loved it and baked all manner of traditional Christmas fare. There were sandwiches and cakes, bright wobbling jellies, trifles and sweets. Here is my grandmother's own sponge cake.

Quantity: 1 9-inch sponge

8 oz/1⅓ cup sugar
1 teaspoon finely grated lemon peel and 1 tablespoon of lemon juice, or a few drops of lemon extract

8 eggs, separated
8 oz/2 cups cornflour/cornstarch

1 Preheat the oven to 250°F (130°C, Gas Mark ½).
2 Have the eggs at room temperature.
3 Place the sugar in a bowl, together with the lemon peel and juice. Add the egg yolks and stir them in with a wooden spoon; then use a whisk or beater to beat the mixture until it lightens, becomes foamy and then fluffy.
4 Gradually add the cornflour/cornstarch, stirring and mixing it until it is blended in.
5 Beat the egg whites until they stand up in peaks and, using a spatula, gently but thoroughly fold them into the yolk and flour mixture. Do not over-stir, otherwise the air trapped in the whites will escape.
6 Lightly butter a 9-inch cake pan, large enough for the mixture to fill it half-way (to allow for rising), and pour in the mixture.
7 Bake for 45 minutes, or until the cake is risen and firm. Cool on a rack.

Notes: A little icing/confectioners' sugar may be sieved over the top. If you wish the cake to be served to guests, you may place a paper doily on top and then sieve the icing sugar on to the cake. Remove the doily straight up into the air, or it will move and spoil the pattern.

9

DINING OUT AND IN

•

Ladies' night at the officers' Mess and dinner parties at home

Apropos of dinner-parties, I think I deserve some pity for being an inaccurate Celt, without any bump for officialdom or ability to remember anyone's official position or title, far less their "grades" and "steps", which is often a dreadful handicap. I don't even possess a copy of the Indian bible of precedence, which I suppose I ought to study, as it tells us all where our proper place, socially or otherwise, is in the official hierarchy.

Lady Wilson, Sarkesar, 1889, *Letters from India*

That night was regimental guest-night. Our white mess-kits and winking buttons seemed to find their point of focus in a Major-General with an incredible row of miniature decorations. The Colonel of the Rutlandshires had a good many, but they didn't overlap like that.

The long vista of dinner-table, with a glittering reef of silver trophies running down its centre, was an imposing sight. At one end sat the Mess President, and at the other end the Vice-President. I watched the small army of our servants in spotless white. The way they avoided colliding with each other reminded me of a flock of seagulls hovering over something in the water, whose wing-tips never touch. Running diagonally across each man's turban was a ribbon in the regimental

---

1. Officers of RAF station, Vizagapatam on the Mess veranda, 1943; 2. Banquet given by the Nawab of Gachin; 3. A waiter; 4. Before the party, Punjab, 1916; 5. Coconuts suspended from a wayside tree as an invitation to travellers to take a long cool drink between Bangalore and Mysore; 6. Vegetable bazaar, Pushkar, near Ajmer; 7. Officers' Mess, Dum-Dum.

colours with a silver regimental badge in its centre. A broad belt of the same ribbon encircled his waist.

Mark Channing, *India Mosaic*

We now come to what is to us the most pleasant of these Notes if only from the fact that it deals with what most people consider "*the*" meal of the day. The black cloud of pessimism through which one viewed this wicked world has been dispelled by the peg at sundown and has given place to the rosy tinted aura of unquenchable optimism – we mean "unquenchable" in the literal not the hot weather sense. The evening game of polo, golf or tennis has caused a pleasant feeling of want in the inner man, which has been further stimulated by the little titbits served at one's Club (just a suspicion more curry with the Prawns please Mr Secretary). It only needs the cocktail to put the finishing touch to one's preparation for the daily climax of the gastronomic world – dinner.

C. C. Lewis, *Culinary Notes for Sind*

In the last one-and-a-half centuries of British rule in India, many cookery books were locally published and aimed at the newly arrived *memsahibs*, who were dazed and bewildered by their legions of domestic servants. They were also perplexed by the unfamiliar foodstuffs of mostly second-rate quality, and horrified by the limitations and squalor of the earth-walled outside kitchens into which, anyway, they were not expected to enter.

Besides laying down rules as to the conduct of the household, the main thrust of the books addressed the all-important business of entertaining, particularly at dinner. For the ability of the *memsahib* to run a good dinner party had quite a significant effect on the career of the *sahib*.

The first thing to be tackled was a thorough study of the "Blue Book" of social precedence within the ranks of the Raj because, without knowledge of that intricate hierarchy, no proper invitations could be sent out, nor the all-important seating arrangement attended to satisfactorily. The informality of the earlier days had coagulated into a systematic and rigid form of social snobbery during Victorian and Edwardian times, which permeated every facet of life. One gaffe, and you were an outcast.

After studying up on social form, *memsahibs* were advised to spend some time composing the menu. At the close of the last century, hostesses were being urged to simplify the hitherto elaborate succession of courses with a premier service and a second service. Colonel Kenney-Herbert, writing under the *nom de plume* of Wyvern in *Wyvern's Indian Cookery Book*, laid out the following:

Soup, fish, a well chosen *entrée*, one joint or its equivalent, game or poultry, a dressed vegetable, one *entremets sucre* or an iced pudding, a savoury instead of cheese, and dessert, will be found, if thoughtfully composed, ample fare for even the most critical of guests.

But a little later on, in his book *Culinary Jottings for Madras*, he urged that the stereotyped "procession of meats" be abandoned and that menus should be composed in the light of whatever was thought best, whatever was in season, and by artistic instinct, and therefore laid down the foundations for the much simplified dinner parties of the next century.

My mother talked about the dinner parties my grandparents would give in the early 1920s. It was a menu order that lasted in India right up to the disappearance of the British Raj. There was a "First toast," which con-

Caviare
Soup
Tomato Soup
Fish
Prawn and Lobster Mold
Entree
Veal Olives
Joints
Glazed Duck
Saddle of Mutton
Pudding
Byculla Soufflé
Savoury
Woodcock Toast
Glacé
Vanilla Ice

Sazghoda, November 14, 1930

sisted of a small preparation on fried bread. Following that was soup, then fish, entrée (some rather complex dish and a chance for the *khansamer* to show his paces), the main dish – a roast, pudding (iced in the hot weather), and then "seconds" or "siccuns," as the Indians called them (see p. 285). There were always fruit and nuts, and little *bowli* glasses or bowls of scented water with rose petals in them to wash one's fingers. There were silver or crystal dishes of fudge and other sweetmeats on the table, and then the port and madeira would be brought round. (In later years, the port was supplanted by cognac and liqueurs.)

My grandparents' dinner table was always beautifully laid: silver candlesticks, crystal glasses and a porcelain dinner service of white bordered in navy blue with a gold edge. There were always flowers on the table. In fact, there were up to thirty vases of flowers throughout the house at all times, which my aunt would arrange daily. The table was generally waited upon by the head bearer (Number One) and the *khitmagar* (Number Two), wearing white jackets with a red and navy cummerbund, and starched white *puggarees* (turbans) with a matching diagonal band with the family crest in the middle. If it was a big party, a third man would be engaged by the *khitmagar* to help. One often invited extra guests at half an hour's notice, so the bearer would run next door and get extra servants. Extra china, cutlery and glass would also be borrowed, and it was quite common to attend a friend's dinner party and look down and see one's own plates and other accoutrements.

Before the dinner party, as on every night, the bearer would move throughout the house with a Flit can or pump and spray all the rooms against mosquitoes; then there would be burning coils of "punk" placed near the tables to prevent any surviving stray insects from biting the legs of the guests.

The sideboard would be fitted with hot cases, which were boxes with grids, lined and with glowing charcoal at the bottom. These would keep the plates and the food hot. You were served in place by the bearers, and the hostess would have a little handbell to signal the servants that the course was ended. (In later years, with the advent of electricity, there was an electric buzzer, sometimes placed on the floor near to the hostess's feet, which occasionally gave rise to misunderstandings!) When the joint came, the host or the cook would carve. My aunt remarked that it was better if it was the cook, as some people took so long.

The *khansamer* always outdid himself over formal dinners. Everything was beautifully presented. Sometimes, they would use pastry or mashed vegetables to form little conceits, such as peacocks, fish, and other similar things. This was really a legacy from the elaborate culinary displays of the Moguls, where almost everything was presented in another form. However, unless restrained, the cooks would carry this disguise of the food to absurd lengths and at the end of the nineteenth century the cookery-book writers were making impassioned pleas for simplicity of presentation. When it came to dessert, however, the cooks were still allowed full licence. As I mentioned before, they displayed great skill with spun sugar and caramel, and a popular presentation was a handled basket of pulled, spun sugar, woven in a lattice and decorated with curlicues and flourishes. These baskets were generally filled with fruit and cream. My mother remembers one dessert with chagrin:

I was a new bride, in fact it was the first dinner party that Daddy and I attended after we were married. It was, of course, the social custom to give the newly married lady precedence over other, more senior women. The dessert was served, and it was the usual large basket of fruit all encased in spun sugar, like Venetian glass. I was in conversation with the man next to me, and the hostess signalled that I should commence helping myself. Still in conversation, I tapped the basket smartly with my spoon, to break off some of the caramel to eat along with my fruit, and it broke ... but it wasn't caramel, it was the real thing, Venetian glass, and there I was, left with this big chunk of valuable glass in my hand!

While dinner proceeded, there was always general conversation, with the host and hostess leading it along. My grandfather was known as quite a raconteur and humorist, and dinner with "Major Whit" was always fun. He was master of the unexpected, and the story goes that at one dinner party, when there was an entrée of minced chicken, he called down the table to my grandmother at the other end: "Gladys, you must tell the *khansamer* to get a new set of teeth. I can hardly eat this chicken!"

Sometimes, conversation would revolve around the lack of a complete command of English that the servants or *babus* had. The *babus* were the clerks who were responsible for the routine paperwork in most government offices and commercial businesses and, while their English was often fluent, they were unable to grasp all the subtleties of the language. One of my grandfather's anecdotes concerned the time when Sir Samuel Hoare was governor of the Punjab. This particular clerk had been asked to go to Government House to see the governor on some minor matter and rushed back to see my grandfather and tell him all about it, full of the importance of the occasion. In my grandfather's words: "The fellow came running in. 'Major Whit! Major Whit!' he said. 'There I am, in Government House, myself, talking to the governor. And while we are talking, talking, this way and that, there is Lady W. sitting at the piano, slowly decomposing.'"

Of such misuse of the English language, there were many anecdotes and instances. There was a tombstone in Peshawar, which recorded the death of a Reverend Isadore Lowenthal, who had met an unfortunate end through misadventure. The inscription read:

ACCIDENTALLY SHOT BY HIS CHOWKIDAR
Well done, thou good and faithful servant

Sometimes my grandparents' dinner parties did not go smoothly, and the event was not caused deliberately by my grandfather. My mother tells it:

It was in Karachi, when we children were still quite young. We used to stay up when Mum and Dad had a dinner party, because the cook used to save the pudding leftovers for us as a treat. Well, we were waiting in the room next door to the dining room and we were bored. Then I looked up at the *punkah* (Karachi had electricity quite a bit earlier than the lesser towns) and got an idea. Perhaps we could get up there and go round on it, like a roundabout. I got my elder brother, Bob, to lift me up and I hung on to the blades. He turned it on slowly and it worked! It was great fun. So then I lifted him up and he had a turn. Then it was little Edgar's turn. We lifted him up and he hung on and then I turned the switch. But I was feeling mischievous so I turned it on full and he went whirling around, hanging on for dear life. Well, the connecting door to the dining room had a glassed fanlight on top. My father was sitting with his back to the door but, at the other end of the table, one of the guests looked up in mid-conversation and saw the incredible sight of a small boy whirling around in the air like a dervish. "Major Whit!" he called. "I think there seems to be something unusual happening next door!" Of course, dinner broke in confusion and we were all soundly beaten by my father.

If there were no *divertissements* of that kind at the table, the normal dinner broke with the ladies retiring after the port, leaving the gentlemen with their glasses, cigars and tall tales, while they "powdered their noses" and were then served coffee in the drawing room.

When the gentlemen later joined the ladies, liqueurs were served and afterwards games were played, such as Sardines or Charades, or members of the party would showcase their talents by playing the piano, reciting or singing. More drinks were served and sometimes a little snack just before the guests departed. Carriages or cars were summoned and the *chowkidar* (night-watchman) would be woken (he was invariably asleep) to light the way and accompany those who lived near by and were on foot.

Melon with chutneyed shellfish

•

This is a lovely appetizer for a hot night in summer. Serve the wedges of melon in individual crystal bowls on beds of cracked ice for maximum effect.

Serves 4

1 honeydew melon, cut into quarters, seeds scraped out

$\frac{3}{4}$ lb (after shelling) shellfish, either prawns or large shrimps, shells reserved

4 fl oz dry white wine

$\frac{1}{2}$ teaspoon salt

$\frac{1}{4}$ teaspoon freshly ground black pepper

2 spring onions/scallions, finely chopped

4 oz/$\frac{1}{2}$ cup mango chutney, mango pieces finely chopped

2 oz/$\frac{1}{2}$ cup pine nuts

sprigs of mint

1   Cut the flesh of each melon quarter cleanly away from the rind and then place it back on top. Wrap the melon quarters in plastic wrap and place in the refrigerator.

2   Place the shells of the shellfish in a small saucepan and cover with water. Simmer until only a third of the liquid is left. Strain the cooking liquid and reserve. Discard the shells. Add the white wine, salt and pepper to the fish liquid and bring to a boil. Add the shellfish and let them cook for 4 minutes. Drain and let them cool.

3   Place the shellfish in a bowl, add the onions, mango chutney and pine nuts; stir thoroughly.

4   Unwrap the melon quarters and place each, with its rind, on a bed of crushed ice. Spoon the shellfish and chutney mixture on to each quarter and garnish with the sprigs of mint.

Notes: The assembled melon quarters may be kept in the refrigerator until serving time.

Potato crêpes of lobster with salmon roe

•

This is a very luxurious-looking appetizer, although the actual cost belies its appearance. The crêpes are ordinary crêpes with a little grated potato stirred in just before frying. Please ensure that the potato is grated at the last minute before adding, otherwise it will discolour and mar the crêpes.

Serves 6

2 oz/½ cup flour	¼ teaspoon paprika
1 large egg, beaten	a dash of freshly grated
4 fl oz milk	nutmeg
3 tablespoons/1½ oz butter, melted	¼ teaspoon salt
	¼ teaspoon white pepper
1 medium potato, peeled and finely grated	1 egg yolk
7 oz cooked lobster meat	4 fl oz double cream
2 tablespoons Madeira	5 fl oz crème fraiche
	2 oz salmon roe

1   Sift the flour into a bowl: Make a depression in the middle, add the large beaten egg, and then the milk and 2 tablespoons of water, beating until the batter is smooth. Stir in a third of the butter, followed by the grated potato.

2   Place a crêpe pan over medium low heat and grease the surface. Pour in approximately 2 tablespoons of the batter and rotate the pan so the surface is covered evenly. Cook the crêpe for 1 minute and then turn it and cook for another minute on the reverse. Accumulate all the crêpes on a plate, with a square of wax paper between each. Cover with a warm, damp cloth until needed.

3   On the top of a double boiler, stir the lobster meat into the remaining melted butter and cook for 2 minutes, until the meat is heated through. Add the Madeira and cook for 2 more minutes.

4   Season with the paprika, nutmeg, salt and pepper. Beat the egg yolk and cream together and add it to the lobster. Stir gently until the mixture thickens. Remove from the heat.

5   Lay out each crêpe and roll it up around 2 tablespoons or so of the

lobster mixture. Lay the crêpes seam side down on a serving dish. Keep them warm in a low oven until you are ready to serve.

6   Stir the crème fraiche and gently add the salmon roe, reserving a little for decoration. Spoon the crème across the crêpes and decorate.

Notes: These seafood crêpes may also be served cold.

Shrimp and cinnamon soup

•

This is a lovely, delicate soup with an unusual taste. It may be served hot or chilled.

Serves 6

½ lb shelled small shrimp	1 spring onion/scallion,
1½ pints fumet	cut crosswise into the
1 3-inch stick of cinnamon	thinnest rings you can
	manage
	12 leaves of coriander

1   Divide the shrimp in half. Place 1 portion in a mortar and pound to a fine paste. Alternatively, chop them finely with a large, very sharp knife or cleaver and then use the flat of the blade to mash them to a paste. Form the paste into little balls, the size of marbles.

2   Heat water in a steamer and steam both the shrimp balls and the shrimps for 3 minutes. Remove them immediately from the heat.

3   Heat the fumet in a large saucepan over medium-low heat, adding the cinnamon stick. Let it simmer for 5 minutes, then add the onion and the shrimp balls and shrimps.

4   Remove the cinnamon stick and discard it. Pour the soup into soup bowls, dividing the shrimp balls, shrimp and onion equally. Place 2 leaves of coriander into each bowl just before serving.

Notes: You may, of course, merely use whole shrimps only in the soup, but the combination of shapes is rather subtle. You could use a little pounded white fish and seasonings to make the balls.

Duck soup with chillied walnuts

•

This is a rich soup with a commanding flavour. It may be made from wild duck instead of the domestic variety but, if it is, the bird should not be too gamey.

Serves 6

1 boned duck breast, complete with its skin

$\frac{1}{4}$ teaspoon salt

$\frac{1}{4}$ teaspoon freshly ground black pepper

$\frac{1}{4}$ teaspoon *garam masala* (sweet spice mix, p. 293)

1 quart duck stock

1-inch piece of fresh ginger root, peeled and cut into hair-thin strips

a 3-inch section of *daikon* (Chinese large white radish), sliced thinly, then into julienne strips

8 walnuts, shelled and cut into quarters

$\frac{1}{2}$ teaspoon cayenne

1 clove crushed garlic

2 tablespoons *ghee* (clarified butter)

1 tablespoon port

salt

1 Preheat the oven to 400°F (200°C, Gas Mark 6).

2 Rub the duck breast all over with the mixed salt, pepper and *garam masala*. Place it on a rack over a baking pan and bake it in the oven for 15 minutes, or until the duck meat is cooked but slightly pink. Remove it and let it cool until it can be handled; then cut off the skin in one piece and any underlying fat remaining and reserve. Slice the breast thinly, crosswise, and then cut the slices into strips about $\frac{1}{4}$ inch in width.

3 Reduce the oven setting to 350°F (180°C, Gas Mark 4). Slice the duck skin into thin strips, about $\frac{1}{4}$ inch in width, and place them in a pan to bake in the oven for about 15 minutes, or until the skin is crisp and curly and the strips have become crackling.

4 Pour the duck stock into a saucepan and add the ginger and *daikon*. Let it come to a boil; then reduce the heat and simmer it for 10 minutes.

5 Meanwhile, place the walnuts, cayenne and garlic in a paper bag and shake it well. Heat the *ghee* in a wok and add the walnuts and any remaining spice powder. Stir-fry the walnuts for 2 minutes, or until they just start to brown. Remove them and drain on paper towels. Put them in an oven-proof dish and place in the oven for 5 minutes.

6   Add the strips of duck from Step 2 to the simmering soup and let them cook briefly, for no more than 2 minutes. Take the soup off the heat and stir in the port. Check and correct the seasoning for salt.

7   Pour the soup into the soup bowls and add the walnuts. Sprinkle the duck crackling on top and serve immediately.

Notes: Instead of adding port, you may like to stir a tablespoon of raspberry vinegar into the soup about 3 minutes before it has finished cooking.

Oysters en brochette

•

This recipe comes from Karachi. I think the cook must have had some exposure to Chinese influences (the use of soy sauce). A dish such as this, using fresh seafood, could equally well have been served in Calcutta or Bombay, since all were cities with access to the harvest of fishermen. In Delhi, and up on the Frontier, we had to make do with tinned oysters and other such delicacies when we could get them, and the occasional freshwater fish.

Serves 4

4 tablespoons freshly squeezed lemon juice	½ teaspoon freshly ground black pepper
4 tablespoons soy sauce (low-sodium if possible)	4 slices of lean bacon
2 tablespoons sweet white wine	2 large green bell peppers, seeds, cores and membranes removed
3 small onions, peeled and chopped	16 medium-sized fresh oysters, shucked, drained and trimmed
1 clove of garlic, smashed, peeled and chopped	16 small mushroom caps
2 dashes Tabasco	2 medium-sized onions, peeled and cut into 8 segments
½ teaspoon freshly grated nutmeg	2 tablespoons melted *ghee* (clarified butter)

1   Mix together the lemon juice, soy sauce, white wine, small onions, garlic, Tabasco, nutmeg and black pepper. Stir well and let the mixture stand for several hours, overnight if possible.

2   Cook the bacon briefly in a greased pan and then cut it into 1½-inch squares.

3   Cut the green bell peppers into similar pieces. Now thread a piece of pepper, a piece of bacon, an oyster, a mushroom cap and a piece of onion on a skewer. Keep alternating the ingredients until each skewer is filled.

4   Have a charcoal barbecue at the point of readiness where the coals are glowing, or preheat the grill. Baste the brochettes with the melted *ghee* and place them close to the source of heat. While they are cooking, baste them repeatedly with the sauce from Step 1. They should be cooked until the oysters curl at the edges and the bacon crisps.

Notes: As a fish course for a dinner party, these are served alone. If you would like them for a supper dish, then serve over a bed of plain rice.

Kerala clam and shrimp coconut soup

•

This is a rich, bright red soup with the bite of chillies tempered by creamy coconut milk. It is a definite appetite stimulator and could happily be followed by another fish dish (maybe whole, stuffed and baked) before the meat course. On the Kerala coast it is served with all the spices and pieces of clam, rather like a red-hot bouillabaisse. But I have refined the recipe for a dinner menu.

Serves 6

2 quarts clams in their shells, washed and scrubbed well

2 stalks celery with their leaves, quartered

1 tablespoon coriander seeds

¼ teaspoon fenugreek seeds

1 teaspoon whole black peppercorns

1-inch piece of fresh ginger root, peeled and finely chopped

2 tablespoons bright red paprika

6 dried curry leaves

2 tablespoons vegetable oil

1 teaspoon black mustard seeds

1 large onion, peeled and chopped

4 cloves of garlic, smashed, peeled and chopped

¾ teaspoon salt

½ lb shelled shrimp	½ teaspoon (or to taste)
the juice of 1 lemon	cayenne
10 fl oz thick coconut milk	2 tablespoons chopped
with its cream	coriander leaves

1   Place the clams in a very large pot and add 14 ounces water and celery. Cover tightly, bring to a boil and hold at boiling point for 5–10 minutes, or until all the clams have opened. Strain the liquid through a large sieve, lined with muslin or a double layer of cheesecloth, and reserve.

2   In a heavy iron pan or skillet, toast the coriander and fenugreek seeds and whole peppercorns until the coriander seeds turn light brown. Empty the seeds into a spice grinder together with the curry leaves and grind everything to a powder.

3   Heat the vegetable oil in a wok or saucepan over medium heat and fry the mustard seeds until they stop popping. Add the onion, garlic and ginger and fry and stir for 5 minutes.

4   Now add the powder from the spice grinder, together with the paprika, cayenne and salt, and stir and fry for 5 more minutes.

5   Pour in the clam juice from Step 1 and bring to a boil. Reduce the heat to low and let everything bubble slowly for 15 minutes. Strain the contents of the pan through a sieve, lined with a single layer of cheesecloth, and discard the solids.

6   Return the spiced clam broth to the heat and bring up to a boil. Add the shrimp and let them cook for 2 minutes. Now add the lemon juice and stir, also adding the coconut milk. Bring the soup back to just under a boil, but do not let it bubble or the coconut milk will curdle. Keep hot until you are ready to serve.

7   Just before serving, stir in the coriander. Pour into soup bowls and bring to the table.

Notes: If you have difficulty buying clams in the shell, try to purchase the jars of clam meat in its own broth. As a short cut, you could use the bottled

clam juice (in which case I would suggest combining it with some home-made chicken stock) but do check the salt ratio in the soup. Similarly, if you do not have the whole spices to toast before grinding, you may use their ground equivalents, browning them *slightly* in a pan. (Watch them with an eagle eye – they burn very quickly.)

Curry leaves are available from Asian foodstores.

Trout baked in an almond jacket

•

This is really a rather spectacular dish so, in a formal dinner sequence, follow it with a simple roast. You will need a salmon or lake trout of about $2\frac{1}{2}$–3 lb and it must be boned for this recipe. Either ask the fishmonger to do it for you, leaving the head on, or tackle it yourself from the instructions below.

Serves 4–6

1 lb white fish fillets (sole, whiting, etc.)	salt and white pepper to taste
$\frac{1}{4}$ lb shelled shrimp, finely chopped	$\frac{1}{2}$ lb flaked almonds
2 egg whites	3 tablespoons/$1\frac{1}{2}$ oz unsalted butter, for the cooking parchment
$\frac{3}{4}$ teaspoon salt	
$\frac{1}{4}$ teaspoon freshly ground white pepper	1 lb fresh mushrooms
1 tablespoon fresh tarragon	2 tablespoons olive oil
	1 tablespoon dry sherry
2 tablespoons chopped parsley	salt and pepper
	1 bunch of watercress, washed and chopped
10 fl oz double cream	
1 $2\frac{1}{2}$–3 lb trout, gutted	4 tablespoons hot chicken stock

1   Chop the fish fillets into small pieces and feed them into a food processor, together with the shrimp. Add the egg whites and process until you have a smooth mousse. Add the seasoning and herbs, while it is still running, and then pour in 4 fl oz of the cream, a little at a time. Refrigerate the mousse for 30 minutes.

2   Lay the trout on its side and cut off the tail. Using a very sharp knife,

cut along, but just *above*, the backbone, pressing the side of the knife against it and following the shape of the rib cage. You will now have separated the first fillet from the backbone.

3   Now cut along *under* the backbone in the same manner. The fillets should now be separated from the backbone. Take a pair of kitchen shears and snip the backbone just behind the head. Discard the backbone. Use tweezers to pick out any bones left behind. Press the filleted trout back into shape.

4   Lay the trout on a board and spread one side with half of the chilled mousse from Step 1. Cover all of it evenly except the head. Place a square of wax paper over the mousse and then turn the fish over. Spread the other side in the same way and cover with another square of wax paper. Chill the fish in the refrigerator for 30 minutes.

5   Preheat the oven to 350°F (180°C, Gas Mark 4).

6   Take a baking tin and line it with a thickly buttered piece of cooking parchment. Remove the trout from the refrigerator. Peel the wax paper from one side and press flaked almonds thickly but firmly on to the surface of the fish so that the mousse is completely covered. Place the fish, almond-side down, on to the buttered parchment in the tin. Press the rest of the almonds evenly on the top of the fish and cover lightly with another square of thickly buttered parchment. Bake the fish for 20 minutes, uncovering it for a few minutes at the end to let the almond jacket brown.

7   Meanwhile, while the fish is baking, chop the mushrooms finely. Heat the olive oil in a pan over a medium setting, add the mushrooms and toss and stir until they start to sweat their juices. Increase the heat to high, add the sherry, stir and cook until all the liquid is reduced. Add the remaining 6 fl oz of cream and cook until you have a thick sauce. Season with salt and pepper and set aside.

8   Remove the fish from the oven and let it sit for a few minutes. Place the watercress in a blender together with the chicken stock, and blend to a purée. Pour the purée evenly on to a serving dish. Place the trout on top of the purée. Spoon the mushroom duxelles close to the trout on either side and bring to the table.

Notes: If you find the head unaesthetic to look at, you may reserve some sprigs of watercress before puréeing it and partially mask the head with them. Serve the fish accompanied by parsleyed new potatoes and a lightly cooked vegetable such as young peas in their pods or green beans.

Veal olives with green peppercorn sauce

•

When Lord Dufferin was Viceroy of India, between 1884 and 1888, he and his wife duly moved up to the hill station of Simla and took over the official residence, the vice-regal lodge called Peterhoff. Prior to his time in India, Lord Dufferin had held posts in both Canada and Russia, and they found the accommodation in Simla very much beneath the standards to which they were accustomed. With the necessary permission from the British government and the aid of the Public Works Department, a magnificent new residence was planned and built on Observatory Hill. The Dufferins moved in and, in August 1888, gave their first formal dinner party.

The menu for such dinner parties probably included beef olives, for it was a popular dish in the nineteenth century. My update here uses veal instead of beef, with a different filling and sauce.

Serves 4

3 tablespoons/1½ oz unsalted butter

6 medium mushrooms, finely chopped

1 small onion, peeled and finely chopped

½ inner stalk celery, finely chopped

½ lb cooked lobster or crab meat, flaked

2 tablespoons finely chopped parsley

1 teaspoon finely chopped fresh tarragon

½ teaspoon salt

¼ teaspoon freshly ground white pepper

1 cup fresh white breadcrumbs

1 tablespoon dry white wine

8 scallops of loin of veal, pounded paper-thin

For the sauce

2 tablespoons/1 oz unsalted butter

3 shallots, peeled and finely chopped

2 tablespoons Armagnac

the juice of 1 lime

5 fl oz cream

2 teaspoons green peppercorns, drained and rinsed

salt and white pepper

1 teaspoon finely chopped parsley

1   Melt 1 tablespoon/½ oz of the butter in a saucepan and fry the mushrooms for 1 minute over medium heat. Add the onion and celery and stir and fry for 2 more minutes. Remove the pan from the heat and stir in the lobster or crab meat, parsley, *half* the tarragon, salt, pepper and breadcrumbs. Combine everything thoroughly and then moisten with the white wine.

2   Lay the scallops flat, one at a time, and place about 2 tablespoons of the filling in the middle of each. Roll them up and secure them with string.

3   Heat 2 more tablespoons/1 oz of the butter in a pan and brown the veal olives over medium heat. Sprinkle them with about a tablespoon of water, cover tightly, reduce the heat to low and let them cook gently for about 25 minutes. Remove them to a low oven and keep them warm while you prepare the sauce.

4   Melt 2 tablespoons/1 oz butter in a pan and sauté the shallots until they are cooked but not brown. Deglaze the pan with the Armagnac and lime juice. Turn the heat low and stir in the cream, blending it well. Let the sauce reduce by half. Mash *half* the peppercorns and stir them into the sauce, adding the remaining ½ teaspoon of fresh tarragon. Now stir in the whole peppercorns. Season the sauce and pour it over the veal olives. Dust the tops with the parsley and serve.

Notes: At the same time that the veal olives are cooking, you may like to add carrots, sliced and cut into flower shapes, and pearl onions to the pan, cooking them and serving them for added garnish.

Glazed duck and stuffed apples in Calvados

•

Because of the high ratio of fat to the total weight of the bird, tart fruits, such as apples, complement duck nicely, and apple brandy adds extra taste. If you cook a larger bird, alter the cooking time accordingly.

Serves 6

1 3½-lb duck, with giblets
1 teaspoon salt
⅓ teaspoon freshly ground
  black pepper
6 cooking apples, washed,
  cored and immersed in
  acidulated water
1 tablespoon/½ oz unsalted
  butter

salt and pepper
3 oz/½ cup sultanas/golden
  raisins
2½ oz/½ cup coarsely
  chopped shelled
  walnuts
16 fl oz Calvados (or
  applejack)
4 oz clover honey

1 Preheat the oven to 500°F (250°C, Gas Mark 9).

2 Wash the bird and pat it dry, reserving the giblets for Step 4. Rub salt and pepper inside the cavity. Fold the posterior flap inside the cavity and truss the legs and tail together with kitchen string.

3 Place the duck breast side up on a rack set inside a large roasting pan, and cook for 15 minutes. Reduce the oven temperature to 350°F (180°C, Gas Mark 4) and rotate the duck to its side on the rack. Cook for 20 minutes. Place the duck on its other side and cook for an additional 20 minutes.

4 Meanwhile, make sure that the apples are properly cored. Finely chop the giblets reserved from Step 2. Heat the butter in a pan over a medium setting and sauté the giblets until they are just brown. Add salt and pepper to taste. Add the sultanas and walnuts, stir, then set the pan aside for the stuffing to cool. Stuff the apples firmly with the mixture.

5 Combine the Calvados and honey in a large saucepan. Place the stuffed apples in the liquid. Bring to a boil and then reduce the heat to low. Cover the saucepan and simmer for 20 minutes, occasionally basting the apples. Remove the apples with tongs and set aside.

6 Increase the heat under the saucepan and reduce the Calvados-honey mixture to 4 fl oz of syrup, stirring now and again.

7 Remove the roasting pan from the oven. Take out the duck and the rack. Pour off all but about 2 tablespoons of fat from the pan. Return the duck to the pan, breast side uppermost, and place the stuffed apples around the bird. Baste both the duck and the apples with the Calvados-honey reduction. Roast for an additional 15 minutes, or until a meat thermometer reaches 180°F (82°C).

8 Transfer the duck to a serving dish and surround it with the apples. Pour the juices from the roasting pan over the duck. Remove the trussing string and serve at once.

Notes: Accompany the duck and apples with the recipe following. It places what would be the stuffing for the bird in a container of red cabbage – at once a vegetable and a receptacle. Red also provides good contrast to the main dish.

Wild rice and sausage stuffing in red cabbage

•

This stuffing can, in fact, accompany any bird which you do not want to stuff.

Serves 6

$1\frac{1}{2}$ pints duck or chicken
  stock
salt and pepper
7 oz/scant 1 cup brown
  rice
$3\frac{1}{2}$ oz/$\frac{1}{2}$ cup wild rice
1 tablespoon *ghee*
  (clarified butter)
1 large red cabbage
8 fl oz red wine vinegar
$\frac{1}{2}$ teaspoon salt
2 tablespoons sugar
4 whole black peppercorns

$\frac{1}{4}$ teaspoon freshly grated
  nutmeg
2 tablespoons/1 oz butter
2 cloves of garlic,
  smashed, peeled and
  finely chopped
1 large onion, peeled and
  finely chopped
$\frac{1}{2}$ lb fresh pork sausage
$\frac{1}{4}$ teaspoon ground sage
2 tablespoons chopped
  parsley

1   Bring the stock to a rolling boil in a large saucepan. Salt and pepper as desired. Gradually introduce both grains so that the stock does not come off the boil. Add the *ghee*. Reduce the heat to low, cover the pan and simmer for about 50 minutes or until the rice is tender and all the liquid is absorbed or evaporated. Remove the pan from the heat, uncover and toss the rice lightly to let the steam escape. Set aside.

2   Cut a thin slice off the base of the cabbage so that it will stand upright. Slice about 2 inches off the top, exposing the inner layers. Carefully hollow out the cabbage with a curved grapefruit knife, leaving a cabbage shell about $\frac{1}{2}$ inch thick.

3   Combine $1\frac{1}{4}$ quarts of water, the vinegar, salt, sugar, peppercorns and

nutmeg in a large saucepan and bring to a rolling boil over high heat, stirring occasionally. Invert the cabbage, cavity side down, and drop carefully into the boiling liquid. Cover the pan, turn the heat to medium, and boil for 5 minutes. Uncover and turn the cabbage with tongs so that the cavity is uppermost. Cover again and cook for 5 more minutes. Remove the pan from the heat, drain the cabbage and set it aside to cool.

4   Melt the butter over medium-high heat in a large pan and fry the garlic and onion for a few minutes until the onion is a light golden-brown. Add the pork sausage and stir to break up the meat. Season with the sage and continue frying until the pork is just browned. Pour the cooked rice from Step 1 into the pan and stir to mix everything thoroughly. Correct the seasoning and add *1 tablespoon* of the parsley to the mixture. Remove from the heat and set aside.

5   Place the cabbage in the middle of a platter. Spoon the stuffing into the cavity of the cabbage and decoratively mound the excess stuffing around the perimeter of the platter. Sprinkle the remaining tablespoon of parsley over the rice and serve at once.

Notes: If you are serving this as a separate side dish to another roast bird or joint, you may like to add sautéed chopped cashews or walnuts to the stuffing. Sautéed raisins would also be a good addition. You would not add them if you serve this with the duck and apples above as that recipe already includes fruit and nuts.

Quails Darjeeling

•

The Indian cook does not in the least understand the treatment of game. When it goes into the kitchen, it is either left lying in a heap on the ground, or hung up in a bunch, most likely by the legs. At the first moment of leisure the cook-boy is set to work to pluck and disembowel the whole game larder, which is then either put to dry in a strong winter wind, or laid out carefully as a fly-trap. When ordered to prepare any for the table, the cook invariably chooses the freshest-looking, and thereafter comes to say, with clasped hands and a smirk, "The rest, by the blessing of God, has gone bad."

F. A. Steele and G. Gardiner, *The Complete Indian Housekeeper and Cook*,
1893

Serves 6

1 lb sliced bacon

4 shallots, peeled and
chopped

1 clove of garlic, smashed,
peeled and chopped

6 chicken livers, chopped

$\frac{1}{2}$ lb mushrooms, 6 of the
caps reserved, the rest,
and the stems of all,
chopped

$\frac{1}{2}$ teaspoon salt

$\frac{1}{4}$ teaspoon freshly ground
black pepper

$\frac{1}{3}$ teaspoon *garam masala*
(sweet spice mix,
p. 293)

2 tablespoons *ghee*
(clarified butter)

6 quail, dressed

4 sprigs of parsley

3 spring onions/scallions

1 bay leaf

a sprig of fresh thyme

2 tablespoons brandy

6 slices of slightly stale
white bread, crusts
removed

4 tablespoons/2 oz
unsalted butter

1 leek, white part only

1 cup freshly brewed
Darjeeling tea

1   Cut 6 of the slices of bacon into small pieces and fry them until they are almost crisp. Drain them over the pan and set them aside. Put the shallots and garlic into the pan and fry them, stirring, for 2 minutes. Add the chicken livers and sauté them for 2 minutes; then add the chopped mushrooms. Put the bacon back in and season everything with the salt, pepper and *garam masala*. Sauté everything for 5 minutes and then empty the contents of the pan into a food processor. Process to a rough forcemeat.

2   Put the *ghee* into a pan large enough to accommodate all the birds. Stuff the quail with the forcemeat and truss them. Heat the *ghee* over a medium setting and brown the birds on all sides. Remove the quail and take the pan off the heat.

3   Line the pan with the remaining bacon in overlapping strips. Replace the quail in the pan. Tie the fresh herbs and spring onions/scallions into a bouquet garni and put it in the middle. Sprinkle the brandy over the top of the birds. Place the pan over medium-low heat, cover the birds with a circle of buttered cooking parchment and braise them gently for 40 minutes.

4   Meanwhile, trim the slices of bread into rounds as large as possible. Heat the butter in another pan and fry the bread until it is golden brown and crisp. Drain the bread over the pan and place it on a dish in a low oven to keep warm.

5   Flute the 6 reserved mushroom caps and sauté them in the butter remaining from the fried bread. Keep them warm in the oven.

6   Cut the white segment of leek vertically into the thinnest possible slivers and place them in a bowl of cold water and ice cubes to curl.

7   Remove the quail from the pan and keep them warm in the oven. Take the slices of bacon from the pan and curl them into rolls, fastening with toothpicks. Place them in the oven with the quail. Discard the bouquet garni.

8   Place the pan back on heat and deglaze it with the tea. Simmer the liquid until it is reduced to about 2–3 tablespoons. Strain the reduction.

9   Place the fried bread rounds on a warmed serving platter and put a quail on top of each. Glaze the quails with the reduction of tea and pan juices. Arrange the fluted mushroom caps from Step 5 and the bacon rolls from Step 7 in between the birds. Drain the slivers of leek and place a little pile on top of each bird. Serve at once.

Notes: You may like to garnish the dish with sprigs of watercress or parsley. This recipe may be used for any small birds.

The regimental Mess

There is still a reminder of the magnificence that was British regimental India in the heart of every military town across England – the Mess. In both countries, those bastions of tradition were erected within the same span of time, and they bear within their bricks and mortar, stones or whitewash, the architectural pride of the Empire and the reverberations of glory immortalized by Rudyard Kipling.

The regimental Mess of the nineteenth century was almost a secular cathedral, sharing with its consecrated cousin the soaring columns and threadbare battle flags that seem to hold the dying echoes of bugles. The locality of the particular cantonment and Mess within India was almost of no consideration in its design, for local fashion never influenced its traditional form. Invariably, a sweeping drive halted beneath a massive pillared portico, often flanked by a pair of captured cannon mounted on plinths, their history recorded on mirror-bright plaques of polished brass. The portico generally led on to a wide veranda, furnished with long-armed reclining chairs of wood and cane, small tables and reed blinds. Sam Browne belts and *topees* could be deposited there before entering the Mess, or hung with the rows of uniform hats in the large, shadowy entrance hall.

The ante-room was an imposing chamber. Life-size portraits of scarlet-coated, white-whiskered colonels, frozen within their heavy gilt frames, glared down on the flesh-and-blood occupants: often intimidated, newly arrived junior officers, who perched on the edges of the deep armchairs, pretending to immerse themselves in ancient magazines. The gentle click of cue hitting ball would break the hush, as devotees moved around the pools of light on the green baize tables of the billiard room across the hall. A double tier of galleried seats flanked the room, but was overshadowed by rows of looming, dead-eyed trophies – tiger, bear, crocodile, ibex, stag, panther – like carved, snarling gargoyles above vacant choir stalls.

The epitome of military glory was always the dining room. An imposing mahogany table stretched in an unbroken length of timber, like the deck of a ship, its surface mirroring the candelabra in a dark lake. Elaborate regimental memorabilia, intricately wrought to the most minute detail, erupted down its length: scenes of entire hilltops taken with blood and gunpowder – heroic *havildars*, skulking Afridi tribesmen, rearing horses and gallant lancers – frozen for ever in silver. Tattered and skeletal battle flags hung from the walls, yielding their substance to the ravages of time in a slow trickle of dust. The monthly regimental guest nights were celebrated in this room in a climax of red and gold, matched only in magnificence by the glittering annual Ladies' Nights.

My mother described to me the Ladies' Nights of the 1930s:

All the guests arrived, the ladies in evening dresses and long, white gloves, of course; the men resplendent in their regimental Mess-kits – navy-blue trousers with red stripes and scarlet "bum-freezer" jackets. Your father's cummerbund was ten inches wide and of red silk. He used to hold one end of it to himself and turn like a top, and old Umar Khan would hang on to the other end until your father was all wound up, then it would be fastened. It was rather splendid. In later years, when your father was dressed up with all his medals on and his face red from the exertion, he always said he felt like a prize bull.

First we would all have drinks, and then a bugle would sound outside. That was the call to Mess. The commanding officer would take the visiting general's wife in to dinner. It was strict protocol. The table would be laden with all the regimental silver and blazing with candles. All our places had name cards and you were escorted to your chair, behind which stood a Mess servant. Then the dinner would commence. There were at least seven courses, followed by the servants bringing *bowli*-glasses and plates, and fruit, then nuts and sweets would be passed. Then a glass was tapped. The senior officer called, "Ladies and Gentlemen! His Majesty, the King!" And we all stood and drank the toast. After that, the health of the general was drunk, and so it went on.

We played little games at the table, particularly the junior officers at the bottom end. On one occasion I remember a silly game where the men put a little oil on their noses, lit it and then promptly blew it out. I was sitting opposite your father and, when it came to his turn, his dinner companion started talking to him. He put the oil on his nose, lit it and forgot to blow it out. Everyone was calling "Pritch! Pritch!" and shouting with laughter. His nose had a big blister on the end.

At a certain point, the senior lady rose and the women retired. When we all joined up again, the junior officers would lay on a "*tamasha*," a foolish exhibition. Sometimes they'd mount on each other's shoulders and each couple would attack the other with rolled-up newspapers. The aim was to knock the other "rider" on to the ground. Of course, on mess-nights, which were "men-only," the games were far rougher. They would play High Cockalorum – I think it was called that – where they would try and travel around the entire room without touching the floor, even the senior officers. They used the tops of tables and chairs and swung across the windows. There were a lot of furniture breakages and quite a few sprains and bruises, sometimes broken ribs and collar-bones.

Marinated steaks of venison

•

There were so many different kinds of deer in India, from little creatures – such as the poor Bambi my mother shot on a Christmas Day *shikar* with the Maharaja of Bhopal and promptly burst into tears (which rather ruined her Christmas morning and didn't improve my father's either) – to big, moose-like animals that often rampaged through the outlying village crops. Nobody wept when they were shot, least of all the villagers. Consequently, venison was a familiar feature on dinner menus. Sometimes all could be safely left to the cook's expertise with excellent results. On other occasions, after frustrating encounters with large slabs of shoe leather sliding around on the best china, the *memsahib* had to step in and give firm instructions as to how the creature should be cooked. A twenty-four-hour bath of marinade was always a good idea, and here is one such recipe. You could substitute this for the roast-meat course in a formal dinner.

Serves 6

For the marinade
5 tablespoons olive oil
1 large onion, peeled and chopped
2 large carrots, peeled and chopped
6 cloves of garlic, peeled; 3 cloves, unpeeled
8 whole cloves
1 tablespoon black peppercorns, crushed
2 dried red chillies, crushed
3 bay leaves
1 teaspoon dried marjoram
1 teaspoon dried basil
8 fl oz malt vinegar
8 fl oz red wine

1 teaspoon salt

6 venison steaks, $\frac{3}{4}$ inch thick
2 tablespoons *ghee* (clarified butter)
2 tablespoons vegetable oil
$\frac{1}{2}$ lb unsalted butter
1 teaspoon freshly grated ginger root
2 spring onions/scallions, finely chopped
a pinch of *garam masala* (sweet spice mix, p. 293)
$\frac{1}{2}$ teaspoon salt
$\frac{1}{4}$ teaspoon freshly ground black pepper

1 Place a saucepan over medium heat. Add the olive oil and fry the onion, carrots, 6 peeled cloves of garlic, the spices and the herbs for 4 minutes, stirring. Add the vinegar, 8 fl oz of water, the wine and salt and bring to a boil. Reduce the heat, simmer for 30 minutes, strain and cool.

2 Place the steaks in a bowl and pour the marinade over the top to marinate for 12 hours, or overnight. Drain them and pat dry.

3 Heat the *ghee* and vegetable oil in a pan large enough to accommodate half the steaks at a time. Turn the heat low and put in the 3 unpeeled cloves of garlic. Fry them for 10 minutes or until they squash when pressed with a spatula. Set them aside. Turn the heat high, put in the venison steaks and sear them quickly on both sides. Reduce the heat to medium and continue to fry the steaks for 5 minutes on either side. Remove the steaks and keep them warm in a low oven while you prepare the accompanying butter.

4   Squeeze the soft garlic from the cloves into a food processor and add the remaining ingredients. Process everything on high until you have a smooth butter.

5   Remove the steaks from the oven and put them on individual plates. Place a dollop of the butter on each steak and serve.

Notes: Serve with parsleyed potatoes and a selection of fresh vegetables, lightly cooked and still a little crisp.

Braised stuffed veal in a Mogul manner

•

The best cooking was said to be derived from the Mughals, and this Mughlai cooking found its highest expression in the kitchens of the Muslim states.

My grandfather attended many dinners given by maharajas and nawabs and he insisted that it was not a bad idea to fast beforehand because one was expected to taste everything. There was always at least five times as much food as there were people but it was not wasted, for the palace servants ate the leftovers. My parents said that at one dinner, given at Tikamgarh by the Maharaja of Bhopal, there were about twenty different chicken dishes, about thirty different varieties of game prepared in various roasts, ten or fifteen spiced meat dishes, which were *ghoshts* and curries, innumerable *dhals*, trays of pilaffs and *birianis* and so on. Even if one took only a dessert-spoonful of each, one was absolutely stuffed by the end of the meal. Of course banquets of this size were leisurely affairs, lasting over several hours but, even so, it was a gargantuan effort to participate. Everyone staggered home and took large quantities of Andrew's Liver Salts. The next day, quantities of plain soda water and no food were in order.

   This recipe carries with it the taste and technique of Mogul preparations, but it is modified to fit within the framework of a western dinner party.

Serves 8

For the marinade
a boned shoulder of veal,
   about 5 lb
6 oz plain yoghurt

1 large onion, peeled and
   chopped
2-inch piece of fresh
   ginger root, peeled and
   chopped

1 clove of garlic, smashed
   and peeled
a pinch of saffron threads,
   soaked in 2 tablespoons
   warm milk
the grated peel of half a
   lemon
$\frac{1}{2}$ teaspoon salt
$\frac{1}{4}$ teaspoon freshly ground
   black pepper

4 tablespoons *ghee*
   (clarified butter)
6 oz/$\frac{3}{4}$ cup long-grain rice,
   washed and drained
2-inch stick of cinnamon
4 cloves

4 whole cardamom pods,
   crushed
$\frac{1}{4}$ teaspoon freshly grated
   nutmeg
$\frac{1}{2}$ teaspoon ground
   turmeric
8 fl oz chicken stock
2 oz/$\frac{1}{3}$ cup sultanas/golden
   raisins
4 oz/1 cup shelled
   pistachio nuts
8 small white onions,
   peeled
5 fl oz double cream
the juice of half a lemon
salt and pepper to taste
2 tablespoons finely
   chopped parsley

1   Lay the veal flat and cut a deep, horizontal pocket into the inside surface of the meat.

2   Place the yoghurt, onion, ginger and garlic into a food processor or blender and process until the mixture is smooth. Pour it into a large bowl and stir in the saffron and its liquid, grated lemon peel, salt and pepper. Put the veal in the bowl and turn it until it is completely coated with the marinade. Cover the bowl and let the veal marinate for at least 6 hours or overnight.

3   Meanwhile, heat 1 tablespoon of the *ghee* in a saucepan and sauté the rice over moderate heat until the grains are white and opaque. Add the cinnamon, cloves, cardamoms, nutmeg and turmeric and stir for 1 minute. Pour in the chicken stock, add the sultanas/golden raisins and half the pistachio nuts. Cover, bring to a boil, reduce the heat to very low and let the rice simmer for 15 minutes, or until all the moisture is absorbed and the whole spices lie on the surface. Discard the cinnamon and cloves.

4   Preheat the oven to 350°F (180°C, Gas Mark 4).

5   Drain the veal, reserving the marinade, and stuff the rice mixture into the pocket in the veal. If there is any surplus, lay it in the middle of the piece of meat. Roll up the veal tightly and secure it with string.

6   Place a flame-proof casserole on the top of the stove, over moderate

heat, add 2 tablespoons of the *ghee* and lightly brown the veal on all sides. Pour the reserved marinade over the veal and cover the casserole. Place the veal in the middle of the oven and bake it for $2\frac{1}{2}$ hours, or between 25–30 minutes per lb of meat.

7   Twenty minutes before the veal is ready, add the white onions round the meat and close the casserole again. Let them cook with the meat for 10 minutes. Remove the onions and keep them warm. Cook the veal uncovered for the last 10 minutes or so.

8   Turn off the oven. Drain the veal from the gravy and place it on a serving platter in the oven. Put the casserole, still containing the gravy, on top of the stove over a moderate setting and reduce it until it is quite thick, stirring so that it does not burn. Turn the heat low and stir in the cream. Keep stirring until you have a thick, creamy sauce, the consistency of thick custard. Add the lemon juice, stir and adjust the seasoning. Pour the sauce over the veal.

9   Crush the remaining pistachios and quickly sauté them in the last tablespoon of *ghee* until they are lightly browned. Sprinkle them on top of the veal. Place the parsley in a saucer and dip the onion tops so they have green caps. Set them around the meat and serve at once.

Notes: You may substitute blanched slivered almonds for the pistachio nuts.

Vegetable timbales

The small but elegant compositions of whole and puréed vegetables are a fusion between the classic European baked moulds and the Indian panorama of spices. In each, ramekin dishes are lined with slices or pieces of one vegetable and then filled with a spiced purée of another, providing a contrast in tone, taste and texture. I have provided a basic recipe with a variation, and then suggestions to use as a springboard to other vegetable creations.

Timbales of cauliflower and green beans

•

Serves 6

$\frac{1}{2}$ lb green beans, cut in half, lengthwise

2 lb cauliflower, cut into florets

2 teaspoons *ghee* (clarified butter)

$\frac{1}{2}$-inch piece of fresh ginger root, peeled and finely chopped

$\frac{1}{2}$ medium onion, peeled and finely chopped

$\frac{1}{4}$ teaspoon *garam masala* (sweet spice mix, p. 293)

$\frac{1}{4}$ teaspoon ground turmeric

$\frac{1}{8}$ teaspoon cayenne

1 tablespoon chopped coriander leaves

6 fl oz cream

3 eggs

$\frac{1}{2}$ teaspoon salt

$\frac{1}{4}$ teaspoon freshly ground white pepper

butter

8 oz/1 cup hollandaise sauce

1 teaspoon ground cumin

coriander leaves for garnish

1   Place the beans in a sieve and immerse them in boiling water for 3 minutes or until they are tender and pliable. Drain, refresh under cold running water, drain again and set aside.

2   Add the cauliflower to a large pan of boiling water and cook until tender (about 8 minutes). Drain, rinse in cold water, drain again and place in the container of a food processor or blender.

3   Heat the *ghee* in a saucepan over moderate heat and add the ginger and onion. Stir and fry until the onion is cooked but not brown (2–3 minutes). Add the spices and cook, stirring for 1 more minute. Add the contents of the pan to the cauliflower in the processor and process at high speed until everything is very smooth.

4   Place the purée in a saucepan over low heat and stir for 5 minutes or until the excess liquid has evaporated. Stir in the cream, increase the heat and bring the purée to a boil. Reduce the heat again and cook, stirring frequently, until the cream is absorbed and the purée reduces to about 1 pt. Transfer it to a bowl and let it cool for about 8 minutes.

5   Preheat the oven to 375°F (190°C, Gas Mark 5). Beat the eggs until they are silky and blended, but with no bubbles. Gradually fold them into the purée. Season with the salt and pepper.

6   Butter 6 ramekins (add or subtract dishes as you estimate the comparative volumes of whole vegetables and purée). Measure the length of the beans against the sides of the dishes and cut them to fit. Line the dishes with the beans, cut side inward. The butter will help them adhere. Spoon the purée into the middle, then tap gently on to the counter to pack the mixture down and release any trapped bubbles of air. Set the dishes in a roasting pan and add sufficient boiling water to come to a level half-way up their sides. Cover the dishes with buttered wax paper or foil and bake in the centre of the oven until the purée is firm to the touch (about 30–35 minutes), adding more water if necessary (see *Notes* below).

7   Remove the ramekins from the hot-water bath and cool them on a rack for about 6 minutes. Run a knife blade around the inside of each. Invert them over a plate or serving dish and turn out.

8   Add 1 teaspoon of ground cumin to the hollandaise sauce and blend well. Pour the hollandaise around the timbales and serve.

Notes: For compact timbales with a velvet-smooth texture, remember to ensure there is no air trapped in the purée during the mixing. In addition, do not let the hot-water bath come to a boil during the baking (add a little cold water from time to time), or the purée will also bubble and trap small air cavities during the coagulating and cooling.

Timbales of turnips and carrots

•

Follow the recipe above, using 3 medium carrots, thinly sliced lengthwise, and cook them for 15 minutes before lining the timbales. About 1½ lb of young turnips, peeled and diced, will suffice for the purée. Omit the turmeric in their spicing. Boil them for about 12 minutes before puréeing.

Here are some other suggestions for timbales: slices of raw tomato encasing a zucchini purée; asparagus spears guarding a broccoli mousse in the middle; spinach leaves wrapping a beetroot purée core; palisades of blanched red bell peppers outlining a creamy corn purée. Try other sauces as well, such as cream and tomato, or garlic butter, tangy with lime.

Mushrooms stuffed with spinach soufflé

•

An elegant accompaniment to the meat course, these pretty puffed morsels were a speciality of our cook. I also feel he was relieved to find another presentation for the *mali*'s beloved "espinidge," which used to turn up relentlessly in unadorned form at the nursery dinner table.

Quantity: 24 stuffed mushrooms

3 tablespoons/$1\frac{1}{2}$ oz unsalted butter

3 tablespoons olive oil

24 large mushroom caps, wiped clean with paper towels

1 cup cooked spinach, drained and chopped

4 oz/1 cup freshly grated Cheddar cheese

$1\frac{1}{2}$ tablespoons flour

6 fl oz milk

1 teaspoon Dijon mustard

$\frac{1}{4}$ teaspoon freshly grated nutmeg

$\frac{1}{4}$ teaspoon freshly ground black pepper

4 egg whites, chilled

$\frac{1}{4}$ teaspoon cream of tartar

$\frac{1}{2}$ teaspoon salt

1   Preheat the oven to 425°F (220°C, Gas Mark 7).

2   Melt the butter over low heat in a pan and add the olive oil. Use a pastry brush to coat the outside of the mushroom caps with the mixture and set them, cavity-side up, in a shallow, greased baking tin.

3   In a processor, purée the spinach and add all but 1 tablespoon of the cheese. Give the processor a few more turns to mix it in.

4   Increase the heat to medium under the pan containing the remaining butter and oil. Add the flour and stir to mix it in thoroughly and smoothly. Gradually pour in the milk while continuing to stir until you have a smooth white sauce, the consistency of thick custard. Add the mustard, nutmeg and pepper and continue to stir until the mixture thickens even further.

5   Transfer the contents of the pan to a bowl and stir in the purée from the blender.

6   In another bowl, beat the chilled egg whites until foamy. Add the cream of tartar and salt and continue beating until the whites are stiff and glossy. Place about 2 tablespoons of the egg whites into the spinach mixture and stir it thoroughly. Gradually fold in the remainder of the whites.

7 Spoon the filling into each mushroom cap, mounding it slightly. Sprinkle the tops with the remainder of the cheese from Step 3. Bake in the oven for 15–20 minutes or until the filling puffs. Serve hot, at once.

Notes: These would also be very nice served on trimmed rounds of fried bread as first course for a dinner party.

Spiced fried potatoes

•

Again, this recipe borrows from its Indian antecedents in the idea for its composition and in some of the spices used.

Serves 6

12 medium-sized new
   potatoes
3 tablespoons *ghee*
   (clarified butter)
1 large onion, peeled and
   finely chopped
$\frac{1}{2}$ teaspoon ground cumin
$\frac{1}{4}$ teaspoon cayenne
$\frac{1}{4}$ teaspoon crushed garlic
$\frac{1}{4}$ teaspoon *garam masala*
   (sweet spice mix,
   p. 293)

1 teaspoon dried lemon
   peel, ground
1 teaspoon dried mint
$\frac{1}{2}$ teaspoon salt (or to taste)
$\frac{1}{4}$ teaspoon freshly ground
   black pepper
2 teaspoons finely
   chopped parsley

1 Wash the potatoes well and drop them into a large saucepan of boiling water. Cover, reduce the heat, and cook them until they are tender (about 20–30 minutes). Peel them while they are still warm, and dice.
2 In a large pan or wok, heat the *ghee* over medium-high heat and fry the onions, stirring, until they are brown and almost crisp. Add the potatoes and continue to fry, stirring, until they are beginning to form a crust. Mix all the remaining ingredients together, except the parsley, and add them to the potatoes. Continue to fry and stir for another 5 minutes, until the potatoes take on a reddish-brown colour and are mottled with the spices.

3   Drain them and place them in a serving dish. Just before serving, sprinkle them with parsley.

Notes: This is a really piquant way to serve potatoes. You may use your imagination to vary the spices a little. Perhaps add a dash of ground coriander, or substitute orange peel for the lemon. Fresh chopped coriander leaves make an interesting alternative to parsley.

Dinner-party desserts in India

Puddings make the most difficult note to write especially in India. Any and every cookery book you pick up contains a host of dishes under this heading but somehow few of them seem applicable for Sind. Personally we advocate cold puddings (always excepting hot soufflés) both in the hot and the cold weather, of which one of the ingredients shall be fruit. Not a few people favour having no pudding at all, going straight from the joint or game to the savoury and winding up with an ice.

C. C. Lewis, Culinary Notes for Sind

The present fashion of making dessert into a *troisième service*, with the servants perpetually handing round wines and sweets, is detestable. The dinner ends, as it began, with a bustle and clatter of spoons and forks, instead of a calm. So soon, therefore, as the dessert has been once handed round, it should be placed on the table and the servants enjoined not to meddle with a spoon, a fork, or a plate, within hearing of the table. Then comes the time for conversation, and not, as now, for a hurried bolt of the ladies into the drawing-room before the *khitmutgars* have done prancing round with distracting chocolates, pralines, or pickled ginger. *"How can you taste your wine with half a pickled orange in your mouth?"* asked the uncle in *Punch* of the undergraduate nephew, winking wisely over a glass of port! How can you, in like manner, feel that you have had a good dinner if some one is perpetually pressing you to spoil it with a bonbon?

F. A. Steele and G. Gardiner, The Complete Indian Housekeeper and Cook,
1893

As you can see, there was much advice on the manner of completing the menu of a dinner in India, but the consensus seems to have been to simplify things as much as possible. From a combination of memory and what various members of my family have told me, there were two puddings served, mostly cold, and they were either left on the sideboard for guests to help themselves, or placed on the table after being taken around by the servants. I know that both my mother and my aunt always had dishes of fudge, chocolates and nuts already on the table for nibbling after the dessert. But whether one ate them or not was purely a matter of choice and one's degree of a "sweet tooth."

As to the desserts themselves, they were light, nothing too solid, and people took small helpings. In C. C. Lewis's cookery book, the tooth-breaking pride of the Anglo-Indian dinner table, the toffee basket, comes up again, and his description is amusing:

Toffee Basket. – This is the *chef-d'œuvre* of the Indian mistri and surely one of the most inartistic puddings imaginable, that is unless the cook responsible is a real artist. As a rule the toffee part of the affair is a teeth-breaking, rock like, substance which is almost invariably left on the plates of the diners. We can only recall once having tasted a toffee basket with the toffee composed (as it should be) of tiny strands which broke at a touch. The interior is filled with compote of fruit and cream. The only suggestion we have to offer if the hostess desires a toffee basket and her mistri is not a master of his craft is that she sends round with the basket a large axe daintily garlanded with greenery.

Since I feel that, in general, elaborate pulled and spun-sugar edifices are best left to the professional confectioners and caterers, you will probably be relieved to find that there are no instructions on the making of such masterpieces among the dessert recipes which follow.

Ginger soufflé

•

One of our family's most popular desserts. In some way, it is associated in my memory with summer nights in the Punjab, for a hot soufflé was always considered an appropriate dessert whatever the climate.

Serves 6

2 tablespoons/1 oz unsalted butter, plus a little more	a pinch of salt
4 oz/1 cup sugar, plus 1 tablespoon	16 fl oz cream, half of it mixed with an equal quantity of water
2 tablespoons flour	6 oz crystallized ginger, finely chopped

the finely grated peel of $\frac{1}{2}$ an orange	1 tablespoon Grand Marnier
$\frac{1}{2}$ teaspoon powdered ginger	very fine julienne strips, cut from the peel of $\frac{1}{2}$ an
6 eggs, separated	orange, blanched
2 tablespoons dark rum	several times to remove the bitterness, drained

1   Butter a 2-quart soufflé dish with the extra butter, reserving the measured 2 tablespoons. Sprinkle the surface with the 1 tablespoon of sugar, tipping out any excess.

2   Put the remainder of the sugar, the flour and salt into the top of a double boiler and place it over the heat. Gradually stir in the cream and water, mixing it with a whisk. When the mixture is smooth, add the butter and continue to whisk over the heat until the butter is melted and the sauce is smooth and thick.

3   Remove the pan from the heat and stir in the chopped ginger, the orange peel and the powdered ginger. Combine everything well. Beat the egg yolks until they are light and creamy and, replacing the pan on heat, stir them into the sauce. Add the rum and stir until the mixture thickens again. Turn off the heat and let the mixture sit for 1 hour.

4   Preheat the oven to 375°F (190°C, Gas Mark 5).

5   Beat the egg whites until they stand up in peaks and fold $\frac{1}{3}$ of them gently into the mixture. When they are integrated, fold in the remainder.

6   Bake the soufflé for about 45 minutes.

7   Meanwhile, whip the remaining cream until it is stiff and incorporate the Grand Marnier. Chill.

8   Serve the soufflé immediately, decorated with the curls of orange peel and accompanied by the cream.

Notes: This soufflé is also very good with whisky substituted for the rum and Drambuie for the Grand Marnier.

Prune and claret mould

•

One almost hesitates to recommend a dessert featuring prunes but this very old recipe has a wonderfully rich flavour and slips down agreeably after a full dinner.

Serves 6

1 lb pitted prunes	2 tablespoons slivovitz
3 oz/$\frac{2}{3}$ cup sugar	(plum brandy)
$\frac{1}{2}$ bottle of claret	30 blanched slivered
(Bordeaux)	almonds
1 tablespoon lemon peel	8 fl oz double cream,
1 2-inch stick of cinnamon	chilled
1 tablespoon gelatine	

1 Place the prunes in a large saucepan, together with the sugar. Pour in 1 pt of water and the claret and add the lemon peel and cinnamon. Bring to a boil, reduce the heat and allow to simmer for 20–30 minutes, or until the prunes are soft and plump.

2 Discard the lemon peel and cinnamon. Drain the prunes and place them in a processor or blender. Measure the juice and if there is more than $\frac{1}{2}$ pint, reduce it accordingly. Take the pan off the heat. Use about 3 tablespoons of the hot liquid to melt the gelatine. Add the slivovitz to the remaining liquid and pour it into the processor. Reduce everything to a purée.

3 Pour the fruit purée into a bowl and stir in the gelatine and juice. Let the purée chill in the refrigerator until it thickens slightly and then remove it and stir in the almonds. Pour it into a chilled mould and refrigerate for 4 hours.

4 Whip the chilled cream until it is stiff. Place it in a piping bag with a rosette nozzle. Turn out mould on to a silver platter and pipe swirls and rosettes of cream all around its base. Chill again until you are ready to serve.

Notes: This dessert is usually very popular with men because it is not too sweet. (The slivovitz is a dry brandy.) Its black-and-white scheme makes it quite sophisticated and the cream complements the full-bodied dessert.

A variation on this recipe is to simmer the pitted prunes as above but not purée them. Let them marinate overnight in their juice, together with the slivovitz; then drain and stuff them with the slivered almonds and serve them with whipped cream. This latter style reminds me of a culinary oddity my parents used to prepare called "drunken prunes." The prunes were kept in a jar, in the manner of the German preserve, and they would pour the remains of suitable and complementary bottles of liquor into the jar. After about six months, these dizzying fruits were served for dessert.

"Siccuns"

The final course of a formal dinner in India was invariably a little morsel that was not sweet. It was designed to clear and rest the palate after the heavy puddings and to act as a pleasant counterpoint to a final glass of wine. In such capacity, it took the place of a cheese service. It was mandated that the little dish should contain no cream, cream cheese or similar ingredients, for it was considered that an ample quantity of these rich substances would have been incorporated in previous courses.

A plain yet marked taste was deemed a prerequisite, and caviar was the ideal choice. Devils or angels on horseback were also popular, as were stuffed mushrooms and all manner of small preparations on rectangles or rounds of toast. This final course became known as "the savoury." All very logical and functional but, in naming this course, the British Raj did not take into consideration the Indian genius for mutating the English language.

Since hors-d'œuvres, such as canapés or creamed mixtures on toast or meat, poultry, fish or eggs, often made their appearance at the beginning of the meal as "first toast," the Indian cooks habitually referred to this closing course as "second toast," but endearingly transmogrified it into "essikin tose" or even "siccuns."

Since the basic idea is simple, merely requiring a hot preparation mounted on plain toast or fried bread, I shall give no recipes for "siccuns." But for those who would like to perpetuate the tradition, these suggestions from old recipes come to mind: shucked oysters, sprinkled with a little Pernod, wrapped in bacon before grilling and mounting on toast; rounds of cheese pastry topped with anchovy butter; cold game, pounded to a paste with stock and a little butter and thickly spread on toast; shrimp, lightly sautéed in butter, mounted on toast and sprinkled with pepper and mace; grated cheese, melted with a pinch of mustard powder, salt and pepper and poured over very crisp toast.

10

THE RAJ PRESERVED

•

The spices, pickles and preserves of the homesick "old kohais"

It is a sad but true comment on the human condition that when people are in one place and time, they generally wish they were in another and do their best to perpetuate the memories of past experiences, once so commonplace and undervalued. When the Raj were in India, they lived their lives in the best facsimiles of English customs and traditions they could devise, as rose-strewn cottages in Simla, rolling golf links in Ootacamund, comfortable clubs in all the major cities and towns, and a thousand accidentally Indianized English recipes all attest. But when they retired to England, when old age or politics forced them to leave the land for which they had worked so hard – the land upon which they had tried their utmost to impose the essence of Englishness – then, with all the perversity of the human soul, they missed it.

The "nice little Indian restaurant round the corner in Shepherd's Bush" provided a chance to re-experience, happily, the curries about which they had complained so loudly and for so long. The manicured greens of such

---

1. The Royal Bombay Yacht Club; 2. Interior of "the sugar house," Cossipore, *c.*1915; 3. Poona racecourse, *c.*1930; 4. Crawford market; 5. Punjab Club, Lahore. Partly destroyed in the earthquake of November 1937.

clubs as Hurlingham furnished the areas upon which to play polo, the game that they had once described as "quaint, but a little barbaric." Discussions arose in Maidenhead as well as Kensington about the best way to make mango chutney, or to construct an authentic curry powder.

The British went home and preserved their Indian memories. Some of their ex-subjects – the peoples of the Empire, now Commonwealth – followed. The Indians who forsook their warm and vivid heritage sought a continuation of the bond they felt they had with that other misty country, their Motherland. Asian foodstores sprang up like mushrooms overnight in the cities of England. Tantalizing smells of garlic, ginger and fenugreek floated down the traditional high streets, and Indian films invaded the screens of the older cinemas in the peripheral areas of the main metropolises. They were all poignant reminders of the time that had been and was no more.

YAD BAD AN ROS-I GIRAN! YAD BAD, YAD BAD! Remember the days that are gone! Remember, remember!

Indian chutneys

The difference between a pickle and a chutney is merely that in a pickle no sweet ingredients, such as sugar, treacle or raisins, are used. In addition, in chutneys the ingredients are often minced or pounded, whereas in pickles they are cut into large pieces or left whole.

The following remarks are taken from a little old book, by an anonymous author, called *All About Indian Chutneys, Pickles and Preserves*, and are as relevant today as when they were first written.

Chutneys are of Indian origin and invention, and several kinds, for which the receipts are here given, are such as are taken by the natives of India, who find relish in them, the more spicy and pungent they are.

To suit the taste of Europeans, the amount of heating ingredients employed may be lessened to a considerable extent. Indeed, the proportion seems very capricious, and we believe that if the amount of chillies and ginger were reduced to a quarter of the quantity indicated, the chutney would more agreeable to a European palate, and even if it should be found otherwise, any deficiency might be easily remedied by adding more.

It is directed in some receipts that both the syrup and the ingredients should be boiled. Though entailing a little more trouble, this is, no doubt, far better than merely incorporating them uncooked and placing them at once in the sun as other receipts direct. Cooking alone, however, is not sufficient; some of the ingredients, ginger in particular, retain a certain degree of rawness, notwithstanding their having been long submitted to the fire. The rawness passes off only by length of time. Chutneys, therefore, though often fit to be consumed when just made, are in all cases vastly improved by age and exposure to the mellowing influences of the sun.

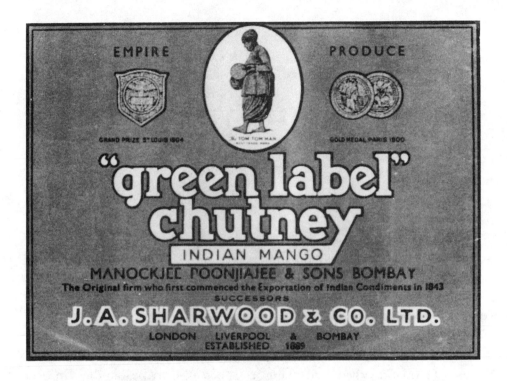

It seems almost needless to mention that the syrup for chutneys should always be made in an enamel saucepan and the scum skimmed off as it rises. The use of copper *degchees* might be attended with dangerous consequences.

Mustard seed should be thoroughly washed and cleansed as well, as should raisins, and afterwards stoned.

Ten good-sized mangoes, when peeled and sliced, are equal in weight, or nearly so, to an English pound.

To which I would add that for some of the following recipes readers must have a measuring scale. Lacking a scale, read only; do not try to cook. Further, in the absence of a sunny climate to mature chutneys, prolonged exposure in a very low oven will have roughly the same effect.

Colonel Skinner's chutney

•

The original recipe instructs that the filled jars of chutney be placed out in the sun for a fortnight! I have made the rather necessary amendments.

Quantity: approximately 2 lb

12 oz dried mangoes
¼ lb garlic, smashed,
   peeled and chopped
½ lb unrefined brown sugar
½ lb fresh ginger root,
   peeled and chopped
½ lb raisins

½ lb salt (original
   measurement; see
   Notes below and adjust
   to taste)
¼ lb chillies (original
   measurement, adjust to
   taste)
2½ pints distilled vinegar

1   Use a food processor with a metal blade to grind all the ingredients (except the vinegar) in several batches, accumulating everything in a large preserving pan.
2   Add the vinegar and stir well. Bring to a boil over moderate heat. Reduce the heat and let the chutney simmer for 1 hour.
3   While it is still warm, transfer it into sterilized jars and seal.

Notes: If you find the dried mangoes too tough to be handled in your processor, you may first soak them until they are pliable. Squeeze out the excess liquid before placing them in the container. The original quantity of salt, which I have given here, seems excessive. It may have been necessary for its preservative qualities in the Indian climate. I suggest you reduce it to your own liking, but do not omit it altogether. Similarly, the chillies are of a quantity to make the chutney quite fiery, but that was how ex-colonials of old liked it. Please adjust accordingly.

Dried mangoes are available from Asian foodstores.

Lime chutney

•

In a way, this reminds me of the great and simple Moroccan preserved lemons because the tang of the rind and oils permeates the whole. It lingers on your palate as well.

Quantity: approximately 6 lb

4 lb limes, quartered
8 oz salt
1 lb raisins
2 oz dried red chillies
6 oz fresh ginger root,
   peeled and finely
   chopped

$\frac{1}{4}$ lb garlic, smashed,
   peeled and chopped
$1\frac{1}{2}$ pints distilled vinegar
$1\frac{1}{4}$ lb sugar

1   Place the limes in something like a large, shallow washbowl and cover them with salt. Try to put them in the sun for 3 days in a row. If you cannot, then place them in a warm (very low) oven every day for about an hour. Whichever method you use, stir them several times a day.

2   The day before you begin to make the chutney, place the raisins, chillies, ginger and garlic in enough of the vinegar (approximately $\frac{1}{3}$ of the total) to moisten them thoroughly and let them macerate for 24 hours.

3   Place the limes and all the other ingredients in a food processor, and process in batches to a coarse mixture, accumulating it in a large, lined saucepan. Add the remaining vinegar and place it over medium heat. Let it come to a boil and then simmer for 45 minutes, or until the mixture thickens.

4   Transfer the chutney into warm, sterilized jars and seal tightly. The jars may be finished off in a hot-water bath if you wish.

Notes: You may macerate the limes longer in the salt, for up to 1 week. If you wish, you may wash off the surplus salt and drain the limes before proceeding further.

Lady MacFarquhar's tomato chutney

•

Although I did include this recipe in another of my cookery books, it is far too good and far too appropriate not to be included here. It keeps extremely well, if your family and guests will allow you to hold some back.

Quantity: about 5 quarts

$1\frac{1}{2}$ lb sugar

24 fl oz white vinegar

$\frac{1}{2}$ lb garlic, smashed, peeled and chopped

$1\frac{1}{2}$ lb fresh ginger root, peeled and coarsely chopped

$5\frac{1}{2}$ lb firm tomatoes, blanched, peeled and quartered

$1\frac{1}{2}$ lb raisins

6 oz sultanas/golden raisins

10 dried red chillies (seeded if you wish to lessen the heat)

salt

1   Bring the sugar and vinegar to a boil in a lined saucepan over medium heat and continue to boil until the sugar is dissolved and a thin syrup is formed.

2   Stir in the garlic and ginger. When the mixture returns to a boil, add the tomatoes, raisins, sultanas and chillies. Bring to a boil once more, stirring. Reduce the heat to low and simmer until the mixture thickens and the solids become very soft. Stir from time to time.

3   Remove from the heat and, when cool enough to handle, salt to taste. Pour into sterilized bottling jars and seal tightly.

Notes: For better keeping, you may sterilize further by immersing the jars in a hot bath for 20 minutes.

Garam masala

•

I have mentioned this sweet spice mix in many of the recipes in this book. Although it can be bought ready-made in Asian foodstores, it is very easy to make one's own mixture and, as the quantities may be adjusted accordingly, it is far better to make small amounts at a time so that the taste is more pronounced.

Quantity: 5 tablespoons

2 tablespoons coriander
seeds
3-inch stick of cinnamon,
broken into small
pieces
1 tablespoon cumin seeds
1 teaspoon whole cloves

1 teaspoon cardamom
pods
1 tablespoon mace
1 tablespoon black
peppercorns

1   Mix all the ingredients together and grind or pound them to a fine powder, using an electric spice grinder or a mortar and pestle.
2   Immediately place in a jar, cap tightly and store in a cool, dark place.

Notes: A coffee grinder works very well for grinding, but you will need a separate one for coffee afterwards, or your coffee will be strangely aromatic. A blender does work fairly well but the mixture will be much more coarse. *Garam masala* may be sprinkled over the top of many dishes towards the end of cooking.

An individual blend of curry powder

•

So much better than using any commercial powder. The whole spices should be freshly roasted and then ground immediately. After grinding it, comparison-test it yourself against any commercial curry powder you have on your shelf.

Quantity: approximately 5 oz

6 tablespoons coriander seeds	¾ tablespoon black mustard seeds
4 tablespoons cumin seeds	2 tablespoons ground turmeric
6–8 dried red chillies	
¾ tablespoon whole black peppercorns	2 tablespoons ground fenugreek

1   Preheat the oven to 300°F (150°C, Gas Mark 2). Line a baking pan with foil and place the *whole* spices in separate heaps upon it (this is done so that you can remove the smaller spices as they are ready). Place the pan on the top shelf of the oven until the spices become aromatic and are slightly browned. Do not over-roast them.

2   Place the roasted spices (in several batches) into a spice grinder, a blender or a mortar and grind or pound to a fine powder. Accumulate them in a storage jar. Add the pre-ground turmeric and fenugreek, cap the jar and shake until the spices are well mixed.

Notes: The spices may also be roasted in a heavy iron pan on top of the stove. Shake the pan well as this is done, and keep your face averted as the smoke from the chillies is extremely acrid and makes your eyes water. Vary the individual quantities of the spices as you wish to make the blend to your own taste.

Home-made spiced tomato sauce

•

Quantity: 1 quart

10 lb tomatoes, blanched and skins removed, chopped	2 dried red chillies, seeded and finely chopped
4 large onions, peeled and diced	1-inch piece of fresh ginger root, peeled and finely chopped
6 large red bell peppers, seeded, cored and diced	1 teaspoon celery seeds
	1 teaspoon ground allspice

1 teaspoon ground cinnamon	½ teaspoon freshly grated nutmeg
2 teaspoons salt	2 bay leaves
½ teaspoon freshly ground black pepper	4 oz/½ heaped cup brown sugar
½ teaspoon ground cloves	10 fl oz white vinegar

1   Mix the tomatoes, onions, bell peppers, chillies and ginger together in a basin. Purée this mixture in several batches in a food processor or blender, accumulating the purée in a large non-stick pan.

2   Add all the remaining ingredients and cook, uncovered, simmering over a low heat for about 3 hours or until the purée thickens to the consistency of ketchup. Stir frequently towards the end of the cooking time, as the mixture thickens, to prevent it from catching on the bottom.

3   While the mixture is thickening, turn the oven to 250°F (130°C, Gas mark ½). Wash and sterilize a couple of 1-pint bottling jars and their closures and put them in the oven to warm.

4   When the sauce is sufficiently thick, remove the bay leaves and ladle it into the jars to within ⅛ inch of the top. Wipe the tops, seal and let them cool. Let them stand for about 2 weeks in a cool, dark, dry place before using.

Notes: You can wrap the jars in foil to preserve the red look of the sauce. Exposure to daylight darkens it.

Essence of chilli peppers

•

In a sense, this is a cousin to Tabasco, or any of the other hot pepper sauces.

Yield: a bottle of chilli essence

2 oz the reddest dried chillies you can find	1 teaspoon salt white vinegar

1   Place the chillies in the sun for 1 hour (a very low oven for 15–30 minutes will possibly do). Then place them in a spice grinder in batches and grind them to a powder.

2   Using a funnel and extreme care, place the powder in a bottle and add the salt. Pour in only as much vinegar as will make a slightly runny paste. Cork or cap the bottle and place it in the sun or in a sunny window for 3 days.

3   Add enough vinegar to turn the mixture into a thick sauce, strain it through a sieve lined with muslin and then re-bottle. Store in a dark place to preserve it.

Notes: Some people like to add a pinch of powdered garlic before adding the vinegar.

Pickled mangoes

•

Locate the green, totally unripe mangoes in ethnic markets.

Yield: 1 large jar of pickle

25 small, unripe mangoes	8 oz fresh ginger root,
6 oz salt	peeled and thinly sliced
$\frac{1}{2}$ pint white vinegar	6 oz white mustard seed
1 tablespoon ground	2 oz garlic, smashed,
turmeric	peeled and chopped
2–4 oz dried red chillies	

1   Cut each mango, making 4 vertical slices to $\frac{3}{4}$ of the way down from the pointed end, leaving the last $\frac{1}{4}$ of the fruit intact. Slightly separate the segments in order to remove the stone. Each mango should now look like a partially opened flower bud. Lay them in a large plastic bowl and sprinkle with the salt. Let them macerate for 24 hours, turning over occasionally.

2   Place the vinegar and turmeric in a saucepan. Bring to a boil, reduce the heat and simmer for 15 minutes.

3   Mix all the remaining ingredients together. Have ready a large, sterilized jar, big enough to hold all the mangoes. Take the mangoes and stuff some of the spice mix inside each one. Place them in the jar, topping them with any remaining spice mix. Pour the hot vinegar and turmeric over the mangoes until they are fully submerged and the liquid comes to within $\frac{1}{2}$ inch of the top of the jar. Seal it tightly and leave for at least 2 weeks.

Notes: Sometimes a little mustard oil is poured on to the top of the pickle to keep it from spoiling. Mangoes pickled in oil are made in the same way, except fresh grated horseradish is added to the stuffing ingredients, the vinegar is omitted and mustard oil used as a substitute.

Brinjal pickle

•

Quantity: approximately 9 lb

8 lb very small brinjals (aubergines/eggplants), halved

6 oz salt

1 lb garlic, smashed and peeled

4 oz dried red chillies

8 oz fresh ginger root, peeled and chopped

3 pints distilled vinegar

2 tablespoons fenugreek seeds

2 tablespoons cumin seeds

4 teaspoons white mustard seeds

1 pint vegetable oil

4 tablespoons turmeric

8 oz/1¼ cups sugar (optional)

1   Place the brinjals in a plastic bowl and sprinkle with the salt. Leave them for 2 hours and then gently press out and drain off the liquid.

2   While the brinjals are marinating, place the garlic, chillies and ginger in a food processor, together with 1 pint of vinegar, and process to a smooth purée.

3   Grind the fenugreek, cumin and mustard seeds to a powder in batches in an electric spice grinder.

4   Heat the oil in a large lined saucepan over medium heat and fry the ground spices and the turmeric for 5 minutes, stirring. Add the purée from the food processor and continue to stir and cook for 5 more minutes.

5   Put in the drained brinjals and stir, adding the remaining vinegar. Bring to a boil, reduce to a simmer and continue to cook everything, stirring

from time to time until the brinjals are soft and the mixture has the consistency of a curry. (During this period, if you desire a sweet pickle you should add the sugar, stirring until it is dissolved.)

6   Spoon the pickle into warm, sterilized jars and seal.

Notes: A lime *kasoundi*, or pickle, can be made by the same method, using 4 lb limes, 4 oz salt, 8 oz garlic, 4 oz dried red chillies, 1 pint vinegar, 2 oz fenugreek seeds, 4 oz mustard seed, 1 packet saffron, and 2 pints vegetable oil. Please note: there is no turmeric, ginger or cumin among these ingredients. To be authentic, use the smallest and hardest limes you can find.

Red pepper conserve

•

This was originally called a marmalade but the term is a misnomer, for this scarlet, tangy conserve is designed to be eaten with hot or cold meats or poultry.

Quantity: just under 2 lb

8 large red bell peppers

6 fl oz freshly squeezed lemon juice

3 fl oz freshly squeezed orange juice

2 fl oz red wine vinegar

2 cloves of garlic, smashed, peeled and finely chopped

3 tablespoons finely chopped onion

1 lb/2 cups sugar

$\frac{1}{3}$ teaspoon cayenne

$\frac{1}{3}$ teaspoon salt

$\frac{1}{4}$ teaspoon dried rosemary

$\frac{1}{4}$ teaspoon dried marjoram

the thin outer peel of 1 lemon, cut into julienne strips

the thin outer peel of $\frac{1}{2}$ an orange, cut into julienne strips

1   Char the skins of the peppers under the grill. Place them in a paper bag to let the steam soften the skins. When they are cool enough to handle, skin, seed and core them and cut them in half. Chop 7 peppers finely and cut 1 into thin, short julienne strips.

2   Place all the ingredients into a lined saucepan and bring to a boil. Reduce the heat to low and simmer for about 5 minutes, stirring from time to time. As the conserve thickens, you will need to stir more often. Cook until it is the consistency of jam. (The temperature will be just under 225°F/110°C on a sugar thermometer.)

3   Spoon the conserve into warm, sterilized jars and seal. Store in a cool, dark place so that the preserve does not fade.

Notes: The look of this conserve is so brilliant, especially if you choose really scarlet bell peppers, and its taste so piquant and unusual, that I suggest you make at least double the given quantity so that you have some jars for gifts.

Guava cheese

•

Quantity: 2 lb

2 lb guavas, peeled and	4 oz butter
sliced	the juice of 4 lemons
14 oz/scant 2 cups sugar	

1   Put the guavas in a preserving pan with $\frac{1}{2}$pt of cold water. Bring to a boil and then reduce the heat to low and cook for $\frac{1}{2}$ an hour. Press the fruit through a sieve and place the pulp in a pan, together with the sugar, butter and lemon juice.

2   Simmer over very low heat for 2 hours, or until the mixture becomes very thick and dry. Stir from time to time.

3   Spoon it into lightly greased moulds. Cover immediately with wax paper, cut to fit. Cover tightly with plastic wrap or wax paper and tie securely. Store in a cool, dark place, such as a well-ventilated cupboard.

Notes: The guava cheese may also be spooned into ordinary jam jars.

GLOSSARY

Historically, there has been no standard convention for the English trans-
literation of the many languages of the subcontinent. Early western attempts
to pronounce and then spell the native words were marked by the particular
nationality of the foreigner and by the spelling conventions of his or her
own language, whether Portuguese, French or English. The mutation and
transmogrification of many Indian words by the British Raj often resulted
from a basic reluctance to learn a foreign language and a certain inherent
snobbery: "If one shouts loud enough in English the fellahs will understand!" Then, too, the British Army has often had the charming habit of
making its own slang from foreign words, and it had plenty of years in
India during which to perfect this trait. The result of these influences has
been an exotic mish-mash of spelling – a salad bar of phonetic options. To
list them all would be to turn a modest glossary into a small book. Therefore,
I have offered merely a single alternative common spelling for most listings.
If your choice is not among them I commend to you *Hobson-Jobson – A
Glossary of Colloquial Anglo-Indian Words and Phrases*.

Adrak	Fresh ginger root
Aloo, alu	Potato
Arak	Distilled palm sap
Arhad, urad dhal	White-hulled split gram bean (whole gram beans have a black skin) (see p. 115)
Atta, ata	Wholewheat flour
Ayah	Nursemaid or lady's maid

1. Bridge over the Hooghly, Calcutta; 2. My father and myself; 3. The sisters and a friend in saris;
4. Punting a boat among the lotus flowers, Kashmir, 1936; 5. The departure from England; 6. My
fifth birthday, Murree, 1940. When everyone knelt Mother could focus the camera.

Babu	Clerk
Baigan	Eggplant, aubergine
Barfi, burfi	Fudge
Behr	Small plum
Besan	Chick-pea flour
Bhindi	Okra, ladies' fingers
Bhisti, bheesty	water-carrier
Bhistra-bund	Bedding roll
Bhugia, bhojia	Spiced stir-fried vegetables
Biriani	A rice pilaff incorporating meat or chicken
Bowli-glass	Finger bowl
Box-wallah	Pedlar (sometimes as a pejorative for an Englishman in commerce)
Brinjal	Anglo-Indian for aubergine (also see *baigan*)
Bul-bul	Nightingale
Burra	Great, big, large
Burra peg	Large drink or double measure of alcohol
Channa dhal	Yellow split peas, also the cooked, spiced dish (see p. 115)
Chapatti, chapati	Unleavened, wholewheat, griddle-baked bread
Char, cha	Tea
Char-masala	Afghani for 4-spices
Charpoy	Wood-framed, woven string bed
Chatti	Spherical earthenware pot
Chaugan	Persian for stick or mallet (original name for polo)
Chenna	Full-cream curd cheese
Chick	Split-bamboo blind
Chickaw	Red-legged partridge
Chota hazri	Little breakfast, early-morning tea
Chota peg	Small drink (often a whisky)
Chowkidar, chokidar	Watchman
Cud, khud	Steep hillside, precipice
Daikon	Japanese name for a large white radish
Dak, dhak	The mail or post
Dalchini	Cinnamon or cassia
Danedar	Milk reduced to granulated solids
Dekshi, degshi	Metal cooking pot with a flat lid
Dhai, dahi	Curds, yoghurt

Dhal, dal	Split pulses and legumes
Dhania	Coriander
Dhobi	Washerman
Dhopiaza, dopiazza	Literally "two onions," double the amount of onions to that of meat
Dhoti	Loin-cloth
Dhow, dow	Arab single-masted vessel
Dhurry	Flat-woven cotton or wool rug
Dolly, dali	Offering tray of edible gifts
Dooley	Box or meat-safe
Doolie, dhooly	Covered litter, palanquin
Dosa	Pancakes
Dudh, dood	Milk
Dumba	Fat-tailed sheep
Durzi	Tailor, dressmaker
Elaichi	Cardamom
Gharry	Four-wheeled carriage
Ghosht	Meat
Gram	Chick-pea (sometimes refers to other varieties of pulse)
Gulab jamun	Fried milk balls in rose-scented syrup
Gur	Unrefined palm sugar, also called *jaggery*
Gurpapedi	Brown-sugar toffee
Gurram or Gurrum	Hot
Haiku	Japanese poetic form
Halva, halwa	Vegetables or fruits with sugar cooked to the consistency of cake or fudge
Havildar	Sepoy non-commissioned officer, corresponding to a sergeant
Hing	Asafoetida
Hissab	Household accounts
Huldi	Turmeric
Jaiphal	Nutmeg
Jarren, jharran	Dishcloth or duster
Javriti	Mace
Jeera	Cumin
Jellaby, jalebi	Crisp batter spirals containing syrup
Jhoonga	Little extra or "make-weight"
Juldi	Quickly

Kabuli channa, safaid — White chick peas, also called *safaid channa*
Kafilas — Caravans
Kali, kala — Black, dark
Kali channa — Unskinned chick peas
Kali jeera, jira — Black cumin seed
Kali mirchi — Black pepper
Karhi — Indian wok, also Tamil for sauce
Kasoundi — Oil-based pickle
Keema — Minced or ground meat
Kesar — Saffron
Kewra — Screw-pine or pandanus extract
Khamir tursh — Afghan wholewheat sourdough starter
Khansamer, khansama — House-steward, cook
Khichri — Cooked mixture of rice and lentils
Khitmagar, kitmutgar — A bearer, waiter
Khoya — Milk reduced to a fudge-like consistency
Khudaah — Exclamation (perhaps from the Persian "Khabar-dar," "Take heed!")
Kibbeh — Arab balls of fried meat or cereal
Kikka — Thorn bush or tree
Kofta — Fried ball of meat or vegetables
Kohai — Literally "Who's there?"
Korma, kurma — To braise
Kulfi — Thick, hard ice-cream
Kurta — Large over-shirt
Kysara — Sanskrit for "a dish for rice and sesamun" (*OED*)
Lal mirchi — Ground red pepper
Lassi — Curd drink
Laung — Cloves
Luddoo — Ball-shaped sweetmeat, often of chick-pea flour
Machan — Elevated platform, hide
Mahatma — Great Soul, Great One
Maidan, mydan — A grassy open space, parade ground
Malai — Clotted cream
Mali — Gardener
Mangi, manjee — Boatman, steersman
Masalchi — Kitchen or scullery boy
Masoor, masar dhal — Pink lentils (see p. 115)
Matar, mutter dhal — Green split pea (see p. 115)

Memsahib	Literally "Lady Sir," lady of the household
Methi	Fenugreek
Mirchi	Pepper
Mofussil	Up-country
Molagu	Tamil for pepper
Mooli	Dish containing coconut milk
Moong, mung dhal	Split mung beans (see p. 115)
Moorgee	Old spelling for chicken
Murgh, murghi	Chicken
Naan	Semi-leavened oven-baked bread
Narga, nurga	Narcissus
Naruel pantua	Coconut sweetmeat
Nautch	Dance
Nawab	Title of distinction, Muslim equivalent of raja
Nimboo-pani	Lime-water or lemonade
Nullah	Ditch or small ravine
Numdah	Embroidered felt rug
Paan	Digestive of betel leaf rolled round lime paste, betel nut, spices and even tobacco
Pakhora, pakora	Fritters
Panch	Hindi for five (corrupted to punch – a drink with 5 ingredients)
Pani	Water
Panir, paneer	Curd cheese
Pansari, punsaree	Chemist or druggist shop
Paratha	Fried, flaky wholewheat bread
Pera	Milk fudge
Picer, paisa	Small-denomination copper coin
Pinki-pani	"Pink water" (permanganate of potash)
Pippali	Sanskrit for pepper
Poppadams, papadum	Flat, round crisp wafers
Powinder	Nomad
Puggaree	Turban
Pukka	Proper
Pulu	Tibetan for ball
Punkah	Suspended swinging fan
Rabadi	Milk reduced to a thick sauce
Raita	Vegetables or fruit in seasoned yoghurt
Rasagullas	Curd cheese balls in rose-scented syrup

Roti	Bread
Rupee	Standard coin of the Anglo-Indian monetary system
Saag, sag	Green leaf vegetables
Sabat moong	Green whole mung beans
Sahib	Master or Sire
Salwar khameez	Traditional Muslim dress of tunic and trousers
Samosa	Meat- or vegetable-filled pastry triangles
Satyagraha	Asserting truth (Gandhi's political belief)
Saunf	Fennel
Seer	Denomination of weight (approximately $2\frac{1}{2}$–3 pounds)
Sepoy	Native soldier
Sev	Fried noodles of spiced chick-pea flour
Shamiana	Canvas awning or flat tent roof
Shikar	Hunt, sport or shoot
Shikara	Kashmiri small boat
Shikari	Sportsman, hunter
Sigri	Small portable stove
Sooji	Semolina
Sowar	Expert rider of horses or camels
Sunt	Dried ginger
Syce	Groom
Tamasha	Big affair, event, occasion
Tamatar	Tomato
Tawa	Traditional iron griddle or frying pan
Teetur	Black partridge
Tejpat	Bay leaf
Thali	Circular metal meal tray
Tiffin	Lunch
Tonga	Light two-wheeled vehicle
Toor, toovar dhal	Yellow lentils (see p. 115)
Topee, topi	Sola (a plant) (corrupted to solar) hat or pith helmet
Tunni	Tamil for water
Vindaloo	Hot, pungent, acidic curry
Wallah	Generic term for person
Wari	Irrigation ditch
Zard Alu	Persian for apricot

BIBLIOGRAPHY

A. C. S., *Memsahib's Book of Cookery*, India, 1894.

Allen, Charles, *A Glimpse of the Burning Plain*, Michael Joseph, London, 1986.

——*Plain Tales from the Raj*, Century, London, 1985.

Anon., *All About Indian Chutneys, Pickles and Preserves*, Thacker, Spink & Co., Calcutta, undated.

Anon., *Manual of Military Cooking and Dietary, 1933*, H. M. Stationery Office, London, 1933.

Apicius, *Cookery and Dining in Imperial Rome*, Dover Publications, New York, 1977.

Barr, Pat, *The Memsahibs*, Allied Publishers Pvt. Ltd, New Delhi, 1976.

Barr, Pat, and Desmond, Ray, *Simla, A Hill Station in British India*, The Scolar Press Ltd, London, 1978.

Beeton, Mrs Isabella, *The Book of Household Management*, Jonathan Cape, London, 1861.

Bradley, John, ed., *Lady Curzon's India*, George Weidenfeld & Nicolson, London, 1985.

Brennan, Jennifer, *The Cuisines of Asia*, Marek, St Martin's Press, New York, MacDonalds, London, 1984.

Channing, Mark, *India Mosaic*, J. B. Lippincott, Philadelphia, 1936.

David, Elizabeth, *Spices, Salt and Aromatics in the English Kitchen*, Penguin Books, London, 1970.

Fay, Eliza, *Original Letters from India*, The Hogarth Press, London, 1986.

Francatelli, Charles Elmé, *The Modern Cook* (1846), Dover Publications, New York, 1973.

Kaye, M. M., ed., *The Golden Calm*, Viking Penguin, London, 1980.

Kenney-Herbert, Colonel, *Wyvern's Indian Cookery Book*, Higgenbotham & Co., Madras, 1869.

Ketab, *Indian Dishes for English Tables*, Chapman & Hall, London, 1910.

Kipling, Rudyard, *Early Verse by Rudyard Kipling*, Clarendon Press, Oxford, 1986.

——*The Works of Rudyard Kipling*, Octopus, London, 1984.

Lewis, C. C., *Culinary Notes for Sind*, C. C. Lewis, Karachi, 1923.

Morrow, Ann, *Highness: The Maharajas of India*, Grafton Books, London, 1986.

Nasa, Shamshad, *Focus on N. W. F. P.*, Hotel Khyber International, Peshawar, date unknown.

Ranhofer, Charles, *The Epicurean*, John Wiley, Chicago, 1920.

Soyer, Alexis, *The Pantropheon*, Constable & Co., London, 1853.

Steele, F. A., and Gardiner, G., *The Complete Indian Housekeeper and Cook*, Bombay Education Society Press, Bombay, 1893.

Tandon, Prakash, *Punjabi Century 1857–1947*, Chatto & Windus, London, 1961.

Theroux, Paul, *The Imperial Way*, Houghton Mifflin Company, Boston, 1985.

Tytler, Harriet, *An Englishwoman in India: The Memoirs of Harriet Tytler 1828–1858*, Sattin, Anthony, ed., Oxford University Press, Oxford, 1986.

Wilkinson-Latham, Robert, *North-West Frontier 1837–1947*, Osprey Publishing, London, 1977.

Wilson, Lady, *Letters from India*, Century, London, 1984.

Yeats-Brown, Francis, *Lancer at Large*, Garden City Publishing, New York, 1939.

Yule, H., Colonel, and Burnell, A. C., *Hobson-Jobson: A Glossary of Colloquial Anglo-Indian Words and Phrases*, Routledge & Kegan Paul, London 1985.

ACKNOWLEDGEMENTS

The author wishes to acknowledge the authors in the Bibliography for their insights and acute observations on the subcontinent and on the British in India. Affection and knowledge shine through their words. Their books are heartily recommended for further study. The publishers and author are also grateful to the following for permission to reproduce material: Century Hutchinson Ltd for Lady Wilson, *Letters from India*, 1984.

Illustration acknowledgements

Billie Love Historical Collection
p. 20, nos. 2, 3; p. 48, no. 2; p. 78, no. 9; p. 178, no. 3; p. 192, no. 1; p. 248, no. 4; p. 286, no. 2; p. 300, no. 1.

Duke of Cornwall's Light Infantry Regiment, Bodmin, Cornwall
p. 78, no. 3; p. 118, no. 1; p. 149, no. 9; p. 248, no. 7.

Douglas Dickins
p. 4, nos. 7–9; p. 20, nos. 1, 4, 5; p. 48, nos. 1, 7; p. 62; p. 73; p. 78, nos. 1, 2, 8; p. 91; p. 113; p. 149, nos. 8, 10; p. 175; p. 178, no. 2; p. 248, nos. 1, 5, 6.

Robert Opie Collection
pp. 23, 25, 81, 289.

Popperfoto
p. 78, no. 7; p. 118, no. 2; p. 178, nos. 1, 4, 6; p. 189; p. 228, no. 9; p. 248, no. 2; p. 286, no. 3.

Author
p. 4, nos. 1–6; p. 48, nos. 3–6, 8, 9; p. 67; p. 78, nos. 4–6; p. 118, nos. 3–9; p. 123; p. 137; p. 145; p. 149, nos. 1–6; p. 162; p. 167; p. 178, nos. 5, 7; p. 192, nos. 2–7; p. 228, nos. 1–8; p. 230; p. 286, no. 5; p. 300, nos. 2–6.

Picturesque Bombay
p. 20, no. 6; p. 149, no. 7; p. 192, no. 8; p. 216; p. 248, no. 3; p. 286, nos. 1, 4.

RECIPE DIRECTORY

Basic recipes

An individual blend of curry powder (pp. 293–4)
Chenna and paneer (pp. 172–3)
Garam masala (p. 293)
Khoya (pp. 170–73)
Rabadi (p. 171)

Starters and snacks

Clam and bacon balls with apricot sauce (pp. 70–71)
Cucumber stuffed with Roquefort and hazelnuts (pp. 204–5)
Mushrooms stuffed with spinach soufflé (pp. 279–80)
Nargisi kofta (pp. 140–41)
Sardine curry puffs (pp. 153–4)
Sev (p. 186–7)

Soups

Camp soup (pp. 157–8)
Cool green almond and watercress soup (pp. 83–5)
Duck soup with chillied walnuts (pp. 258–9)
Kerala clam and shrimp coconut soup (pp. 260–61)

Mulligatawny soup (pp. 85–7)
Shrimp and cinnamon soup (p. 257)
Spiced tomato soup with saffron cream (pp. 82–3)

Salads and dressings

Bloody Mary shellfish mould (pp. 203–4)
Chick pea and smoked fish salad in tomato cups (pp. 160–61)
Cucumber raita salad mould (pp. 87–8)
Marinated paneer and wilted spinach salad (pp. 88–9)
Stuffed pomfret rolls in aspic (pp. 200–201)

Fish and seafood

Bloody Mary shellfish mould (pp. 203–4)
Chick pea and smoked fish salad in tomato cups (pp. 160–61)
Chingree samosas (pp. 124–6)
Clam and bacon koftas with apricot sauce (pp. 70–71)
Devilled shrimp (pp. 58–9)
Kedgeree of smoked haddock (p. 66)
Kerala clam and shrimp coconut soup (pp. 260–61)
Machi kebabs (pp. 91–2)
Melon with chutneyed shellfish (p. 255)
Nowshera fishcakes (pp. 69–70)
Oysters en brochette (pp. 259–60)
Parsee patia (pp. 89–90)
Polo pilaff (pp. 207–10)
Potato crêpes of lobster with salmon roe crème (pp. 256–7)
Sardine curry puffs (pp. 143–4)
Shrimp and cinnamon soup (p. 257)
Spiced scramble in fried-bread cups (pp. 55–6)
Stuffed pomfret rolls in aspic (pp. 200–201)
Trout baked in an almond jacket (pp. 262–4)

Beef

Aloo chops (pp. 144–5)
Braised stuffed veal in a Mogul manner (pp. 274–6)
Eshepherd's pie (pp. 94–7)
Jhalfarajie (pp. 113–14)
Keema mutter in pittas (pp. 161–3)
Spiced beef (p. 142)
Spiced mince with croutons and mashed potatoes (pp. 239–40)
Veal olives with green peppercorn sauce (pp. 264–5)

Lamb

Aloo chops (pp. 144–5)
Baluchi carpet-wallah kebabs (pp. 67–9)
Camp soup (pp. 157–8)
Jhalfarajie (pp. 113–14)
Keema mutter in pittas (pp. 161–3)
Madras Club quoorma (pp. 97–9)
Nargisi kofta (pp. 140–41)
Peshawari pasande (pp. 240–41)
Pish-pash (p. 235)
Railway lamb curry (pp. 165–6)
Saag ghosh (pp. 99–100)
Shami kebabs (pp. 131–4)

Pork and ham

Bacon and coriander pancakes (pp. 60–61)
Clam and bacon koftas with apricot sauce (pp. 70–71)
Ham, lord of the breakfast sideboard (pp. 76–7)
Quails Darjeeling (pp. 268–70)
Raised game pie (pp. 138–9)
Roulade of duck (pp. 206–7)
Sind Club ham in gin (pp. 102–3)
Wild rice and sausage stuffing in red cabbage (pp. 267–8)

Poultry

Game

Variety meats

Rice

Brown rice (p. 101)
Dhal and rice with poached eggs (pp. 237–8)
Kedgeree of smoked haddock (p. 66)
Khuni kitchri (pp. 64–5)
Masala kitchri (pp. 63–4)
Pathan chicken pilaff (pp. 107–10)
Polo pilaff (pp. 207–10)
White pilaff with pine nuts (p. 213)
Wild rice and sausage stuffing in red cabbage (pp. 267–8)

Eggs

Devilled eggs (pp. 53–8)
Dhal and rice with poached eggs (pp. 237–8)
Drappit eggs with herbs (pp. 57–8)
Ginger soufflé (pp. 282–3)
Indian masala omelette (pp. 59–60)
Nargisi kofta (pp. 140–41)
Prairie oyster (p. 227)
Spiced scramble in fried-bread cups (pp. 55–6)

Bread dishes and cooked cereals

Aloo parathas (pp. 130–31)
Bangalore Club sandwiches (pp. 182–3)
Carrot and raisin spirals (p. 184)
Chapattis with butter and marmalade (pp. 71–2)
Keema mutter in pittas (pp. 161–3)
Naan bread (pp. 128–9)
Poppadams (pp. 242–3)
Sooji (pp. 75–6)

Vegetable accompaniments and side dishes

Baigan masala (p. 159)
Brown rice (p. 101)
Dhal churchurree (pp. 114–16)
Spiced fried potatoes (pp. 280–81)
Tamatar bhugia (pp. 92–3)
Timbales of cauliflower and green beans (pp. 277–8)
Wild rice and sausage stuffing in red cabbage (pp. 267–8)

Sauces

Clam and bacon koftas with apricot sauce (pp. 70–71)
Essence of chilli peppers (pp. 295–6)
Home-made spiced tomato sauce (pp. 294–5)
Veal olives with green peppercorn sauce (pp. 264–5)

Puddings and desserts

Baked rose custard (pp. 156–7)
Bombay pudding (p. 117)
Byculla Club soufflé (pp. 215–17)
Ginger soufflé (pp. 282–3)
Khansamer's lemon pudding (pp. 243 4)
Kulfi malai (pp. 244–5)
Prune and claret mould (pp. 284–5)
Stewed brandied apricots (pp. 145–6)
Tipsy laird (pp. 214–15)

Cakes, scones and cookies

Droppies (pp. 184–5)
Flagstaff House chocolate éclairs (pp. 187–90)

Granny Whitburn's pound cake (pp. 190–91)
My grandmother's sponge cake (pp. 246–7)
Rawalpindi potato scones (pp. 185–6)

Sweets and sweetmeats

Jellabies (pp. 175–6)
Luddoos (p. 174)
Peras (p. 173)

Chutneys and pickles

Brinjal pickle (pp. 297–8)
Colonel Skinner's chutney (p. 290)
Coriander chutney (p. 141)
Lady MacFarquhar's tomato chutney (p. 292)
Lime chutney (p. 291)
Pickled mangoes (pp. 296–7)
Red pepper conserve (pp. 298–9)

Jams and preserves

Granny Whitburn's Scottish whisky marmalade (pp. 72–4)
Guava cheese (p. 299)
Nimboo curd (pp. 74–5)

Drinks

A classic gimlet (p. 220)
Athol brose (pp. 226–7)

GENERAL INDEX

CULINARY INDEX

See Recipe Directory (p. 310) for names of dishes.